BEHAVIORAL PORTFOLIO MANAGEMENT

HOW SUCCESSFUL INVESTORS MASTER THEIR EMOTIONS AND BUILD SUPERIOR PORTFOLIOS

BY C. THOMAS HOWARD, PhD

HARRIMAN HOUSE LTD
3A Penns Road
Petersfield
Hampshire
GU32 2EW
GREAT BRITAIN

Tel: +44 (0)1730 233870
Email: enquiries@harriman-house.com
Website: www.harriman-house.com

First published in Great Britain in 2014
Copyright © Harriman House 2014

The right of C. Thomas Howard to be identified as Author has been asserted in accordance with the
Copyright, Design and Patents Act 1988.

ISBN: 9780857193575

British Library Cataloguing in Publication Data
A CIP catalogue record for this book can be obtained from the British Library.

FOLLOW US, LIKE US, EMAIL US

@HarrimanHouse
www.linkedin.com/company/harriman-house
www.facebook.com/harrimanhouse
contact@harriman-house.com

 Harriman House

"Professional money managers and investment advisers alike will find Tom Howard's thought-provoking exploration of the practical implications of investing in a world where emotional crowds dominate the determination of prices to be an interesting and engaging read."

Jim Peterson, Chief Investment Officer,
Charles Schwab Investment Advisory, Inc.

"By rethinking the basic challenges of equity investing from a behavioral viewpoint, Professor Howard has arrived at some totally fresh insights into what it takes to be an outstanding long-term investor. Though aimed at professionals in the field of investment management, many of the ideas presented in this highly readable book will be invaluable to a wider audience."

Andrew Cox, Director, Janus Capital Group

"Tom Howard masterfully bridges the gap between the insights of behavioral finance and the demands of portfolio management, and he explains behavioral data investing in a forthright and engaging style. Advisors and investors alike stand to benefit from this book."

Philip Lawton, Ph.D., CFA, Research Affiliates, LLC

"There has been a glaring hole in the study of behavioral finance, namely, how to incorporate its caveats and principles into successful investment management. *Behavioral Portfolio Management* helps to fill the gap left behind by theorists with its creation of a unique framework for investment managers."

Jason A. Voss, CFA Institute Behavioral Finance Content
Director, author of *The Intuitive Investor*, retired investment manager

"Tom Howard was the most inspirational and influential professor in my master's programme. His proven ability to harness behavioral factors and rigorously apply them to the portfolio management process makes this book a fascinating read!"

George Spentzos, Managing Director, Société Générale, London, UK

"Tom Howard demonstrates how the traditional tools of the investment industry, like modern portfolio theory and investment style boxes, combine with investor emotions to distort portfolios and asset prices. This book can teach you the proper strategy, consistency, and conviction to harness these distortions in your portfolio for higher returns and avoid the Cult of Emotion."

John Nofsinger, Ph.D., Seward Chair in Finance,
University of Alaska, author of *The Psychology of Investing*

"This book is a game-changer; as early adopters of Behavioral Portfolio Management, we found this to be an oasis in the desert of Modern Portfolio Theory. I know of no better way to beat the market then to do what this book tells me to do; and no book says it better than this. The reasons for our outperformance transcend time and trump the competition, 'rational' or otherwise. Of course we are emotional investors--now we can profit from that!"

Karl Frank MA, MBA, MSF, CFP,
President, A&I Financial Services LLC

"Dr. Tom Howard has taken the principles of Behavioral Theory and applied them to investing in his new book *Behavioral Portfolio Management*. Beyond theory he has applied these precepts to actual portfolios with considerable success. He examines 'What If' we take advantage of human behavior and use that knowledge to enhance portfolio returns. An excellent read that takes us to the next stage in the investing arena."

Philip Hartwell, CFP, Royal Alliance

"Traditional finance assumes that investors are rational. Behavioral finance rejects that notion and studies how emotions and psychology affect investors and the financial markets. Most academics have rejected behavioral finance because of the perceived lack of practical applications. In this book, Dr. Howard shows how his methodologies can incorporate behavioral finance concepts into a very successful investment strategy. His evidence may give behavioral finance the academic credibility it deserves."

Maclyn Clouse, PhD, Professor of Finance,
Daniels College of Business, University of Denver

CONTENTS

FREE EBOOK VERSION

As a buyer of the print book of *Behavioral Portfolio Management* you can now download the eBook version free of charge to read on an eBook reader, your smartphone or your computer. Simply go to:

http://ebooks.harriman-house.com/behavioralportfolio

or point your smartphone at the QRC below.

You can then register and download your free eBook.

ABOUT THE AUTHOR

DR. HOWARD IS co-founder of AthenaInvest, a Greenwood Village-based SEC Registered Investment Advisor. He led the research project that resulted in Behavioral Portfolio Management, the methodology which underlies AthenaInvest's patented investment approach. Since 2002 he has managed Athena Pure Valuation/Profitability, Athena's signature equity offering, which has been recognized by PSN and Barron's as a top US active equity portfolio. He oversees Athena's ongoing research, which has led to a number of industry publications and conference presentations. Dr. Howard currently serves as CEO, Director of Research, and Chief Investment Officer at Athena.

Dr. Howard is a Professor Emeritus at the Reiman School of Finance, Daniels College of Business, University of Denver, where for over 30 years he taught courses and published articles in the areas of investment management and international finance. For many years he presented stock analysis seminars throughout the US for the American Association of Individual Investors, a national investment education organization headquartered in Chicago. Dr. Howard has been a guest lecturer at SDA

Bocconi, Italy's leading business school and at Handelshojskole Syd in Denmark and was a 2004 summer lecturer in international finance at EMLYON in France.

He consulted with a number of firms, most recently First Data Corp and Janus Capital Group, and served for ten years on the Board of Directors for AMG National Trust Bank N.A., a financial counselling and investment management firm headquartered in Denver.

After receiving his BS in Mechanical Engineering at the University of Idaho, Dr. Howard worked for three years at Proctor & Gamble as a production and warehouse manager. He then entered Oregon State University where he received an MS in Management Science, after which he received a Ph.D. in Finance from the University of Washington.

PREFACE

EMOTIONS PLAY A central role in financial markets – this is an uncontroversial statement for most market participants. However, for some it borders on intellectual heresy. They argue that, while emotions are present, their impact is mitigated by the arbitrage activities of rational investors and thus markets correctly price assets. But markets do not correctly price assets and indeed emotions trump arbitrage. Emotion is the proverbial elephant in the room of financial theorists. It is time to elevate emotions to their proper place in the pantheon of factors to be considered when making investment decisions.

This book explores the role emotions play in every aspect of financial markets, from how huge sophisticated markets price securities, to the conventional wisdom doled out by investment professionals, to the investment decisions made by individuals and professionals. Over the last 40 years, numerous studies in behavioral science have increasingly challenged the notion of humans as rational decision-makers. It is startling how difficult it is to find any significant amount of rationality in these studies! Markets are human institutions, so it is not surprising they too are driven by emotional decision-making.

While emotions are the focus, the analysis presented in this book is quantitative and objective in nature. My own background is quantitative, with degrees in mechanical engineering, management science, and finance. So as it became increasingly apparent to me that emotions play a central role in how securities are priced, I turned my attention to the behavioral science literature and how the impact of emotions could be objectively measured. This is a quantitative process that leans on many of the careful statistical techniques in current use by academics and higher-level practitioners. Whenever possible, I support my conclusions with my own large sample statistical studies as well as those conducted by other academics.

EMOTIONAL CROWDS AND BEHAVIORAL DATA INVESTORS

I present an alternative way of thinking about financial markets and how to go about investing in them. It draws upon the growing behavioral science literature as a challenge to the foundations and predictions of Modern Portfolio Theory. Viewing the world through the lens of investor behavior challenges much conventional wisdom regarding how to make investment decisions.

Throughout this book, I will focus on the interplay between two important groups: *Emotional Crowds* and *Behavioral Data Investors*. The story is set in the stock market, but its lessons are applicable to any market where Emotional Crowds play a dominant role. As information and events swirl about the market, Emotional Crowds respond by coalescing around the currently popular fearful or exciting scenarios. Humans are hardwired for myopic loss aversion and to herd, so it is not surprising that Crowds dominate, producing a stock market fraught with excess volatility and pricing distortions. Rather than making things safer, as in our evolutionary past, myopic loss aversion and herding instead destabilize financial markets.

Behavioral Data Investors (BDIs), on the other hand, step away from the Crowd and systematically determine where the market is providing opportunities, building successful portfolios based on their analysis. They release their emotional brakes and uncover the behavioral price distortions (and sometimes information opportunities) provided by Crowds. That is, Crowds and BDIs engage in a complex dance about the market.

Market events may exist for a short time, but the resulting emotions last well past the event that triggered them. Thus the emotional opportunities provided by the Crowd are measurable and persistent. BDIs know this, harnessing the resulting price distortions.

POWER OF RELEASING AND HARNESSING

Successful investing is emotionally difficult. It often requires waiting for long-term results when your portfolio was recently pummelled, recommending an investment when others think it is a dog, investing when volatility is high, and often looking and acting different from the Crowd. To be a successful investor, you must make a conscious decision to control your natural reactions and instead focus on decisions that flow from careful and thoughtful analysis. Staying disciplined in an emotionally-charged, 24-hour news cycle world is a challenge.

I believe that releasing your emotional brakes and then harnessing the price distortions created by the cognitive errors of others are the two most important things you can do in building a successful portfolio. The primary focus of this book is how to avoid becoming part of Emotional Crowds and, instead, develop into a successful BDI. In short, **release** and **harness**. The motivation for doing so is simple: on average Crowds underperform while their counterparts, BDIs, reap superior returns.

Behavioral science has introduced new terminology that aids in this transition, with concepts such as representativeness, availability cascades, loss aversion, peak-end memory, WYSIATI (what you see is all there is), anchoring, mental accounting, myopic loss aversion, social validation, phantastic objects, and many more. An important step in releasing your emotional brakes is to adopt this new terminology. It gives you the ability to see emotional decision making for what it is and reduce the chance of being swept away by the Crowd.

To be clear, this book is not about banishing emotions, for they play a central role in decision making and, without them, we would not have survived as humans and would be unable to function today. Rather, this book is about mastering your emotions and at the same time uncovering the role emotions play at every level of the investing process. You can be a very spiritual and emotional person, as am I, while at the same time making investment decisions based, not on emotion and intuition, but on careful, data-rich analysis. Such an approach leads to success in the world of investing.

Along the way I will discuss why it is important to shed many a conventional wisdom and instead look underneath the hood to determine what is really going on. Often conventional wisdom is catering to investor emotions and provides the basis for industry *best practices* (read *emotional catering*). Digging into the data and seeing for yourself what is really going on often reveals quite a different story.

So the steps to become a BDI are:

1. understand the dynamics of Emotional Crowds;
2. understand how an emotional investor makes decisions;
3. release your own emotional brakes, the first step of which is adopting a new terminology;
4. avoid the emotional conventional wisdom of the investment industry; and
5. harness behavioral price distortions.

This brings up an important consideration when becoming a BDI. By its very nature, you are often thinking and speaking differently than the Crowd. If social validation is important to you, then this will be a very difficult transition to make. I have been in this role my entire career. My wife frequently reminds me that I am tough to take out in polite company, since my views are so often different from the typical person. I bite my tongue often in social situations, but my being this way pays off handsomely in the stock market!

A PROFESSIONAL JOURNEY

In the early 1970s, I took a course that forever changed the way I thought about the world around me. It was a basic economics course taught by Professor Billy Hughel Wilkins. In his soothing Texas accent, he showed us how economists think about the world. What I found so fascinating was that many things did not turn out to be as they seemed. That is, conventional wisdom regarding economic matters and the United States in general were often wrong. By carefully looking at the evidence on important economic issues facing the US, we came to conclusions that were at odds with those frequently reported by the press and which were generally accepted.

This approach fascinated me and led to a career in which I seldom accept at face value what I am told about the economy and markets. Instead my modus operandi became exploring the underlying data in order to figure out what was really going on. I was struck with how often what was stated as truth about a situation was incorrect. I was hooked on the economist's way of thinking from that time on and spent the remainder of my graduate program focused on the tools used for testing empirically the explanations put forward regarding the economy and markets.

Many years later I read Steven Levitt and Stephan Dubner's *Freakonomics*, which fitted hand in glove with my own view of how best to understand complex issues. They explore everyday matters by uncovering relationships using data that virtually everybody else ignores when trying to understand what is really going on. They examine issues such as illicit drug-selling organizations and the decline of crime over the last several decades, coming up with often surprising and controversial conclusions.

Levitt and Dubner's view of economics is that if morality is how we would like people to act, then economics is how they actually act. In their view, incentives are the cornerstone of modern economic life and to understand why people or organizations do what they do, you need to understand the incentives driving them. This turns out to be incredibly important for understanding financial markets and, in particular, the institutions that have grown up around these markets.

RELUCTANTLY REJECTING MPT

I received my PhD in 1978 at what I now realize was the peak of Modern Portfolio Theory (MPT). Having a strong quant background, I was thrilled to see firsthand the launch of a simple, concise theory of capital market equilibrium. The rational behavior model, first proposed by Bernoulli in 1738, had become the standard within the social sciences and now, with the emergence of MPT, it was being placed at the very heart of finance.

But quickly it became apparent that MPT was not living up to its advanced billing. As I graduated, the small firm effect was being reported by Banz and the low PE effect was being reported by Basu. These two anomalies simultaneously challenged the Efficient Market Hypothesis (EMH) as well as the Capital Asset Pricing Model (CAPM), two pillars of MPT. Since then it has only gotten worse, with the CAPM now thoroughly discredited and the EMH riddled with gaping holes.

What is more, I now realize that the third pillar of MPT is built on emotionally-driven market volatility. That is, mean-variance optimization places emotions at the center of portfolio construction. Thus it is surprising to discover that, by focusing on volatility in building long-term portfolios, both emotions and returns are reduced while risk is increased. By using what is one of the most widely accepted portfolio models (its creator was awarded an Economics Nobel Prize in 1990), you are actually succumbing to the Crowd.

As my career progressed, the growing body of empirical evidence has led me to reject MPT in its entirety. In the spirit of Levitt and Dubner, I found conventional wisdom in the form of MPT to be wrong. The underlying data point to a much different reality – that is behavioral finance in which investors make emotional rather than rational decisions. In a variation on Levitt and Dubner's economics versus morality observation, it turns out that if MPT is the way investors ought to act, behavioral finance is the way they act in reality. Thus I concluded, with some nostalgia for the less messy way of viewing financial markets, that building portfolios based on MPT concepts is hazardous to your wealth. I view BPM as an alternative to MPT.

A PERSONAL JOURNEY

The material presented in this book is as much a personal journey as it is a professional one. I talk about releasing the emotional brakes that prevent us from building successful portfolios. You can have the best investment strategy, but if your emotional brakes are set, then you will ultimately fail.

My personal journey within – as they say, the scariest journey of them all – began about 25 years ago. During my 20s and 30s I kept saying to myself there were personal issues I needed to think about, but I was too busy with family and career, so put off this effort. But when I reached my 40th birthday I began this journey, the actual trigger for which is lost in the haze of time.

One of the books I read at the time was particularly influential: Scott Peck's *The Road Less Traveled*. It turns out that I've taken that road less traveled in thinking about investment decisions, as well as a range of other matters. With the help of 20/20 hindsight, I realize that I could not have made the professional journey that produced *Behavioral Portfolio Management* without also making the personal journey. As a result, I have been able to release many of the emotional brakes that I will discuss in the early part of this book, allowing me to build successful portfolios based on BPM concepts. In its own right, BPM is a road less traveled.

Lest I should be appearing to suggest I have completely mastered my emotions, let me confess to one of my emotional failures. I suffer from acrophobia, an unreasonable fear of heights. Take me up in a tall building and put me in front of a large window and I dissolve into an irrational panic, at times having difficulty even standing.

Twice my wife and I have gone up the Eiffel Tower. We took the elevator to the second level and she continued to the third level alone, leaving me trembling on the second level, unable to bring myself to take what I was convinced was the perilous journey to the third level. Twice she wrote our names on the wall on the third level without me, which took a little romance out of the Parisian experience. My acrophobia is a constant reminder of the challenge one faces when trying to master emotions; don't expect it to be easy.

ABOUT THIS BOOK

Two threads run throughout *Behavioral Portfolio Management*. First, conventional wisdom regarding the markets and how to invest in them is often wrong. As Einstein said, "Common sense is nothing but a collection of misconceptions acquired by age eighteen." As I will argue, common sense and conventional wisdom rarely lead to good investment decisions.

Second, to discover what works requires the careful analysis of large data sets over extended time periods. This kind of diligent effort is essential to uncovering those factors important for building successful portfolios. Put another way, what Daniel Kahneman calls System 1 thinking – dependence on anecdotal information and virtually automatic decision-making – is a sure route to underperformance. To be successful, it is important to turn on your slow and deliberate System 2 in order to tease out those behavioral factors critical to building successful portfolios.

As is frequently the case when discussing new ways of thinking about the world around us, it is easier to describe the final outcome than the process one needs to follow to get there. Most of the book is focused on a new way to think about financial markets and creative ways to build portfolios based on behavioral factors.

I will provide aids to help understand how to implement BPM. First, wherever possible I will provide practical suggestions on how to implement such things as releasing your own emotional brakes, as well as the emotional brakes of your clients. Much is being written about these processes and so I expect that you will have a number of suggestions available to you beyond this book.

Second, I will summarize the research underlying the transition from MPT to behavioral finance and then on to BPM so that you will not need to trace this journey for yourself by spending a great deal of time reading dense academic papers. For those who want to dig in further, I provide a comprehensive bibliography of the underlying BPM research at the end of the book.

This book is based on my 35 years in teaching, research, and actual portfolio management. I hope you find what I present useful in building a successful portfolio. And, finally, I leave you with the investor's blessing: may you always buy low and sell high (or at least 60% of the time)!

C. Thomas Howard
Denver, Colorado, 2014

ACKNOWLEDGEMENTS

IN BUILDING THE case for BPM, I frequently reference three books: Daniel Kahneman's *Thinking, Fast and Slow*, Nassim Taleb's *Fooled by Randomness*, and Hersh Shefrin's *Behavioralizing Finance*.

Kahneman, winner of the 2002 Nobel Memorial Prize in Economic Sciences, does a masterful job of presenting the major conclusions of Behavioral Science, providing numerous insights into how individuals actually make decisions using shortcuts and heuristics. The rational model it is not. Behavioral science came of age during the same time period over which MPT became the de facto standard in the investment management industry. I came to wish my own education and early experience would have included much more behavioral science and much less MPT, but it is better to be late than never as they say.

Taleb provides an eminently readable exposition on the challenge facing individuals in mastering one of the most difficult realties of the world: the random nature of events and markets. He contends that the complex and random nature of the investing world we face has outrun our brains' evolutionary hard wiring. To be successful, an investor must think of the world in terms of probabilities and previously unobserved dramatic events (*black swans* in his parlance). This requires a dose of heavy-duty analytic thinking – what Kahneman refers to as System 2 thinking. The BDI spends most of the time engaging the cerebral cortex portion of the brain and little time engaging the intuitive limbic portion of the brain.

Shefrin, in *Behavioralizing Finance*, provides a systematic analysis of how behavioral assumptions impact various aspects of modern finance theory. He posits a world in which investors begin with unequal wealth endowments, have different probability assessments of future events (some are pessimistic, some are optimistic, some are overconfident, and some are rational, with probability assessments changing over time), and have different risk preferences.

The result is a composite probability distribution of future events which differs in important respects from the true probability distribution. The differences between composite and true probabilities leads to pricing distortions. Individual securities, as well as market-wide indices, can go from being undervalued to overvalued and back again. Shefrin believes that "the future of finance will combine realistic assumptions from behavioral finance and rigorous analysis from neoclassical finance." I hope to take a step in this direction by showing the implications of such a dynamic pricing model for how investing decisions should be made in light of emotional investors.

I must mention Robert Haugen and his book *The Inefficient Stock Market*. In the mid-90s as I was actively questioning the validity of MPT, I came across this excellent book which confirmed many of the things I was thinking at the time. It provided arguments and empirical results challenging the pillars of MPT. He essentially posited a behavioral market in which pricing distortions were common. He captured these distortions by means of a multi-factor proxy model based on PE ratios, growth rates, debt ratios, and other company characteristics. I used his book in my securities classes at Daniels for nearly 20 years. Haugen provided an important stepping stone on my journey to BPM, and for that I am thankful.

I would like to thank Craig Callahan, friend and colleague, for posing the initial questions and providing support for the research project which has produced one surprising result after another and is the basis for this book. Gary Black of Janus Capital saw early potential in this project and provided initial research funding. For many years I have enjoyed and benefited from my conversations with my friend and industry veteran Andrew Cox. Academic colleagues Russ Wermers, Levon Goukasian, Hersh Shefrin, Oliver Boguth, Russ Goyenko, Randy Cohen, Malcolm Baker and Gene Fama have provided useful insights over the years. Jeff Wurgler, Ken French and Jay Ritter generously provided data for testing purposes. This book would not have been possible without the support and infrastructure development provided by my colleagues at AthenaInvest: Andy Howard, Joel Coppin and Lambert Bunker.

And most importantly, the unwavering love and support of my wife Mitch has been indispensable. She has stood by me for 40 years, through the trying years of the PhD program and now through the trying years of launching a new business. To her I dedicate this book with love.

EXECUTIVE SUMMARY

IN THIS EXECUTIVE summary I present the most important features and conclusions of my research, broken down by chapter so that readers can navigate to topics of interest. This Executive Summary thus acts as a more detailed contents page – helping you find your way to specific areas – and also provides a guide to the most significant conclusions that I present.

* * *

Behavioral Portfolio Management (BPM) is presented as a superior way to make investment decisions. BPM's first basic principle is that Emotional Crowds dominate the determination of both prices and volatility, with fundamentals playing a small role. The second basic principle is that Behavioral Data Investors earn superior returns. The third basic principle is that investment risk is the chance of underperformance. (See Chapter 1.)

Emotions and heuristics dominate our decision process – they act as brakes on our investing, preventing us from making good decisions. How do we avoid falling prey to emotionally-driven and ineffective heuristics?

This is a challenge since money and market volatility stir up strong emotions and so we have to constantly work to not let them control our thinking. (See Chapter 2.)

We do not have the ability to intuitively identify trends in financial time series. Thus a successful market timing approach must be based on rigorous analysis, revealing both statistical and economic significance. The identification of such a process is complicated by investor myopic loss aversion, driving us to seek relief from short-term losses, while making us susceptible in any number of poorly tested timing techniques. Achieving a DNA level understanding of randomness is a critical step to becoming a successful Behavioral Data Investor. (See Chapter 3.)

The investment industry is dominated by a Cult of Emotions in which investors make emotional decisions and the industry does little to discourage them to do otherwise. Particularly pernicious are the Cult Enforcers who use the emotional tools of MPT to keep investors from building superior portfolios. (See Chapter 4.)

The typical emotional, anecdotal investor makes poor decisions. Myopic loss aversion interacts with social validation which interacts with availability bias which interacts with mental accounting and so on, leading to the careful creation of inferior portfolios. (See Chapter 5.)

Like any good scientific, rational, truth-seeking organization, the finance profession has chosen to reject the world rather than reject the empirically discredited MPT. Now that we have spent the last 40 years, essentially my entire professional career, waiting for evidence supportive of MPT to appear and seeing none, it is time to move on. Luckily an alternative is emerging: behavioral finance. (See Chapter 6.)

Diversification, remembering the name of the stock in which you invested, and the price you paid for it, are a few of the things that lead to poor investment decisions and should be avoided. (See Chapter 7.)

The traditional mountain chart for representing investment performance is an emotionally-driven, random representation of portfolio returns. Instead, return histograms and matched returns are a more meaningful way to present what an investor can expect when making an investment. Equity return distributions are self-healing in that negative returns are more than offset by matching positive returns within the distribution. Investor patience is rewarded by this self-healing feature. (See Chapter 8.)

Among active equity mutual fund managers, style drift is part and parcel of superior performance. Without style drift, a manager cannot produce superior investment returns. The ill-conceived, leaderless stampede that is the style grid is a major contributor to active equity underperformance. The consistent pursuit of a narrowly-defined equity strategy, while taking high-conviction positions, produces both superior performance and style drift. (See Chapter 9.)

In the pantheon of investment virtues, diversification is right up there. It is so widely accepted that nary an objection is raised against it. I feel much differently and, in fact, I believe there are very few situations in which diversification makes sense. It is akin to bubble wrapping your portfolio. (See Chapter 10.)

While emotions are part and parcel of human nature, responding to gut-wrenching volatility by exiting the stock market hurts both short-term and long-term portfolio performance. At the very least, clients should stay the course in the face of rising volatility, and maybe even increase equity exposure. In short, they should avoid falling into the Volatility Trap. (See Chapter 11.)

It is important to distinguish between emotions and investment risk so that good decisions are made. Most currently used measures of risk are really measures of emotion. As it stands, finance academics have almost nothing meaningful to say about measuring true investment risk. (See Chapter 12.)

When building a successful strategy, it is necessary to identify a limited number of behavioral factors upon which to focus. Superior portfolios are created by consistently pursuing a narrowly-defined investment strategy while taking high-conviction positions. What matters in executing a strategy is not consistent returns and not a consistent set of stock characteristics such as market cap and PE, but rather the consistent pursuit of the strategy. (See Chapter 13.)

Stock picking skill is common among active equity mutual funds. Much of that skill resides among buy-side analysts with portfolio managers displaying less skill. Best and worst stocks are identified using the relative holdings of active equity managers. (See Chapter 14.)

Superior performance is driven by the consistent pursuit of a narrowly-defined strategy, while investing in a small number of high-conviction positions that have been identified based on a small set of measurable and persistent behavioral price distortions. (See Chapter 15.)

Dividends provide valuable information regarding future company performance and, as a result, stock performance, while at the same time providing signals about future volatility. These are good reasons to consider dividends when analyzing, buying and selling stocks, and dividends should play a prominent role in an equity strategy. (See Chapter 16.)

The best markets are identified by means of deep behavioral currents in contrast to trying to time the choppiness on the surface. The goal is to uncover behavioral measures that are predictive of expected market returns. The resulting expected market returns are then used for executing a behavioral market timing strategy. (See Chapter 17.)

Behavioral price distortions will persist for a very long time. Throughout my career, my professional colleagues attempted to explain the anomalies bedeviling the EMH, but things have only gotten worse, with more anomalies than ever. So I've decided to be the student picking up the $100 bill on the sidewalk and not the professor spouting the rationality model. (See Chapter 18.)

CHAPTER 1: BEHAVIORAL PORTFOLIO MANAGEMENT

ON THE FIRST day of my securities class, I would lay out a $1, $5, $20 and $100 bill on the front table. I would then ask the class which they would choose. I got puzzled looks from the students, wondering whether this was some kind of trick or whether I had lost my marbles.

After some assurances from me, they all agreed that they would pick the $100 dollar bill. I then explained that the four bills represented the expected payoff on four different *investments*, with the same holding period and equal initial investments. Not surprisingly, they all again chose the $100 investment.

I further explained that each of the four investments represented somewhat different levels of risk, with the $100 investment the least risky (this last point being contrary to conventional wisdom, as I explain further in Chapter 12). But the real difference across the four investments was that there was considerably more emotion associated with the ever larger payoffs. Now the choice was not so clear. It was obvious that they were trying to conduct some sort of return, risk, emotion trade-off.

The four *investments* are proxies for choices typically available to investors. The $1 bill represents an investment in default-free treasury bills, the $5 bill an investment in bonds, the $20 bill an investment in the stock market, and the $100 bill an investment in an active equity portfolio earning an excess return. The payoffs roughly capture the relationship of ending values for each of these investments over a long time period, say 30 years.

I then challenged the students by stating that over their investment lifetimes few will choose the $20 investment and a countable, small number will choose the $100 investment. Instead, most will build portfolios heavily made up of $1 and $5 investments. They will do this because they apply emotional brakes during the investment process and, what is worse, will be encouraged to do so by the emotion enablers that currently dominate the investment industry.

Consequently the typical investor leaves hundreds of thousands if not millions of dollars on the table during their investing lifetime, because they aren't able to release their emotional brakes and the industry does little to encourage them to do otherwise.

THE TRIUMPH OF REALITY OVER RATIONALITY

Consider the following allegory:

> The finance professor and his student are walking to lunch one day and come upon a $100 bill lying on the sidewalk. The student leans over to pick it up but is restrained by the professor with the admonition "Do not bother to try to pick it up, for if it were real, it would have already been scooped up. So our eyes must be playing tricks on us." The student responds "With all due respect professor, I do not believe in your rationality model," then leans over to pick up the bill and stuffs it into his pocket.

Ten years ago I was the professor and now I'm the student picking up the $100 bill and stuffing it in my clients' pockets.

Behavioral Portfolio Management (BPM) is set in a world in which prices rarely reflect underlying fundamentals – instead they are driven by emotional crowds who are unable or unwilling to release their emotional brakes. BPM focuses on how investors, advisors and asset managers can go about releasing their own emotional brakes and harnessing the behavioral price distortions uncovered by means of careful research.

BPM is based on my research and the research of other behavioral and finance academics, as well as my experience in managing active equity portfolios. Along the way, BPM rejects the rationality-based concepts and methods of Modern Portfolio Theory, the primary tools used by those industry professionals who I will refer to as Cult Enforcers. The most important conclusion of BPM is that *building high performance portfolios is surprisingly straightforward but emotionally difficult.*

MY BPM TRANSFORMATION

I began my career steeped in the concepts of MPT. Early on, I was able to release my emotional brakes to the point of being able to concentrate my investment portfolio in the $20 investment (i.e. 100% allocation to equities). For many years I continued to believe that hiring an active equity manager was the triumph of hope over reality, so I invested in equity index funds rather than in actively managed funds. More recently, my ideas began to change, based on my research and the research of others, and I am now a strong believer in active management.

In July 2002 I began managing what has become AthenaInvest's flagship concentrated stock portfolio, Athena Pure Valuation/Profitability, earning a nearly 25% compound annual return over a 12-year time period. During 2013, it produced a greater than 60% return. One needs to remain humble whenever reporting results like these, since, as 2002 Nobel laureate Daniel Kahneman of Princeton University reminds us, "reversion to the mean can be just around the corner."

But I am encouraged that we are heading in the right direction in that our other portfolios, among them mutual fund allocation, equity dividend, ETF, hedge fund, and global tactical ETF, are all producing superior returns. Like Pure, each portfolio is based on harnessing behavioral factors that have been identified through careful research as measurable and persistent emotionally-driven price distortions.

We do not attempt to out-analyze or outsmart other professional investors by creating a superior information mosaic for the investments we make. Instead, we attempt to understand the emotional crowds that dominate market pricing and, in managing our portfolios, exercise the consistency and persistence necessary to earn superior returns. In short, we practice BPM.

At first I was rather surprised by my portfolio performance. But as I conducted additional research and carefully reviewed the finance literature, I found that building a successful portfolio is not uncommon within the industry and the way in which I had been managing Pure is very similar to the way others who are successful manage their portfolios. Thus over time my methodology became embedded in a broader research stream which I will report on in the remainder of this book. The rest of this chapter is devoted to the foundational concepts underlying BPM.

EVOLVING MARKET PARADIGM

Equity market theory has passed through two distinctly different paradigms over the last 80 years and currently is experiencing the rise of a third. The first paradigm was launched in 1934 when Benjamin Graham and David Dodd of Columbia Business School published *Security Analysis*, the first systematic approach to analyzing and investing in stocks. Graham and Dodd (GD) argued that it was possible to build superior stock portfolios using careful fundamental analysis and a set of simple decision rules. These rules were based on behavioral price distortions as identified by fundamental analysis. The success of GD is all the more impressive as their book appeared in the depths of the Great Depression, when stocks were crashing and market volatility reached levels not seen before or since.

GD's dominance lasted 40 years, until it was pushed aside in the mid-1970s by the ascendency of Modern Portfolio Theory. MPT accepted the fact that there were many emotional investors, but argued there existed enough rational investors to arbitrage away any resulting price distortions and therefore market prices were *informationally efficient*. A prediction of this theory was that it was not worth conducting a GD type of analysis, nor any analysis for that matter, and instead an investor should buy and hold an index portfolio.

MPT immediately ran into problems in the late 1970s when S. Basu of McMaster University published a study demonstrating that low PE stocks outperformed high PE stocks and Rolf Banz of Northwestern University published a study in the early 1980s demonstrating that small stocks outperformed large stocks. MPT had no answer for these anomalies and so in order to save the model the two anomalies were sucked in as *return factors*. Never mind that it was never determined whether these represented risk or opportunities and that recent studies show these two effects disappearing. It was better to have them inside the theory rather than outside challenging the theory's credibility. It has been downhill ever since for MPT, with study after study uncovering one pricing anomaly after another.

As MPT was rising to prominence, a parallel research effort was studying how individuals actually made decisions. The conclusion of this behavioral science research stream was that emotions and heuristics dominate decision making. It is amazing how little rationality was uncovered in these studies!

Because of the many problems facing MPT and the growing awareness of provocative behavioral science results, we are witnessing the decline of MPT and the rise of behavioral finance. Among other things, this transition brings back Graham and Dodd as an important way to analyze the market's faulty pricing mechanism.

BEHAVIORAL PORTFOLIO MANAGEMENT

Behavioral Portfolio Management, henceforth referred to as BPM, is an approach to managing investment portfolios that assumes most investors make decisions based on emotions and shortcut heuristics. It posits that there are two categories of financial market participants: Emotional Crowds and Behavioral Data Investors.

Emotional Crowds are made up of those investors who base decisions on emotional and intuitive reactions to unfolding events and anecdotal evidence. Human evolution has hardwired us for the short run, loss aversion, and social validation, which are the underlying drivers of today's Emotional Crowds. Emotional investors make their decisions based on what Daniel Kahneman refers to as System 1 thinking: automatic, loss avoiding, quick, with little or no effort and no sense of voluntary control.[1]

On the other hand, Behavioral Data Investors, henceforth referred to as BDIs, make their decisions using thorough and extensive analysis of available data in order to tease out stable pricing relationships. BDIs make decisions based on what Kahneman refers to as System 2 thinking: effortful, high concentration, and complex. BPM is built on the dynamic interplay between these two investor groups.

MPT, as the prevailing theory of financial markets, posits that even though there are numerous irrational investors (think emotional, heuristic investors), the price discovery process is dominated by rational investors who quickly arbitrage away any price distortions. This implies a number of things regarding markets, such as prices fully reflecting all relevant information, the lack of excess returns to active investing, and the superiority of indexed portfolios over their actively-managed counterparts. In short, MPT contends that rational investors dominate the financial pricing process.

What if it is the other way around, that is, what if emotional investors dominate? Put another way, what if emotion trumps arbitrage? If this were the case, then price distortions would be common and could be used to build superior portfolios relative to the corresponding indexed

---

[1] Daniel Kahneman, *Thinking, Fast and Slow* (Farrar, Straus and Giroux, 2012).

portfolios. Active management could generate superior returns. In fact we would see the impact of emotions in every corner of the market and they would have to be taken into account when managing investment portfolios.

There is now ample evidence, which I will review shortly, supporting the argument that Emotional Crowds dominate market pricing and volatility. Emotional Crowds drive prices based on the latest pessimistic or optimistic scenarios. Amplifying these price movements is a market in which trading is virtually free and so there is little natural resistance to stocks moving dramatically in one direction or the other. "If anything is worth doing, it is worth overdoing," is the market's mantra.

Rational investors, or what I call BDIs, react to the resulting distortions by taking positions opposite the Emotional Crowd. But they are not of sufficient heft to keep prices in line. As a consequence, the resulting distortions are measurable and persistent. BDIs are able to build portfolios that harness these distortions as they are eventually corrected by the market, either rationally or simply because the Crowd is now moving in the other direction.

THE EMOTIONAL CROWD, BDI INTERPLAY

BPM is built on the dynamic interplay between Crowds and BDIs. Crowds more often than not dominate market pricing and it is only by chance that individual security prices fairly reflect underlying value. Price distortions partially offset one another when aggregated across all securities, but even at the market level significant distortions remain. Thus prices more commonly reflect emotions than they do underlying value.

The events that trigger Crowd responses may be short lived, but the subsequent emotions are long lasting. As a result, price distortions are both measurable and persistent. This provides BDIs with an opportunity to identify distortions and build portfolios benefiting from them. Even though a BDI portfolio will outperform, building such a portfolio is emotionally difficult because the BDI is frequently going against the Crowd. The need for social validation acts as a powerful deterrent for most investors. Given the difficulty of behavior modification, there is little reason to believe that this situation will change any time soon. So I contend that BDIs will have a return advantage relative to Crowds into the foreseeable future.

BDIs depend upon Emotional Crowds for generating superior returns. But the impact of emotion is felt well beyond this relationship. Market professionals, such as portfolio managers, mutual funds, hedge funds, institutional funds, consultants and financial advisors are also impacted. Viewing the world through the lens of BPM reveals that the decisions made by these professionals are often based on faulty emotional analysis. It appears that much of what passes as professional analytics and due diligence is a way to rationalize emotional catering.

In this book, I focus on managing *equity* portfolios as a way to illustrate the three basic principles of BPM, with the proviso that these principles apply to managing portfolios in other markets as well.

1. BPM's first basic principle, that Emotional Crowds dominate market pricing and volatility, is presented along with supporting evidence.

2. The second basic principle, that BDIs earn superior returns, is presented along with supporting evidence from the active equity mutual fund research stream. I also discuss the evidence regarding average equity fund performance and reconcile these two results.

3. The third basic principle, that investment risk is the chance of underperformance, is presented alongside the argument that emotions need to be carefully distinguished from investment risk.

I now discuss each of these basic principles in more detail.

THE BASIC PRINCIPLES OF BPM
Basic Principle I: Emotional crowds dominate pricing

The dynamic interplay between Emotional Crowds and BDIs is the focus of BPM. In contrast to MPT, I posit that the Crowd more often than not dominates the price discovery process. This means that prices infrequently reflect true underlying value and, even at the overall market level, price distortions are the rule rather than the exception.[2]

For many market participants, the first principle is uncontroversial. The chaotic nature of the stock market shows few outward sign of rationality as prices swing wildly based on the latest events or rumors. For many investors, the contention that prices are emotionally determined is consistent with their market experiences. But it is necessary to go beyond what a majority of investors believe and examine what stock price data tell us regarding the importance of emotions in the price discovery process.

There is considerable evidence that stock prices are driven by something other than fundamentals and that emotions play a major role. I now discuss what I believe are the two most germane research streams. The first stream deals with excess stock market volatility. Robert Shiller of Yale – 2013 Nobel laureate – highlighted excess volatility in 1981 and since then it has been hotly debated. But after 30 years of empirical efforts to explain excess volatility and thus resurrect the Efficient Markets Hypothesis, Shiller stands by his initial assertion:

> "After all the efforts to defend the efficient markets theory there is still every reason to think that, while markets are not totally crazy, they contain quite substantial noise, so substantial that it dominates the movements in the aggregate market. The efficient markets model, for the aggregate stock market, has still never been supported by any study effectively linking stock market fluctuations with subsequent fundamentals."[3]

---

[2] Shefrin (2008) introduces the concept of "knife edge" market efficiency which exists only with the occurrence of a rare combination of wealth and investor emotions. Thus he argues stock prices rarely reflect underlying fundamentals.

[3] Robert Shiller, 'From Efficient Market Theory to Behavioral Finance', *Journal of Economic Perspectives* 17 (2003), pp. 83-104.

The fact that noise, rather than fundamentals, dominates market price movements is clear evidence that Crowds dominate stock pricing.

The Equity Premium Puzzle research stream provides additional evidence that emotions play a prominent role. The long-term equity risk premium should be associated with long-term fundamental risks. Rajnish Mehra of the University of California, Santa Barbara and 2004 Nobel laureate Edward Prescott of Arizona State University report that the US stock market has generated a risk premium averaging around 7% annually from the 1870s to the present. They argue that this premium is too large, by a factor of two or three, relative to fundamental market risk, so they coined the term *Equity Premium Puzzle*.[4] Over the last 25 years, there have been numerous attempts to find a fundamental explanation of this puzzle, but with little success.

However, Shlomo Benartzi of UCLA and Richard Thaler of the University of Chicago provide an emotional explanation:

> "The equity premium puzzle refers to the empirical fact that stocks have outperformed bonds over the last century by a surprisingly large margin. We offer a new explanation based on two behavioral concepts. First, investors are assumed to be "loss averse," meaning that they are distinctly more sensitive to losses than to gains. Second, even long-term investors are assumed to evaluate their portfolios frequently. We dub this combination "myopic loss aversion." Using simulations, we find that the size of the equity premium is consistent with the previously estimated parameters of prospect theory if investors evaluate their portfolios annually."[5]

The observed 7% equity premium is thus the result of short-term loss aversion and the investor ritual of evaluating portfolio performance

---

[4] R. Mehra and E. Prescott, 'The equity premium: A puzzle', *Journal of Monetary Economics* 15 (1985), pp. 145–161and R. Mehra and E. Prescott, 'The Equity Premium in Retrospect', NBER Working Paper No. 952 (February 2003).

[5] S. Benartzi and R. Thaler, 'Myopic Loss Aversion and the Equity Premium Puzzle', *Quarterly Journal of Economics* 110:1 (1995), pp. 73-92.

annually, rather than the result of fundamental risk. Putting these two results together leads to the conclusion that both stock market volatility and long-term returns are largely determined by investor emotions.

Beyond these two emotion-driven results, numerous other pricing distortions have been uncovered. Many of these have been linked to the decision errors documented in the behavioral science literature. David Hirshleifer of the University of California, Irvine provides three organizing principles to place the price distortion phenomena into a systematic structure:

1. People rely on heuristics because people face cognitive limitations. Owing to a shared evolutionary history, people might be predisposed to rely on the same heuristics and therefore be subject to the same biases (read *Emotional Crowds*).

2. People inadvertently signal their inner states to others. This means that nature might have selected for traits such as overconfidence in order that people signal strong confidence to others.

3. People's judgments and decisions are subject to their own emotions as well as to their reason.

Santa Clara University's Hersh Shefrin, in *Behavioralizing Finance*, provides an excellent summary of four behavioral finance studies, including David Hirshleifer, mentioned above, along with Nicholas Barberis of Yale University and Richard Thaler; Malcolm Baker of Harvard, Richard Ruback of Harvard, and Jeffrey Wurgler of NYU; and Avanidhar Subrahmanyam of UCLA. He also presents a comprehensive list of behavioral finance articles.

THE INEFFECTIVENESS OF ARBITRAGE

A key difference between BPM and MPT is the extent to which arbitrage is effective in eliminating stock price distortions. Research over the last 40 years has shown that arbitrage has not been able to eliminate such distortions, termed *anomalies* since they are inconsistent with

Efficient Market predictions. There are three possible reasons for this lack of effectiveness:

1. the difficulty in identifying arbitrage opportunities,

2. arbitrage is costly and risky, or

3. there are few if any market participants willing to engage in arbitrage.

Clearly stocks are difficult to value and so there is validity to the first reason. But even when the price distortion can be accurately estimated, such as with closed-end funds, the distortions persist. Cost and risk clearly make arbitrage difficult, but one would think that there is sufficient incentive to attract a large number of arbitragers into the stock market.

However, recent results by Bradford Cornell of the California Institute of Technology, and Wayne Landsman and Stephen Stubben, both of the University of North Carolina, are discouraging in this regard. They find a tendency for both mutual funds and sell-side analysts to exacerbate sentiment-driven price movements, rather than dampen them as one would expect of supposedly rational investors. That is, institutional professionals tend to join the Emotional Crowds rather than act as BDIs.

David McLean of MIT and Jeffrey Pontiff of Boston College explore the limits when arbitraging academically-identified anomalies. Starting with a sample of 82 such anomalies, they find that two-thirds of resulting excess returns remain even five years after publication. Furthermore, they find that the effectiveness of arbitrage has not improved in recent years, even with steep declines in transaction costs and the greater dominance of supposedly rational institutional investors.

Indeed, emotion trumps arbitrage.

Finally, Hersh Shefrin's insightful observation is of interest:

> "Finance is in the midst of a paradigm shift, from a neoclassical based framework to a psychologically based framework. Behavioral finance is the application of psychology to financial decision

making and financial markets. Behavioralizing finance is the process of replacing neoclassical assumptions with behavioral counterparts. ... the future of finance will combine realistic assumptions from behavioral finance and rigorous analysis from neoclassical finance."[6]

Thus Basic Principle I, that Emotional Crowds dominate pricing, is a logical first step in building an effective decision process for investing.

Basic Principle II: Behavioral data investors earn superior returns

Basic Principle I would seem to open the door for BDIs to earn superior returns by taking positions opposite the Crowd. This is not necessarily the case, since even though there is little doubt emotions increase volatility, the resulting distortions might be random and unpredictable, making it difficult if not impossible to take advantage of them. So beyond the fact that emotions drive prices, it is necessary to show that the resulting distortions are measurable and persistent.

The behavioral finance literature is full of examples of measurable stock price distortions.[7] It would therefore seem easy to build superior performing portfolios, but in order to do so means taking positions that are different from the Crowd. The powerful need for social validation acts as a strong deterrent for many investors, discouraging them from pursuing such an approach. It is tough to leave the Emotional Crowd and become a BDI. Thus price distortions are measurable and persistent, but building a portfolio benefiting from these distortions is emotionally difficult.

In order to demonstrate that it is possible to earn superior returns, I turn to active equity mutual fund research. This group of investors is one of the most studied in finance because of the availability of extensive, long-

---

[6] Hersh Shefrin, *Behavioralizing Finance* (Now Publishers Inc., 2010).

[7] See the behavioral finance summaries in Shefrin (2010), Hirshleifer (2008), Barberis and Thaler (2003), Baker et al. (2007), and Subrahmanyam (2007).

time-period data. One stream within this large body of research reveals that active equity funds are successful stock pickers.[8] Rather than focus on long-term fund performance, these studies examine individual fund holdings and confirm that a fund's top stock picks produce superior returns.[9] The most compelling results are reported by Randy Cohen, Christopher Polk and Bernhard Silli (CPS), and these are reproduced in Figure 1.1.

FIGURE 1.1: ANALYSIS OF FUNDS' TOP STOCK PICKS

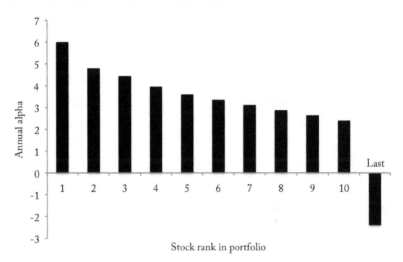

Based on Graph 3 in Cohen, Polk, and Silli (2010). The graph shows, over the subsequent quarter, the average six factor adjusted annual alpha for the largest relative overweighted stock in a mutual fund portfolio, the next most overweighted, and so forth. Based on all active US equity mutual funds from 1991 to 2005.

Figure 1.1 reveals that a fund's best idea, as measured by the largest relative portfolio weight, generates an average six factor, annualized after-

---

[8] See articles by Alexander, Cici, and Gibson (2007); Baker, Litov, Wachter and Wurgler (2004); Chen, Hong, Jegadeesh, and Wermers (2000); Cohen, Polk and Silli (2010); Collins and Fabozzi (2000); Frey and Herbst (2010); Kacperczyk and Seru (2007); Keswani and Stolin (2008); Kosowski, Timermann, Wermers, and White (2006); Pomorski (2009); Shumway, Szeter, and Yuan (2009); and Wermers (2000).

[9] There is another research stream that shows truly active managers are able to earn superior returns. See Amihud and Goyenko (2013); Brands, Brown, and Gallagher (2006); Cremers and Petajisto (2009); Kacperczyk, Sialm, and Zheng (2005); and Wermers (2010).

the-fact alpha of 6%. What is more, the next best idea stocks also generate positive alphas. This is evidence that it is possible to build a superior stock portfolio. CPS did not explore the source of these returns, but it is reasonable to conjecture that much of the return is the result of fund BDIs (buy-side analysts and portfolio managers) harnessing behavioral factors. Probably of less importance is the investment team's ability to build a superior information mosaic for the stocks in which they invest.[10]

RECONCILING TWO STOCK PICKING SKILL RESEARCH STREAMS

A better known conclusion from this line of research is that the average active equity mutual fund earns a return that is less than, or at best equal to, the index return.[11] That is, the average fund earns a zero or negative alpha. This leads to the oft-stated conclusion that equity fund managers lack stock picking skill, which is in fact the opposite of what was just presented.

One would think that professional investors, such as mutual funds, hedge funds, and institutional managers, would be BDIs. Indeed, the analysts within such organizations are most often BDIs, but the further up one goes in the organization and the larger the fund, the more like the Crowd it becomes.

In order to grow AUM, funds must attract and retain emotional investors, which means the fund often caters to client emotions and thus ends up taking on the features of the Crowd. As the fund grows in size, it increasingly invests in those stocks favored by the Crowd, since it is easier

---

[10] It is an open research question to determine the source of these excess returns, that is, what portion is due to harnessing behavioral factors and what portion is due to generating a superior information mosaic. It is difficult to untangle these two return drivers, so for now we are left with the plausible supposition that emotionally-driven prices are the most important source of excess returns for fund managers.

[11] See Bollen and Busse (2004); Brown and Goetzmann (1995); Carhart (1997); Elton, Gruber and Blake (1996); Hendricks, Patel, and Zeckhauser (1991); Jensen (1968); and Fama and French (2010).

to attract and retain clients by investing in those stocks to which clients are emotionally attached.[12] What often starts out as BDIs harnessing behavioral factors ends up with a fund morphing into something that is acceptable to the Crowd, a process I refer to as "bubble wrapping" the portfolio. Such behavior is rational on the part of the fund, as revenues are based on AUM.[13] Consistent with this argument, others have found that returns decline as the fund grows large.[14]

The combination of the many documented price distortions and the excess returns earned by active equity mutual funds on their best idea stocks provides empirical support for basic principle II. But many investors will find it more difficult to assimilate principle II than principle I, since the emotional barrier of social validation must be overcome in order to build a successful BDI portfolio.

Basic Principle III: Investment risk is the chance of underperformance

There is no more confusing issue regarding the role of investor emotions than how to measure investment risk. Those measures currently used to capture investment risk, once carefully examined, are mostly measures of emotion. As an example take *volatility*, as measured by return standard deviation. Earlier I reviewed the evidence regarding stock market volatility which concludes that most volatility is generated by Crowds overreacting to information flowing into the market. Indeed, almost none of the current volatility can be explained by changes in underlying economic fundamentals at both the market and individual stock level. So

---

[12] Other possible reasons why a fund might purchase other than best idea stocks, as the fund grows in size, is mimicking the index to lock in a past alpha and becoming a closet indexer to avoid style drift and tracking error.

[13] J. B. Berk and R. C. Green, 'Mutual Fund Flows and Performance in Rational Markets', *Journal of Political Economy* 112:6 (2004), pp. 1269-1295.

[14] See Chen, Hong, Huang, and Kubik (2004); Han, Noe, and Rebello (2008); and Pollet and Wilson (2006).

volatility is mostly a measure of emotions and not necessarily investment risk. This is also true of other measures, such as downside standard deviation, maximum drawdown and downside capture.

Investment risk is the chance of underperformance. Measuring underperformance depends on the time horizon of the investment and the specific goal of the investor. For example, if the goal is to have a fixed amount at a fixed time in the future (e.g. $100,000 in two years), risk is measured as the chance of ending up with less than $100,000 in two years. In this case, short-term volatility is an important contributor to risk.

In cases where there is a specific long-term need (e.g. $1,000,000 in 30 years), risk is measured as the chance of not meeting this goal. In the cases where there is no specific time horizon, however, the appropriate benchmark is the highest expected return investment being considered, since over long time periods the actual return should approximate the expected return due to the law of large numbers. Most long-term investment situations fall into the latter.

Another important consideration is that short-term volatility plays an ever smaller role as the time horizon lengthens. This is because the short-term emotionally and economically-driven price changes tend to offset one another over the long run, to the tune of reducing long-term volatility by a factor of three to four relative to short-term volatility.

RISK AND VOLATILITY ARE NOT SYNONYMOUS

The widely used mean-variance optimization methodology for constructing portfolios was first introduced in 1952 by 1990 Nobel Prize laureate Harry Markowitz of the Rand Corporation:

> "We first consider the rule that the investor does (or should) maximize discounted expected, or anticipated, returns. This rule is rejected both as a hypothesis to explain, and as a maxim to guide investment behavior. We next consider the rule that the investor does (or should) consider expected return a desirable thing and

variance of return an undesirable thing. This rule has many sound points, both as a maxim for, and hypothesis about, investment behavior."[15]

Unfortunately, the industry took this approach and mistakenly began building portfolios by minimizing *short-term* volatility relative to *long-term* returns. This places emotion at the very heart of the long horizon portfolio construction process. In the context of BPM, the reason this approach became so popular is that it legitimizes the emotional reaction of investors to short-term volatility. I refer to this as the unholy alliance between mean-variance optimization, on the one hand, and emotional investors on the other. This is a classic case of catering to client emotions.

Currently, risk and volatility are frequently thought of as interchangeable. One of the ironies is that, by focusing on short-term volatility when building long-horizon portfolios, it is almost certain that investment risk increases. Since risk is the chance of underperformance, focusing on short-term volatility will often lead to investing in lower expected return markets (e.g. low expected return bonds versus higher expected return stocks) with little impact on long-term volatility.[16] Lowering expected portfolio return in an effort to reduce short-term volatility actually increases the chance of underperformance, which means increasing risk.

A clear example of this is the comparison of long-term stock and bond returns. Stocks dramatically outperform bonds over the long run, so by investing in bonds rather than stocks, short-term volatility is reduced at the expense of decreasing the long-term return and, in turn, increasing long-term investment risk. Equating short-term volatility with risk leads to inferior long-horizon portfolios.

The cost of equating risk and emotional volatility can be seen in other areas as well. It is known that many investors pull out of the stock market when faced with heightened volatility, but research shows that this is

---

[15] H. Markowitz, 'Portfolio Selection', *The Journal of Finance* 7:1 (March 1952), pp. 77-91.

[16] Higher return variance lowers an investment's long-term compound return, but this impact is small compared to the impact of investing in lower expected return markets.

exactly when they should remain in the market and even increase their stock holdings, as subsequent returns are higher on average while volatility declines.[17]

It is also the case that many investors exit after the market declines only to miss the subsequent rebound. This was dramatically the case following the 2008 market crash when investors withdrew billions of dollars from equity mutual funds during a period in which the stock market more than doubled. The end result is that investors frequently suffer the pain of losses without capturing the subsequent gains.[18] Again this is the result of not carefully separating emotions from risk and thus allowing emotions to drive investment decisions.

ASSIMILATING BASIC PRINCIPLE III

Principle III will likely be the most difficult to assimilate. It involves redirecting the powerful emotion of loss aversion, while acting contrary to the hardwired tendencies of thinking short-term and social validation. For a number of investors, this may be too much to ask. But for others, progress may be possible. A first step is calling things as they are. Rather than labelling everything risk, be careful to identify and separate that portion which is really emotion. There are risks that must be taken into account when making investment decisions but don't muddy the water by carelessly lumping emotions and investment risk together into a single number, as is the case for many popular *risk* measures.

A flying analogy may help think about the separation process. All of us who fly have experienced turbulence, which can range from being unnerving to downright frightening. When asked about their flight, many travelers will comment on the amount of turbulence they

---

[17] See French, Schwert and Stambaugh (1987).

[18] Several studies confirm that the typical equity mutual fund investor earns a return substantially less than the fund return because of poorly timed movements in and out of the fund.

encountered. However, we know from years of FAA (Federal Aviation Administration) research that turbulence rarely causes injury or death. Instead, pilot error (over 50%) and other human error are the leading causes of plane crashes.

What if the FAA had instead listened to passengers to determine the risk of flying? Rather than meticulously studying each accident and uncovering the true cause, the FAA would have spent considerable time trying to reduce turbulence, as requested by passengers, thus missing the critical role of human error in accidents. By focusing on short-term turbulence, they would have actually made flying more dangerous. Luckily they did not and as a result 2012 was the safest year in commercial flight since the dawn of the jet age.

We are not so fortunate in the investment industry. Rather than carefully separating risk from emotions, the industry provides a mixed bag of *risk* measures that exacerbate the emotional aspects of investing. As I argued earlier, this means many long-horizon portfolios are built to reduce short-term volatility, while at the same time increasing portfolio risk.

So to make the transition, it is necessary to allay the fears of clients while at the same time disregarding many a conventional wisdom. Unlike those who have a fear of flying and only have themselves to change, the investment professional has to confront both clients and the investment establishment. Sadly, the *risk* measures put forward by the industry are more emotional measures than they are investment risk measures.

Summarizing the three Basic Principles

Behavioral Portfolio Management focuses on the behavioral aspects of financial markets to help make better investment decisions. BPM's first basic principle is that Emotional Crowds dominate the determination of both stock prices and volatility, with fundamentals playing a small role. This means that more often than not prices reflect emotions rather than underlying value, a consequence of arbitrage failing to keep prices in line with fundamentals. As a result, price distortions are the rule rather than the exception, making it possible for BDIs to build superior portfolios, which is the second basic principle.

Volatility and risk are not synonymous. In the case of meeting short-term financial goals, volatility is an important contributor to investment risk, as measured by the chance of underperformance, and this is the third basic principle. On the other hand, volatility plays a much less important role when building long-horizon portfolios. By focusing on short-term volatility when building long-horizon portfolios, the investor injects emotions into the portfolio construction process. It is important to distinguish between emotions and investment risk so that the best decisions can be made.

The bottom line is that building successful investment portfolios is straightforward but emotionally difficult. Making decisions based on price distortions created by the Emotional Crowd and ignoring short-term volatility when building long-horizon portfolios presents significant challenges for investment professionals. This is because such a strategy is frequently going against the Crowd, thus depriving the client of social validation, and in turn asking them to set aside the strong emotions associated with volatile prices.

Consequently, it is necessary to mitigate the impact of client emotions. Emotion mitigation is a fact of life in the investment industry and both advisors and investment managers should develop such skills. The goal is to be sensitive to the emotional reactions of clients while minimizing the damage to their portfolios. Developing an approach that keeps clients in their seats while building superior portfolios is important for clients, advisors and investment managers alike.

SECTION 1: THE CULT OF EMOTION

CHAPTER 2: EMOTIONAL BRAKES

EMOTIONS AND HEURISTICS dominate our decision process – they act as brakes on our investing, preventing us from making good decisions. A heuristic is a shortcut approach to making decisions and, while it often leads to good decisions, in the world of investing such an approach can be highly problematic. How do we avoid falling prey to emotionally-driven and ineffective heuristics? An important first step is to gain an understanding of how the typical investor makes decisions.

When making investment decisions, we often engage what Kahneman refers to as our System 1, a part of our brain dominated by emotions and heuristics. Evolution has shaped this system to allow us to survive as humans and make the thousands of decisions that we face daily. Most are made automatically, with little conscious effort on our part. Unless we deliberately guide our brains in a different direction, System 1 becomes the primary way we make investment decisions.

We need to apply these lessons to how we make decisions and turn on what Kahneman refers to as System 2 thinking. This is a challenge since money and market volatility stir up very strong emotions and so we have to constantly work to not let these emotions control our thinking. Again, work on releasing your emotional brakes, not eliminating the underlying emotions.

BPM, as a way to navigate around this automatic yet faulty decision process, focuses on the dynamic interplay between Emotional Crowds and BDIs (Behavioral Data Investors). Crowds dominate stock pricing and the resulting price distortions make it possible for BDIs to build superior portfolios. So we want to avoid being part of the System 1-driven Crowd, and instead build an investment strategy that harnesses the resulting price distortions.

INVESTOR COGNITIVE ERRORS

To make this transition from being part of the Crowd to pursuing a strategy that takes advantage of distortions caused by the Crowd, it helps to construct a multi-faceted image of how the typical person makes decisions, particularly investment decisions. Based on behavioral science research, here are the important cognitive errors made by investors.

Myopic loss aversion (MLA)[19]

A game pays $1.10 if a fair coin comes up heads and costs $1 if it comes up tails. You can participate in this game as often as you wish, as long as you hold up a dollar bill prior to each flip to ensure you are good for the potential loss. Would you participate? In answering this question, it might help to know that the expected return on each round is $0.05 or 5% of our one dollar "investment". Does this change your decision regarding whether or not to participate?

It turns out that very few of us would participate. This is because we experience far greater pain from losing one dollar than joy from winning $1.10. What is more, the fact that the game can be played multiple times seems to have a limited impact on the decision. It appears we view each round as a separate event.

---

[19] This term was first coined by Benartzi and Thaler (1995).

How large must the return to heads be in order to attract the typical individual? Research has shown that the amount is somewhere around $2, which means that the ratio of gain to loss is *2-to-1*. That is, short-term *loss aversion* is twice as strong a feeling as the positive feelings regarding a comparable sized gain.

This ratio has a pervasive effect in the world of investing. It appears that we are myopic even when the investment horizon is supposed to be long term, such as saving for retirement. Rather than viewing such situations as 20, 30 or 40-year time periods, we view them as a series of days, months, quarters, or years. We evaluate performance in each short time period and apply 2-to-1 loss aversion to our gains and losses in each period. Thus if an investment loses money during our short measurement period, we may decide to get out of that investment and into another. This is true even if high short-term volatility is offset by high long-term returns.

The choice of time period over which to apply the 2-to-1 loss aversion is arbitrary. There are no guidelines for deciding on this length and so different investors choose different lengths, with no rhyme or reason. While there are analyses that can lead to buying and selling a particular investment, there is rarely a time frame that makes logical sense as part of this analysis. *Almost all time periods in investment analysis are arbitrary and the length decided upon is based on emotion rather than on logic.* This means that many of us are unable to reap the benefits of time diversification, where the volatility of the investment diminishes as period to period movements offset one another over time.

A closely related cognitive error is known as the *fallacy of composition*. We believe that in order to do well over the long-run, we must do well in each and every period. We then set about trying to accomplish this and end up doing poorly over the long run. The so-called *absolute return* funds seem to play into this fallacy, which is to a large extent driven by MLA. The only investment of which I am aware that produces positive returns every period is cash and we all know how well that works for building long-term wealth.

Social validation

Think of your most stylish pair of shoes. When was the last time you wore them? Let's say it was to a wedding and the subsequent wedding dance. How long did you keep these shoes on? Did you take them off during the wedding? How soon after the start of the wedding dance were you shoeless? My experience reveals that a large portion of the audience is shoeless early in the evening. Why? Because those stylish shoes are painful to wear!

Social validation is the culprit here. Style is defined arbitrarily, often by what famous people do and wear. This arbitrary example of social validation is so powerful that we can be convinced that those shoes, which we know will be painful to wear for any length of time, are worth the outrageous price we pay for them. It is amazing how easily we can be convinced to spend big bucks on an item that will cause us considerable pain.

Social validation, sometimes referred to as herding, is a powerful, hardwired behavior. It is observed in nearly all species, including geese, deer, fish, and insects. Herding is frequently critical for survival, so to go contrary to it is incredibly difficult. The lesson of our past is that sticking out from the crowd by doing something different is dangerous. At the first sign of danger sensed by any member of the herd, we all bolt and hope we are not the slowest member of the group.

It is only natural that we carry this into our investment decisions. We buy the investments that others are buying; we listen to conventional wisdom provided by so-called experts and celebrities; when presented a new investment opportunity we ask who else has invested in it; and we like to join the herd by investing in large funds rather than small funds.

Social validation is the primary reason why harnessing the market's emotions is so difficult. It frequently requires taking a position opposite the very large, emotional crowd and most often going against conventional wisdom. When we move in that direction, the ancient warnings of danger when sticking out from the crowd, along with a racing heartbeat and the natural impulse to flee the situation, can overwhelm us.

Stories

The US economy is huge, complex and constantly changing. It provides the foundation upon which we build our lives, careers and portfolios. So it is natural for us to want to know how the economy is doing and what the future holds. The government, as well as many private organizations, churns out a steady stream of economic statistics. But rather than gather and analyze this information, most of us would rather hear a story about the economy.

We judge the story's validity by the reputation of the storyteller and whether an explanation is logical to us. Generally the more detailed the story, the greater the validity that is attached to it (when, in fact, more detail increases the chances the story will be wrong). Social validation also plays a role as the story is viewed as more believable if it agrees with other stories that we have heard. All of this may have little to do with the validity of the story.

Stories allow us to summarize complex situations and are, as a result, easier to remember than these situations. But there is little reason to expect the right details will be retained. Emotions drive us to remember those aspects of the situation that were the most emotional. When retelling the story, we report on these aspects, as well as other details that are easy to recall. The peak-end memory process, discussed later in this chapter, plays an important role as well. Just as in that situation, the story may have little to do with what actually happened. The unreliability of eye witnesses in court confirms this, but true to human nature, eye witness testimony is held in higher regard than circumstantial physical evidence. This is the legal equivalent of personal experience trumping data.

Stories, besides frequently being incorrect, omit many important details. Analysis of such detail requires turning on our energy sapping System 2 and, being lazy, we are reluctant to do this. For example, in order to conduct a financial analysis, it is necessary to gather and analyze large amounts of data. In teaching this topic, I found that when presented with financial statements, most students' eyes glazed over. This was their System 2's way of saying it did not want to expend the energy necessary to process pages of numbers. I would tell them they needed to learn to concentrate and tease out the important results from the numbers. Due diligence is difficult to do properly and very few are good at it.

Stories play another important role. When something happens, we want to know why it happened. The truth is that in many situations knowing why does not help or there is no reasonable explanation, but we do not like these responses and thus seek out an answer in the form of a believable story.

Every day the stock market either goes up or down. Careful research reveals that, in general, we cannot identify the reasons for these movements, other than collective human emotions. Most of us do not accept this though – we want to know why, on this particular day, the market went up. There is no shortage of market observers willing to provide the day's market story. The validity of the story is judged by the reputation of the source, how logical it is and whether it agrees with other things we have heard that day (social validation). The truth is that the story teaches us nothing useful about the market but, nonetheless, satisfies our innate need for an explanation.

Leaving things unexplained is unsettling and at times scary. We have survived by achieving a better understanding of what is happening around us and acting accordingly, but that does not mean every explanation is valid. In many cases, like the stock market example above, we are fulfilling an emotional need for an explanation. In such situations, it is best if we accept the fact there is no plausible explanation and move on.

From time to time I am asked to comment on what happened in the stock market that day. My response is always the same: "Sometimes the market goes up and sometimes it goes down and I do not know why it does either. It goes up more often that it goes down and over the long run, it is driven by the economy, producing a long-term compound return of around 10%. And that is all I know about that." I regard this as the only reliable comment I can make, as saying anything further would be to fall foul of the human bias towards storytelling. Needless to say, I am not regularly asked to comment on the market.

Anchoring

It is logical to start an analysis with an estimate based on the best information available at the time, then adjust that estimate as additional information is obtained. Statistically this is known as Bayesian inference, named after the 18th century mathematician Thomas Bayes. This is a statistically rigorous method for combining the best prior estimate with new information, weighted by the confidence with which each estimate is held.

The problem is that the initial anchor is frequently irrelevant to the task at hand. Studies have shown that arbitrarily saying a number, for example "153", prior to asking a group to estimate the number of jelly beans in a jar drives the group's estimates towards that number. If a second group is asked to provide estimates for the same jar and the number "233" is mentioned instead, the resulting estimates will be closer to 233. In fact, studies have shown that the average estimate in the second group will be in the range of 40 points higher than in the first, that is, 50% of the 80 points difference in the initially mentioned numbers. Distressingly, arbitrary anchors easily and frequently distort decisions.

The world of investing is full of arbitrary numbers that become decision anchors. These include recent stock and market highs and lows; one, three, five and ten-year performance; the price paid for a stock; and the amount invested in a portfolio. I will discuss later why these and other numbers represent irrelevant anchors. The fact is that we cling to these anchors and it is incredibility difficult, if not impossible, to abandon them.

Availability bias

How important is the price of gasoline as an economic issue? For some it is very important, but for most it is not, although everyone, save for an oil company, would like to see a lower price. However, if we watch the news we would think it very important, since its level is reported daily and it is often the topic of lengthy news stories.

Why is this the case? It is because the price of gas is posted on many street corners and so its level is available and continuously updated. When we think about the economy or our personal financial situation, the price of gasoline is something that comes easily to mind. We might even conclude that as the price rises, the economy is worse off, as well as our own personal financial situation. Is the price of gasoline really so important that it deserves such an exalted position in the pantheon of economic variables?

The price of gasoline is an example of the *availability bias*. When asked to think about a particular issue, we often focus on what is most available to us at the time or can be most easily recalled. Closely related is that the degree of confidence we have in our conclusion is connected to how easily the facts can be recalled: the easier the recall, the more confident it is. What researchers have found is that what is available and how confident we are has little to do with the quality of our analysis. In this respect, System 1 provides little guidance on the quality of our analysis.

Availability bias actually goes a step further, uniting the entire market in a false sense of certainty regarding events. A single reporting of an event may trigger the availability bias, while multiple reportings trigger an *availability cascade*. In such cases, multiple reports have an overpowering influence on individuals, driving them into the Emotional Crowd. Consequently, it is extremely difficult to come to an independent judgment in that everywhere we turn, the event is being reported and people are overwhelmed by the event.

Natural and manmade disasters are examples of cascades, with considerable media time devoted to reporting such events. There are those who believe that legislation is unduly influenced by emotionally-driven cascades, with small risks taking on outsized importance in the minds of the public and, in turn, politicians. Financial markets are highly susceptible to availability cascades, being continuously dominated by one cascade or another. Cascades are important drivers of Emotional Crowds.

Representativeness

Past performance is no indication of future performance. We have all read this statement many times. Every prospectus and investment performance report is required to include such a disclaimer. Numerous academic studies confirm that past performance is not predictive of future manager performance and if anything, it is a negative predictor, with poor past performance predicting superior future performance.

So with all the warnings and the evidence against using past performance in selecting managers, what does everyone do: use past performance! The emotional attachment to past performance overwhelms the compelling evidence of its lack of predictive power.

This is a classic example of *representativeness.* We make judgments using our internal image of what the person or situation should look like. In the case of an investment manager, since the manager has performed well in the past, we easily jump to the conclusion that performance will be good in the future. That is, past performance is representative of future performance, even though it is not predictive. This is not unique to investing, as representativeness plays a major role everywhere, particularly in sports where contracts are negotiated based on last year's performance.

We make many judgments based on representativeness. We cast our presidential vote for the person who looks presidential; people who are attractive are judged to be more intelligent; people who are good speakers are judged to be smarter; and CEOs tend to be taller than average. These are just a few of the manifestations of representativeness. Stereotypes are an example of representativeness. We have a preconceived image of a librarian, police officer, minister, professor, criminal, and many more. Stereotypes provide a shortcut for decision making, for both good and bad. Non-discrimination laws are intended to counteract some of the more damaging aspects of representativeness.

Besides past performance, another powerful representativeness bias in the stock market is the idea that a good company is a precursor to picking a good stock. That is, if the company is well run, with quality management, carries little debt, is innovative, and has grown large, it must be a good stock to buy. The qualities of the company are representative of the investment qualities of the stock. On the other hand, a weak company with lots of debt, teetering on bankruptcy, with weak management and falling sales, must be a bad investment. Similarly, if we like the company's products, we are inclined to invest in its stock. Representativeness plays a large role in investment decisions.

WYSIATI

WYSIATI is a term coined by Kahneman which stands for *What You See Is All There Is*. For example, the Federal Reserve announces that they will continue to purchase long-term bonds. The stock market is up for the day and so that evening the word on the street is that the market's strength was due to the Fed announcement. Never mind that thousands of pieces of information descended upon the market during the day, many good but also many bad. The Fed was the most visible, so garnered the headlines. Never mind that research shows current daily events have little or no consistent impact on current stock prices.

WYSIATI is based on the notion that we gather much of our information from what we observe personally, in particular what we observe right now or have seen recently. We place considerable weight on these observations, while placing no weight on what is not directly observed. This puts probable but unobserved events at a distinct disadvantage to improbable but recently observed events. From a technical standpoint, this means that individuals place too much weight on recent sample data and too little on base rates, which is a violation of Bayesian inference. This makes it very difficult for individuals to correctly estimate true probabilities, even with good information regarding possible events.

We see this in a number of situations. When asked how many bad drivers are on the road, most will suggest that the percentage is high. In fact, most will say they are an above average driver, which is of course impossible, unless we live in Garrison Keillor's mythical Lake Wobegon, where everyone is above average. Careful observation of traffic reveals that there are very few bad drivers – most motorists are courteous and drive carefully.

The reason the percentage of bad drivers is overestimated is that they are more noticeable than good drivers and so we tend to remember them. When we return from a trip to the store, we don't say "I saw hundreds of good drivers," but we might say "You won't believe the guy that cut me off and then raced down the street ahead of me!" Emotional events are better remembered, thus reinforcing the biases resulting from WYSIATI.

Peak-end memory

I often present a graph (see Figure 10.1 later in the book) showing the wealth generated by investing \$10,000 in the stock market, the bond market and the T-bill market relative to inflation since 1950. Stocks soar in this graph, producing a portfolio worth over \$5m, compared to the bond and T-bill portfolios worth well less than \$500,000. The latter barely beats inflation. All in all, there has been a dominant performance by stocks over this time period.

A strange thing happens when I show this graph. Instead of focusing on the \$5m+ result, most cannot take their eyes off of the two steep declines that occurred over the last ten years. Of course these are factored into the ending value of the portfolio, as are the other 60 or so years of annual performance. It is as if the other years disappear in the minds of those who observe the chart, in light of the 2000 to 2002 and 2008 market declines. As a result, many prefer the stable but much lower return graphs of bonds and cash to the bumpier but higher return graph of stocks.

This is an example of *peak-end memory*. What research has shown is that human memory is not an additive or cumulative process, but instead focuses on what was the ending experience and the peak emotional experience, whether good or bad, during the time period. So rather than remembering that the average annual compound stock market return over this 62-year period was 10.6% and that the ending portfolio value was over \$5m, instead investors remember that the market dropped nearly 40% in 2008 and that the last ten years in the stock market generated little return. The highly emotional events of 2008, along with the recent so-called *lost decade*, comprise the peak-end memory of the stock market. No amount of data seems able to alter this perception.

Kahneman observes that we have two people inside us – the experiencing self and the remembering self –and the two are strangers. What we remember is only remotely related to what we experience. Memories are constructed by the remembering self on the basis of peak-end experience, while the experiencing self participates in everything that comes its way.

Earlier I discussed the 2-to-1 ratio in which research has shown that we feel twice as bad regarding a loss as compared to the equivalent gain. This means that we are more likely to remember losses than gains, since losses produce a much stronger emotional regret. This hampers our ability to view investments like stocks, in which positive returns are more frequent and larger than negative returns, leading to substantial wealth accumulation over time. Since we tend to remember the peak emotional events rather than cumulative results and with 2-to-1 we are more likely to remember losses, we cheat ourselves out of potentially large payoffs.

Personal experience trumps data

Many news stories start with a personal interest slant in order to introduce a topic at the individual level. This is done to fit into the way we come to conclusions: from individual experience to general observations.

For many, the assessment of how the economy is doing is based to a large extent on our personal financial situation. Expectations of future market returns are based on our own portfolio's recent return. Personal experiences, along with the personal experiences of those with which we have spoken recently, are the most important information used in making decisions. In short, *personal experience trumps data*.

One morning, I was talking with a group at coffee and the topic of what I do came up. I was asked what investments I recommended and I said I am a real fan of the stock market and that over time the market had produced an average return of 10%. I also quoted the $10,000 growing to over $5m over the last 60 years.

Both of the people with whom I was speaking rejected my answer, since their experiences in the market were not good. Both were old enough to have invested throughout most of the period I mentioned, but it was clear that, like so many others, they had moved in and out of the market and had managed to be in when the market did not do well and out when it did.

Not surprisingly, they were not at all interested in the long data set that I described. One explained to me that he had invested in low-rate municipal bonds and was very happy with his consistent return, even though it was considerably lower than the stock market return. My morning coffee conversation was a clear case of *personal experience trumping data*.

The typical investor is anecdotal emotional, making decisions based on their personal experiences as well as anecdotal information gathered from those around them, including strangers, and the emotional response to the situation they face. This approach is hardwired into us as a result of millions of years of evolution during which we lived in small groups and every outsider was considered an enemy to be killed. No wonder it comes naturally for us to gather information only from those around us and, in turn, distrust everyone outside our small group.

Conclusions based on careful, data-intensive research are a recent phenomenon, which has played a critical role in the amazing advances of the last few centuries. The typical investor is a long way from adopting this approach for making decisions. The emotional anecdotal approach is still preferred over data-driven investing.

Confidence in anecdotal information unjustifiably grows rapidly. When we hear something for the first time it is interesting, when we hear it the second time it is a fact, and when we hear it for the third time it is a trend worth following. Such overconfidence is the basis for many a bad decision.

Finally, what is the plural of anecdotal information? Answer: no data.

Substituting an easier question for a harder one

You are asked "Do you think _____ will be a good President of the United States?" and you answer, "I like _____ so I am going to vote for him." Notice you did not answer the question. Instead of providing an assessment of the candidate's skills, personality and beliefs, and whether or not these will allow the person to be a good President, you said that you liked the candidate. You have just *substituted an easier question for a harder one.*

The world is a complex, dynamic place with few simple answers. Answering realistic questions requires effortful System 2 thinking, but by our very nature we are lazy and loathe to turn on this energy sapping activity. Instead, we substitute an easier question that we can answer by quickly recalling information from memory. So not only do we answer the wrong question, we also have great confidence in our response, since it was easily recalled from memory. As they say, often wrong but never in doubt!

Stock analysis is fraught with this problem. When asked if *xyz* stock is a good investment, we might answer that we like their products. Or we think their advertising is very cool. Or we heard their CEO speak on TV and he was articulate. Or we have never heard of them and we never invest in a company with which we are not familiar. Or we do not invest in small stocks. In each case, we have substituted an easier question for the more difficult one. In each case we are overly confident in our answer.

Fallacy of information

Economic and market information is served up to us 24/7 by a bewildering array of media outlets. We feel pressure to keep up with all of this information and organize it into a cohesive picture of what is currently happening in the market. There is a sense that if we do this, we will make better investment decisions.

This is the *fallacy of information* at work. The more information we have the better, right? Maybe yes, maybe no. If we are one of those heavily-resourced firms that have carefully sifted through the historical data to identify persistent patterns, are able to process huge amounts of data, and have the ability to respond quickly, then the answer might be yes. Might be, but no guarantee. If it is insider information, the answer is definitely yes, but probably illegal, at least in the US. If we are not particularly well resourced and do not have the ability to organize large amounts of data, which is the case for the vast majority of investors, then the answer is no. In this case, we are most certainly suffering from the *fallacy of information*.

Our brains have an amazing capacity, mostly automatic, to process large amounts of information about our immediate surroundings. Again, evolution has hardwired this skill for survival. The process of gathering as much current market information as possible fits intuitively into these mental circuits. The problem is that we are competing against millions who are hardwired in the same way. While this ability allowed our ancestors to avoid being eaten by a saber-toothed tiger, it is much less likely that it will allow us to outsmart our fellow investors. The caliber of competition has ratcheted up dramatically over the last million years or so!

Obviously, information can be useful, but only in a carefully researched framework of a BDI. Otherwise gathering copious amounts of information is simply an emotional adventure of our System 1 thought process.

Fallacy of control

When asked how we wish to choose lottery ticket numbers, we often want to choose our own, maybe a birthday, maybe a favorite sequence, rather than have them chosen randomly. We believe that by choosing them ourselves we have increased the chances that we will win. Incredibly, people also believe that if you choose the same numbers every week you increase your chance of winning as these numbers will have to come up eventually. This is an example of overconfidence in our own abilities. Of course, picking our own numbers does not change the odds of winning, but we feel better about the experience. This is a well-known example of the *fallacy of control*. We have this innate belief that if we are in control things will work out better for us.

I was an undergraduate engineering major and had the idea that I could do most things myself and arrogantly believed that I could do them better than others could do them. Just after college I built some of my own furniture and did the repair work on my car (back in the dark ages of the 1970s when cars were not all electronic and it was possible to do your own maintenance!). Over time I realized that there were very few things I was good at, least of all car repair. After several attempts at fixing my own car and then having to take it to the mechanic to really get it fixed, I quit working on my car! One mechanic had a sign on the wall that read: "labor rate $50 an hour, $70 an hour if you watch, $100 an hour if you want to help". I have long since disabused myself of the notion that I can fix things and I now turn to the experts to do this for me.

We have a much harder time giving up control of our investments than giving up control in other areas of our life. It is common to think that this is our hard-earned money and no one will manage it as well as we can. Driven by MLA, we not only want to manage the money ourselves, but also monitor it continuously. We prefer to have our foot on the brakes so we can move decisively when there is a need to sell one investment and buy another.

The fallacy of information and the fallacy of control are closely related. Evolution has again hardwired us to gather information and control the situation around us. System 1 is operating at this level continuously, with most of this process conducted automatically and with little effort on our part. When something different is detected, energy is focused on the possible danger. It is only natural that in investing, where information arrives continuously, it is easy to shift this system into overdrive.

Mental accounting

Clients have a hard time thinking in terms of the overall portfolio, but instead set up a mental account for each investment. Clients then expect each to generate a positive return and are disappointed when they do not. The concept of diversification is lost when thinking this way with respect to a portfolio. Clients think that the portfolio does well only if each individual investment does well. A loss on any one investment is felt strongly, independent of the performance of the portfolio as a whole. They are applying *mental accounting* to their portfolios.

MLA plays an important role here as well. Rather than focus on the portfolio as a whole, we drill down to individual funds or stocks to see how they are doing. We then apply MLA to each individual investment, expecting each to perform well. The fallacy of composition strikes again! Like time diversification, the reason why we diversify across markets and securities is to reduce the risk and volatility in our portfolio. This is all for naught if we fall into mental accounting by applying MLA to the short-term performance of individual investments, rather than focusing on the long-term performance of the portfolio as a whole.

Framing

A food item is advertised as being 90% fat free. A similar item is advertised as being 10% fat. Based on fat content, which item would we choose? Many would choose the first even though they have the same amount of fat because the first is stated in a way that is more appealing to us, and so we make the decision to purchase it instead of the second item.

Framing is used skillfully by those attempting to sell us stuff. They know that how a product, service or issue is framed impacts the way we view it and ultimately whether or not we will purchase it or agree to their side of the argument. System 1 easily gets fooled by framing, so it is necessary to engage System 2 to determine that the two choices are the same with respect to fat content in the example above.

In financial markets, framing is particularly important when chances of a loss are discussed.

Phantastic objects

When we were young, we had a vivid imagination allowing us to be whatever we wanted to be. We could be a prince or princess, a super hero, an astronaut, incredibly wealthy, a singer, an actor, a technology super star, or any number of other celebrities. Right now my two-year-old granddaughter thinks herself to be Disney's mermaid Ariel and demands to be called Ariel rather than her real name. Most of us do not achieve these early dreams, but the wonderful emotions we experienced when thinking about these possibilities remain deep within us, even as we grow up.

Then something comes along that triggers these dormant emotions and that thing takes on a life of its own. This is known as a *phantastic object*. It is no longer viewed in the frame of everyday life, but instead begins to embody the hopes and dreams of childhood. It is an exhilarating experience, which blinds us to the realities of the situation.

Recently, Apple grew to be the most valuable stock on the planet. During the run-up, it was the stock that everyone had to own. While many warned the stock might be overpriced, the demand for the stock remained strong. For many, Apple stock became a phantastic object, taking on a highly emotional state by triggering, more than likely subconsciously, the hopes and dreams of childhood. The possibility of increased wealth can trigger these latent emotions and encourage us to make some very bad decisions.

AN ABSENCE OF RATIONAL DECISIONS

To make sense of a complex world, we rely on an intricate web of emotions and heuristics. Within this web, MLA interacts with mental accounting, which interacts with the fallacy of control, and so on. The resulting decision process evolved over millions of years, allowing us to survive as humans.

Over the last couple of centuries, the world of investing has outpaced our hardwired decision-making capabilities. Unless we make the effort to turn on our System 2, there is a strong chance that we will make many investing mistakes. Unfortunately, intuition and reliance on emotions are poor tools for building successful investment portfolios.

CHAPTER 3: RANDOMNESS

WE AS HUMANS have a strong desire to understand the world around us, a consequence of millions of years of evolution. For the vast majority of time humans have inhabited the earth, life was short and brutish. To survive, our brains evolved to understand how to get out of trouble rapidly and have progeny. Life got even shorter if we did not quickly identify the dangers in our immediate environs and respond to them correctly.

Our current confusion regarding randomness comes from the fact that we have evolved out of our historical habitat faster, much faster, than have our genes. Thus it is not surprising that we have a built-in need to understand everything that's going on around us. So when someone tells us that what is being observed is random and thus there is no particular explanation for why it's happening, we find that very unsettling.

In order to be a successful investor, it is important to understand randomness, along with its undesirable interaction with emotionally-driven System 1 reactions and, in turn, put this knowledge to work when making decisions. There are three important skills that need to be developed.

First, as described above, you need to get comfortable with not understanding why things happen, just that they do. Prices are largely driven by collective market emotions which, by definition, are unexplainable. To attempt to unearth an explanation for every price change is at best a wasted exercise and at worst a recipe for very bad decision-making. The US economy and financial markets are huge, with millions of participants, and in fact we understand very little about the complex interactions among participants and the resulting mechanism that determines prices. The ultimate goal is to understand a few critical behavioral factors upon which you can build an investment strategy and, in turn, assign everything else to unexplainable randomness.

Second, you need to be able to extract the signals used for making investment decisions from a sea of surrounding noise. This requires careful analysis to determine the validity of a signal. Often this requires conducting large sample, long time period statistical analysis. The null hypothesis in such tests is that the markets are random and that there are no measurable and persistent pricing relationships. So when a relationship is said to be statistically significant, this means it has passed the test and what you are trying to measure rises above the noise that dominates markets. Besides being statistically significant, the relationship should also be economically significant and able to cover the transaction costs of implementing the strategy.

Once a set of signals have been identified, it is critical that you have the discipline to execute a strategy in the world of highly emotional and random markets. It does little good to conduct a careful analysis to identify profitable signals and then allow the benefits of the strategy to be dissipated by responding to random information and events. As Kahneman says, trust the numbers and not your intuition. If you find yourself making decisions based on statements beginning with "I feel" or "I think", you are headed down the road to emotional and intuitive portfolio management. Portfolio management is a dispassionate, hard-nosed process that does not respond to the random noise permeating markets. This makes you a rather narrowly focused and uninteresting person, but it allows you to produce superior returns.

Third, you need to insulate yourself from short-term volatility and see tail events as opportunities rather than risk to be avoided. Volatility is largely driven by emotion and engenders emotional reactions in investors. To be a successful hard-nosed investor, you need to remove volatility as a portfolio management issue. Closely related to volatility are tail events, those extreme negative and positive investment returns that happen from time to time. Positive tail events outweigh negative tail events, so a strategy that eliminates both reduces your total return. In the case of concentrated portfolios, the exceptional returns are often associated with tail events. So tail events should be sought rather than eliminated.

RANDOMNESS OR LOGICAL EXPLANATION?

Consider two descriptions of a day of market action:

1. **Today's market**: Technology stocks led the stock market's slide today as traders registered their disappointment in a profit forecast from Google that heightened concerns about the upcoming earnings season. The Dow Jones Industrial Average gave up 38 points by the close.

2. **Today's market**: Market observers were disappointed today as Brent Smith slipped while selecting the -38 ball from the DJIA urn. Those close to the action thought his hand was heading towards the +49 ball just before the fateful mishap.

The second description to many will seem absurd. These are large sophisticated markets with millions of participants who continuously buy and sell stocks and thus determine stock prices. Participants gather thousands of pieces of information, conduct sophisticated analysis and deploy trillions of dollars into their favorite stocks, so it seems logical that there ought to be an explanation of why prices do what they do. However, the startling result is that the two market descriptions above cannot be distinguished from each other.

First, a consistent relationship between information flowing into the market and changes in market prices has not been unearthed. Second, price changes can be nicely modelled as being drawn randomly from a roughly normal distribution. So with all of the activity within the market on a daily basis, we could save ourselves time and money if, rather than having those guests ring the opening bell, they draw from the normally distributed set of bingo balls. The market could then shut down until the next day, when that day's guest draws a bingo ball.

Of course, we need markets so that stocks and other financial securities can be traded. So the suggestion that we can replace the markets with a set of bingo ball machines is tongue-in-cheek. It does drive home the point that little can be said about price changes over short time periods, daily, monthly, and, to a large extent, yearly stock returns are random. In general it is not worth the effort to try to explain them and build a strategy based on the explanations.

Be that as it may, many investors long to understand why prices move up and down and spend considerable time trying to uncover an explanation. This is driven by the evolutionary-based need to understand what is currently happening around them. As a result, many judge you a poor investment manager if you are not able to explain what they see happening in the markets on a daily basis. This is an uncomfortable disconnect resulting from you understanding randomness in a world where few do.

UNEASY ROOMMATES: RANDOMNESS AND THE HUMAN MIND

During the many years I taught, I ran a simple exercise to see if it's possible to distinguish a truly random series from a series of stock market prices. I handed out a piece of paper which displayed four histories of the S&P 500 (see Figure 3.1). I would ask the students to spend a few minutes examining all four histories and then vote on which was a random series and which was a real series. At least one of the series is real and at least one of the series is random, generated by drawing returns from a normal distribution with the same mean and standard deviation as the real series (I provide the answer in Chapter 7).

I ran this exercise many times over the years and not once did the class correctly identify which series were random and which were real. In a class of 30 or 40 students, there might have been one or two who correctly distinguished real from random. Of course, this is what you would expect from pure chance.

I would then designate those who identified correctly as the experts in market forecasting and suggested that the rest of the class seek their advice when it came to future market movements. Of course this was tongue-in-cheek, as their ability to distinguish random from real was a result of pure chance. This exercise demonstrated the random nature of the stock market and the perils of trying to make short-term predictions.

FIGURE 3.1: ACTUAL S&P 500 PRICE SERIES OR CREATED BY RANDOM DRAWINGS FROM A PROBABILITY DISTRIBUTION? (EACH SERIES ORIGIN IS SET AT 500 FOR COMPARABILITY)

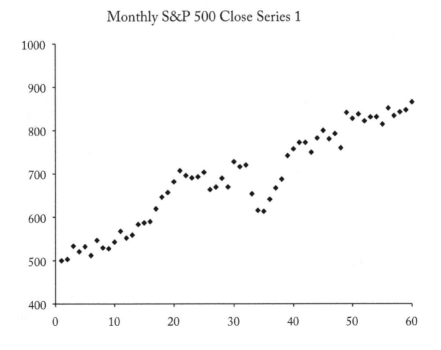

Monthly S&P 500 Close Series 1

Monthly S&P 500 Close Series 2

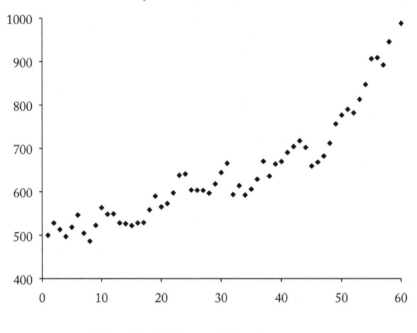

Monthly S&P 500 Close Series 3

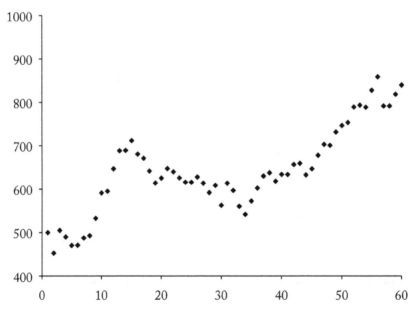

Monthly S&P 500 Close Series 4

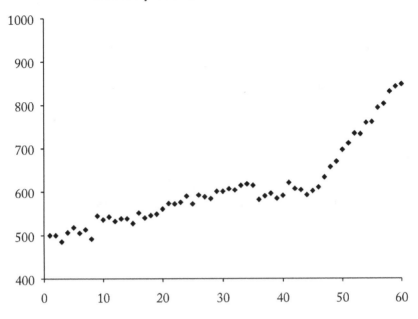

By the way, the same exercise has been run with market professionals, rather than with students, and the same results were obtained. The professionals could not distinguish the made up series from the real stock market series any better than could the students.

I ran another exercise in class in which I asked the students to replicate a fair coin flip with a 50-50 chance of heads or tails. In one case, they were asked to actually flip a fair coin 25 times and record the flips. I emphasized that they should not create this series without actually flipping a coin. I referred to this as the real coin flip series.

I then asked them to recruit a spouse or friend to generate a series of 25 coin flips by calling out "heads" or "tails" until 25 events had been recorded. I suggested that if the subject looked at them as if they were a bit nuts, they were to say that their slightly crazy professor had asked them to conduct the exercise, so just humor the old guy.

So each student came to class with a list of 25 real coin flips and 25 made up coin flips. Heads were given the value of +1 and tails were given a value of -1, and a cumulative real and the made up series of coin flips each were created. An example of such is shown in Figure 3.2.

I then ran various statistics such as the mean, standard deviation, serial correlation and a runs test. Consistently the made up series was not truly random and in fact had significant mean reversion, as can be seen in Figure 3.2 (highly significant first-order serial correlation of -0.16).

On the other hand, the real series had more long runs (29 of 5 or longer) than did the made up series (5 of 5 or longer). The students were surprised that the real series looked less random than did the made up series. But the statistical analysis verified that the real series was truly random and the made up series displayed a predictable pattern.

FIGURE 3.2: CUMULATIVE REAL AND MADE UP COIN FLIP SERIES

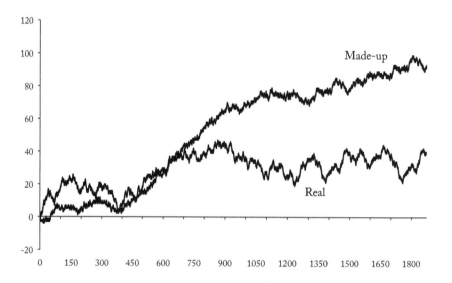

This simple exercise uncovered two problems the human mind has in dealing with randomness. First, the mind interprets ups followed by downs as being random. In other words, a negatively serial correlated series is interpreted as being more random than is a truly random series. Second, a truly random series has much longer runs than the human mind intuitively thinks it should, and so finds trends where none actually exist.

This clearly shows that the untrained human mind cannot be trusted to identify real trends. This is not to say real trends don't exist in financial and economic time series, but they cannot be successfully identified without careful statistical analysis. We do not have the ability to intuitively identify trends in financial time series.

A further complication is our desire for an explanation even when experiencing a truly random event. A large industry has emerged to meet this need, as a number of radio, TV, and internet channels spew forth a constant stream of commentary. However, to be helpful, the useful information must be culled from the background noise. This is possible only through careful large sample, long time period statistical analysis. This requires a great deal of effort, so many investors simply accept the anecdotal explanations offered by the media and, along with their lack of understanding of randomness, make poor investment decisions.

CHALLENGING TAIL EVENTS

Investors have a particularly hard time dealing with tail events. In the case of investment returns, tail events are those that are either very large or very small, sometimes referred to as two, three, or higher standard deviation events. In the case of the stock market, the average return over time has been somewhere between 10% and 12% annually, with a standard deviation of about 15%. Negative tail events would be those annual returns of -20% or worse, while positive tail events would range upward from 40%.

In the period 1928 through 2012, there were six years in which the stock market return was worse than -20% and five years in which returns were greater than 40%. The highly negative annual returns are particularly impactful because of MLA. These returns take on an outsized role when making investment decisions and are remembered much longer than the very large positive returns, even though large positive returns easily offset the negative returns.

We are currently experiencing the impact of MLA as the pain of 2008 is seared into investors' memories and often becomes the primary focus when making investment decisions. Even five years after the 2008 meltdown, potential clients continue to ask me how we did in 2008. My response when they ask about 2008 is "Why ask me about 2008, 2009 or 2006, or any other year for that matter?" Our flagship portfolio Pure produced a 300% return in the months after March 2009, so why not ask about that. Even this impressive performance is insufficient to offset the negative emotions of the 2008 market crash. Thus the painful emotions of a negative tail event often overshadow the good emotions of a positive tail event.

Tail events present other problems for investors. Research shows that individuals either significantly overestimate or underestimate the chance of rare events. The -39% return the stock market experienced in 2008 was the second worst in the last 140 years of stock market history. By this metric, the chance of this event is about 1 in 70. Yet many investors, to this day, continue to build their portfolios as if this event is very likely to occur again in the near future. Thus they overestimate the probability of such an event; a cognitive error that is typical of many individuals.

The probability of rare events is overestimated when they have occurred recently. On the other hand, if they have not occurred recently, individuals often assign a zero probability even though clearly there is a positive probability of occurrence. This is one of the more significant cognitive errors made by individuals. It is exacerbated in financial markets as money triggers strong emotions and extreme money events trigger even stronger emotions. Our brain is not cut out for nonlinearities. Our emotional apparatus is designed for linear causality. Owing to this nonlinearity, people have a hard time comprehending the nature of the rare event.

MENTAL ACCOUNTING STRIKES AGAIN

By our very nature, we are short-term oriented and have difficulty focusing on the big picture. Instead we conduct our analysis on individual securities, setting up a mental account for each. Randomness causes problems in this regard, since as the time frame grows shorter and the individual security becomes the unit of analysis, the larger becomes the noise-to-signal ratio. Most of the daily information on individual stocks is of little help for making investment decisions, as randomness plays an increasingly important role as one considers shorter time periods and less portfolio aggregation.

A serious problem here is that over a short time increment, one observes the variability of the portfolio, not the return. Our emotions are not designed to understand the point. If my brain can tell the difference between noise and signal, my heart cannot. Again, this is not a very comfortable situation for investors, forcing them to move away from their intuitive, preferred habitat.

THE LAW OF SMALL NUMBERS

As discussed earlier, personal experience trumps data. Since individuals operate in a very small universe, their personal experience, by definition, is a small sample. Small samples are subject to large measurement error. So randomness strikes again as the preferred information gathering approach of individuals is subject to serious cognitive errors.

It is much better to rely on large samples when analyzing a situation. A well-known statistical concept is the law of large numbers. It states that the larger the sample, the more representative is the sample, and the more accurate are the resulting estimates. Instead, individuals rely on limited personal experience and therefore end up with very inaccurate estimates. This has been dubbed the law of small numbers. The following description of a "hot hand" study among professional basketball players may help you appreciate this problem.

> After careful study, it was determined that there is no such thing as a "hot hand" in basketball. The chances of making the next shot are related to the player's long-term shooting accuracy but not to how many shots made recently. After studying the results, all those

associated with the team rejected the statistical analysis and reaffirmed their belief in hot hands.[20]

This belief in hot hands is termed a *prior* in the terminology of statistics and the new evidence that they really don't exist should be used to modify the prior and come up with a posterior belief. In the case of the player and coach rejection above, the prior belief was held so strongly that the careful study of a large amount of basketball data could not change minds.

This rejection of statistical analysis is common, an example of the cognitive error of personal experience trumping data. As Nassim Taleb of New York University's Polytechnic Institute reminds us, most results in probability are entirely counterintuitive, so in order to understand the randomness surrounding us we need to turn on our System 2 thinking and not rely on our intuitive, anecdotal System 1 thinking. To do otherwise is to invite being confused by randomness.[21]

The *law of small numbers* shows up regularly in investing:

- "I once bought a stock and it went down over the next month, so I am never buying a stock again."

- "I noticed that the stock market went down the last two Februaries so I am selling my stocks at the end of January this coming year."

- "The Fed said they would continue buying bonds and the bond market went up, so bond movements must be driven by Fed announcements."

And the list goes on. Investors freely extrapolate to general relationships based on very little empirical evidence. In addition, they hold these beliefs with great certainty since their scant evidence is fully consistent with their conclusion. One piece of evidence, one conclusion.

---

[20] Daniel Kahneman, *Thinking, Fast and Slow* (Farrar, Straus and Giroux, 2012).

[21] Nassim Taleb, *Fooled by Randomness* (Random House, 2nd edition, 2004).

IS FORMAL EDUCATION NECESSARY?

My own experience with understanding randomness began in graduate school when I took several probability and statistics courses. Once I took those courses, I never viewed the world the same. As I encountered different events, what often hopped into my head was a statistical distribution. Instead of trying to explain the event, I viewed it as a random draw from this distribution. To this day, I view daily, monthly, and even annual stock returns as being randomly drawn from a distribution.

The question is *can people understand randomness and not be confused by it if they have not studied it at some point in their education?* My experience with most students who take statistics is that they view it as incomprehensible and boring. This is their lazy System 2 telling them that it did not want to do the heavy lifting necessary in order to understand these challenging concepts.

So can someone understand randomness and not be confused by it if they have not taken such courses? An open question for sure, but it is a critical step if one is to become a BDI. Kahneman is one who believes that formal education is a prerequisite for understanding randomness. My statistics and probability courses were the most difficult I took in graduate school but I thoroughly enjoyed them and continue to use many of these concepts in my research.

If one does not gain an appreciation of randomness, then one is sentenced to be a prisoner of anecdotes, WYSIATI and availability bias. So each of these cognitive errors are the result of not appreciating the random nature of events and therefore uncritically accepting what is presented to you. This is the System 1 thinking that can be so destructive of investment performance. Unless you understand randomness at the DNA level you are doomed, as argued by Taleb, to be continually fooled by it.

60/60/60

When we talk with clients about the performance of their portfolios, we frequently reference the 60/60/60 concept. The stock market produces a positive monthly return 60% of the time (actually 63%), our portfolios outperform the market in 60% of the months, and our individual stock picks outperform 60% of the time. These are very attractive odds and result in superior performance over long horizons.

But as the percentages indicate, there is no guarantee of short-term positive returns. This means that in any one month there is a 40% chance the stock market will generate a loss, there is a 40% chance that our portfolios will underperform, and there is a 40% chance that an individual stock selection will underperform.

Those with MLA and a lack of an understanding of randomness often overreact when these 40% events occur. Clients need to appreciate that at each level the odds are tilted in their favor and they need to remain patient, taking a long-term perspective. The randomness of 60/60/60 works in their favor long-term, but creates short-term emotional anxiety. An understanding of randomness is critical to building long horizon wealth.

CHAPTER 4: CULT ENFORCERS

I HAVE JUST explored the impact of emotions and randomness on investment decision-making and concluded that cognitive errors are pervasive. Indeed, emotions and randomness interact in unfavorable ways, producing even worse decisions. Beyond the cognitive errors made by investors, there is an army of professionals and regulators who enforce this situation, which I call the Cult of Emotion (COE). The tools and analysis they use encourage, rather than discourage, investors from stepping on their emotional brakes and thus encourage clients to remain in the Cult.

To a large extent the Cult is driven by how difficult it is to get clients to avoid cognitive errors, since the decision process is hardwired by millions of years of evolution. It is easier to tell clients what they want to hear rather than what they need to hear. Another important driver is the conversion of investor emotions into business risk for the advisor or investment manager. As much as we try, investors still make emotional decisions that can lead to money being withdrawn from the firm. It is understandable that advisors and investment managers want to avoid this business risk.

The challenge of leaving COE, then, is made much more difficult by the fact that the industry reinforces emotions rather than helping clients to avoid cognitive errors. Leaving COE is transformed into a two-step process: first, the investment professional has to release their own emotional brakes as well as those of their clients, and, second, much of what is used by industry professionals when analyzing portfolios and investments has to be discarded. This makes it even more difficult to release emotional brakes and to become a BDI.

CATERING VERSUS MITIGATING

There are two basic choices for dealing with emotional decision-making. The first choice is to cater to emotions, which means that they are accepted and even reinforced. This means clients are encouraged to step on their emotional brakes and even push down harder, rather than release them. The other choice is to work to mitigate the emotional damage done to client portfolios. Research shows that the biggest drag on long-term wealth creation is the emotional mistakes made by investors. Helping clients avoid such mistakes is the most important thing an advisor can do and is a major justification for the fees charged.

The reality is that there are times when all that can be done is cater to client emotions. Investment professionals are constantly balancing between guiding clients in the right direction versus being accused of badgering.

Indeed it may not be possible for some clients, maybe many clients, to make this transition. Kahneman himself is pessimistic regarding the possibility of avoiding emotionally driven cognitive errors. Anyone who has tried behavior modification knows how difficult it is. So there is only so much that can be done to help clients change the way they make decisions.

As professionals we should at the very least work to release our own emotional brakes and then develop the skill to help clients do the same. We want to encourage clients to release their emotional brakes – or on the other side, we don't want to be a Cult Enforcer (CE).

MPT: THE CE TOOLKIT

MPT provides the CE's toolkit by placing emotion at the center of the portfolio construction process. MPT began with the work of Harry Markowitz and his mean-variance optimization model.

We have already seen (in Chapter 1) how Markowitz's work signaled the move towards volatility as a measure of risk and the basis for making investment decisions was launched. However, volatility is really a measure of emotion since it is the result of investor emotions driving prices up and down. What is more, volatility is created by emotion and on the other side stirs up strong emotions in investors.

Obviously there are risks associated with investing, but volatility has little to do with these risks. In spite of this, the investment profession has moved forward as if volatility and risk are one and the same. Using mean-variance optimization places emotion at the very center of portfolio construction.

The suggestion that volatility be considered when making investment decisions permeates modern finance. Portfolio managers are asked to reduce volatility under the guise that this is risk reduction. For investors who suffer from MLA, volatility is perceived as risk. For those investors who have successfully ridded themselves of MLA, volatility is an uncomfortable aspect of building long-horizon portfolios, but in general is not risk. For such an investor, risk is the chance of underperformance.

If one starts with $100,000, what is the chance of ending up with less than that over the investment horizon? If the portfolio is a mixture of asset classes, what is the chance of ending up with less than if it had been invested in a single high expected return asset class? These are the measures of risk of interest to long-term investors. For short-term investors, volatility does contribute to risk and such portfolios are built to either minimize or completely eliminate volatility, but most investors are or should be thinking long term. Thus in most investment situations volatility represents emotion and has little to do with risk.

Investment professionals regularly focus on volatility when making investment recommendations. In turn this heightens client sensitivity to volatility and reinforces MLA. Other measures that also exacerbate this problem are max drawdown, downside volatility, upside capture, downside capture, and the Sharpe ratio. The latter is particularly pernicious since it is a return-to-emotion ratio and thus reinforces MLA. All of these measures are based on short time periods, thus ignoring the benefit of time diversification over long time periods. So not only is MPT built on emotion, it makes matters worse by focusing on short-term volatility.

One of the more bizarre features of MPT is the introduction of tracking error for measuring investment performance. The first step is to assign an arbitrary benchmark, such as small-cap value. It is arbitrary since it has little to do with the investment strategy being pursued by the fund. When the style grid was first introduced, the hope was that the assigned box would somehow match up with the strategy being pursued by the fund, but this has turned out not to be the case. To heap insult on injury, the fund is asked to track this arbitrary benchmark and then, laughingly, expected to beat the benchmark. The resulting tracking error is calculated and, incredibly, it is referred to as risk. This arbitrary way to categorize funds and measure performance not only hurts performance, but has created a highly misleading measure of risk – that is, tracking error.

Another tool that is used in measuring investment performance – CAPM beta – is based on individual stock volatility relative to market volatility, as well as the stock's correlation with the market, so it really is a measure of emotion and not risk. Indeed, the empirical tests of whether beta is priced by the market as a measure of risk have uniformly failed to find a positive relationship between expected return and beta. This seems to confirm that market participants do not view beta as risk as is predicted by CAPM.

Gene Fama of the University of Chicago and Ken French of Dartmouth College contend that there is no empirical evidence supporting beta as a measure of risk and therefore recommend not using it in real-world investment management.[22] Even more damning, Malcolm Baker of Harvard, Brendan Bradley of Acadian Asset Management and Jeffrey Wurgler of NYU have called beta the greatest anomaly in finance.[23] A measure of risk it is not, a measure of emotion it is.

As mentioned earlier, I began my career anchored in MPT and the concise way it represented markets. So to discover that MPT, rather than being a rigorous framework for thinking about investment management, is a framework built on emotion that discourages investors from releasing their emotional brakes, was both surprising and very disappointing. Sadly MPT has degenerated to the point of being the primary source of CE tools.

To a man with a hammer every problem looks like a nail. To an analyst armed with MPT, every emotion looks like a risk.

FAUX DUE DILIGENCE

When analyzing an investment manager one should focus on determining whether or not the manager is good at selecting investments. This is a difficult question to answer. So what often happens is that an easier question is substituted for this harder one; questions such as how much money is being managed and for how long.

The assumption is that if there is a lot of money under management and the manager has been at it for a long time, they must be good. On the contrary, research reveals that the larger the fund and the longer it has been around, the worse its performance. It is emotionally easier to sell a manager to clients whose fund is large and old, so selecting a manager with these characteristics is often the triumph of emotion over reality.

Much due diligence is based on MPT and thus thrusts emotion into the center of the selection process. For example, it is not unusual for an investor or advisor to select a manager based purely on max drawdown.

---

[22] Eugene F. Fama and Kenneth R. French, 'The Capital Asset Pricing Model: Theory and Evidence', working paper (January 2004).

[23] Malcolm Baker, Brendan Bradley and Jeffrey Wurgler, 'Benchmarks as Limits to Arbitrage: Understanding the Low Volatility Anomaly', working paper (2010).

Very likely these investors and advisors are strongly afflicted by MLA and trade off lower returns for reduced emotions.

Beyond the arbitrary concepts of AUM, age, and the emotional measures of MPT, a popular gauge of investment skill is past performance. Investors believe that if the fund has performed well over time periods of one, three, five and ten years, for example, it will continue to do well going forward. However, particularly for equity fund managers, the evidence overwhelmingly shows that past performance is not predictive of future performance. In fact regulators require investment managers to clearly state that past performance is not indicative of future performance on all past performance materials presented to clients.

In spite of the fact that both evidence and regulators agree that past performance is not predictive, virtually all fund analysis, whether it is conducted by an individual or professional, relies heavily on past performance. If you were beamed to Earth from another planet and saw this process and was familiar with the evidence you would be dumbfounded that investment professionals use past performance at all.

The reason past performance is so heavily used both by individuals and professionals who should know better is that it appeals to the cognitive errors of availability bias and representativeness. Past performance is widely available and it is assumed that managers who have performed well in the past will continue to perform well in the future. So strong are these cognitive biases that it is virtually impossible to convince anyone to do otherwise.

Much like the basketball players and coaches discussed in the last chapter who rejected the evidence that there is no such thing as a hot hand, investors and professionals reject the evidence that past performance is not predictive of future performance. Using past performance to select investment managers is the clearest evidence that emotions trump data. Data doesn't have a chance.

THE LAWYERS PILE ON

Our society as a whole is litigious and this is mirrored in the financial services industry. Lawsuits are frequently brought when something is done differently than everyone else is doing it. The prudent man rule is such an example in the world of investing. So what does a prudent man do? He does the same thing as everyone else does, that is, social validation. The legal profession takes up its post, along with MPT, as a CE. This is accomplished by setting standards that if something is done differently than everyone else is doing and it doesn't work out, this becomes grounds for a lawsuit. Since pretty much all investors are making cognitive errors and emotional decisions, such legal rules enforce the Cult. My own experience in the industry, and I am sure the reader's experience as well, is that people will not do things differently for fear that they will be sued as a result of the prudent man rule.

Not everything is a problem with the legal profession, for there are unscrupulous people in the industry and as a result investor protections are critical. The ability of an investor to sue over fraud is essential to the integrity of the market. As is often the case though, what is worth doing is worth overdoing and unfortunately this is the situation with the cult-enabling aspects of the legal profession.

IT IS HARD TO LEAVE THE CULT

The Cult of Emotion is strongly fortified. For most individuals, System 1 thinking dominates the investment decision process. The hardwired emotions and reactions that allowed us to survive as humans are triggered by market volatility and, as a result, thoughtful, data-driven analysis is thrown out the window.

The industry has evolved to encourage these emotions and reactions rather than help investors move beyond primitive decision-making. The current paradigm, MPT, provides the emotion-based toolkit used by the many Cult Enforcers. Further, as often happens within an industry, case law has evolved to protect the Cult.

It seems a formidable challenge to leave the Cult, so why even try? The reward is the ability to build superior portfolios for growing long-horizon wealth. The effort required is worth it.

CHAPTER 5: HOW THE CULT OF EMOTION INVESTS

ONE OF MY favorite comic strips growing up was Pogo, written by Walt Kelly. I found his mixture of humor, satire, and political commentary both entertaining and insightful. His most famous quote has proved enlightening in many situations I have faced:

"We have met the enemy and he is us!"

This is no more the case than when we examine how individuals and professionals alike make investment decisions. By applying any number of emotional brakes, investors do serious damage to their portfolios. If only we could get out of our own way, portfolio performance would improve significantly. As they say, "No matter where I go, there I am." The thought that we act differently when making investment decisions than we do in other situations is a naïve assertion.

To begin with, it is important to inventory the emotional brakes stepped on when making investment decisions. A Coean is someone who constantly steps on emotional brakes when making investment decisions and is thus a member of the Cult of Emotion (COE), the suffocating environment that currently envelops the investment industry.

THE INVESTING HABITS OF A COEAN

Let's have a look at the traits of a Coean when they are investing.

Developing investment strategy

Coeans develop an investment strategy based on the following:

INTUITION AND ANECDOTAL INFORMATION

Investment markets are complex and it is a challenge to analyze them properly. Basing your decisions on intuition is a recipe for poor decisions. As Kahneman says, trust the numbers never your gut. If you find yourself saying things like "I feel" or "I think" when making investment recommendations, you're clearly heading down the emotional investing road. If anecdotal information plays a major role in your investment strategy, then you are depending upon a small and often unreliable sample. "*I heard it from Fred and then heard it from Paul, so it must be a trend.*" The law of small numbers strikes again. Intuition and anecdotal information are clearly part of System 1 thinking and are very Coean.

PURCHASING "BRAND" STOCKS

Brands play a prominent role in modern economic life. Learning about products and services is time-consuming, so purchasing a brand is a convenient shortcut. Brand also represents social validation, as you are doing something that many others are doing. So it's a short step to using the branding concept for investment decisions.

Since it's so easy to buy a brand stock rather than slog through a careful stock analysis, it's not surprising that brand stocks often underperform. At AthenaInvest, when we examine potential client stock portfolios we invariably see the same 50 stocks. Without careful direction by an investment manager, investors tend to buy the same small number of stocks. Buying brand-name stocks is emotionally reassuring, but often results in a portfolio of performance dogs.

CURRENT ECONOMIC EVENTS

Economic information is reported daily. Analysts provide estimates of what they think a particular series, such as the unemployment rate, will be as the market waits breathlessly for the number to be reported. Once reported, the information is analyzed endlessly. So it's no wonder that many investors believe they must understand what's happening in the economy today and on an ongoing basis.

But it turns out that the stock market is largely unrelated to what is happening in the economy right now. In fact studies show that the stock market is a predictor of economic activity six to nine months hence. So unless you are able to forecast the economy that far ahead, economic information is of little value in building a portfolio. Indeed, the Economic Conditions strategy is one of the worst performing US strategies of the ten that have been identified by AthenaInvest, consistent with the notion that top-down economic strategies perform poorly.

Even so, given all of the talking heads, there is a strong desire by investors to use current economic information for making investment decisions. They believe that doing so is the right thing to do.

HOLDING MORE THAN 20 STOCKS

In a 1968 study, John Evans and Stephen Archer, both of the University of Washington, showed that the benefits of adding additional stocks to a portfolio drops off rapidly and provides little diversification benefit when more than 20 are added to a portfolio.[24] So adequate volatility reduction is obtained with a relatively small number of stocks.

It is surprising, therefore, that so many in the industry believe that adequate diversification is only obtained with a very large number of stocks. When presented with a portfolio made up of a small number of stocks, many immediately jump to the conclusion that the portfolio is

---

[24] John Evans and S.H. Archer, 'Diversification and the reduction of dispersion: an empirical analysis', *Journal of Finance* 23 (1968), pp. 761-767.

overly volatile. But it is not. Holding more than 20 stocks in a portfolio is a Coean approach to equity portfolio construction.

OVERLY FOCUSING ON DEBT

Debt is an emotional issue. Since the last group standing in the event of economic failure are the debt holders, many jump to the conclusion that debt was the problem. When the bond was first issued or the bank initially granted the loan, both borrowers and lenders had every expectation that the debt would be repaid. Then subsequent economic and market events led to a company unable to meet its obligations. Companies go out of business, not because of too much debt, but because of unforeseen economic and market events, which might have been exacerbated by poor management decisions.

In most circumstances, leverage is positive for a company as the interest payments are tax deductible (in the US at least) and it is more than likely the company took on the debt believing the return on their investment opportunities exceeded the interest payments on the debt. Thus leverage can add significant value for shareholders. An emotional fixation on debt as always being bad is Coean.

THE PRICE PAID

The price paid for a security represents an investment anchor. So rules like selling when the stock drops by, say, 20% or selling when it increases by 20% are common. There is little evidence to support the profitability of such strategies. In fact, Hersh Shefrin and Meir Statman of Santa Clara University proposed the disposition effect in 1985 when they noted investors sold their winning stocks too soon and held on to their losing stocks too long.[25]

---

[25] Hersh Shefrin and M. Statman, 'The disposition to sell winners too early and ride losers too long: theory and evidence', *Journal of Finance* 40 (1985), pp. 777-790.

Investors wish to experience the positive feelings associated with a gain while deferring the regret of a loss. This is an MLA-driven response, as remembering the price paid creates an anchor, leading to the disposition effect. In order to avoid this Coean aspect of portfolio management, it is important to forget the price paid. While this may seem startling to many, it allows you to avoid many of the emotion-based decisions plaguing investment management.

HOLDING A STOCK UNTIL IT GETS BACK UP TO THE PRICE YOU PAID FOR IT

I've always felt that this was the ultimate grudge match with your portfolio: I will get even with the stock for going down by holding until the price gets back up to the purchase price. Of course this is driven by the powerful emotion of loss regret, but it has the undesirable result of making decisions based purely on emotions rather than on a carefully developed strategy. It locks you into a position, making it impossible to sell a stock which is no longer attractive and buying one that is. Investment management is about investing in the best ideas going forward and not dwelling on the mistakes of the past. It is so Coean to continue holding a stock to avoid recognizing a loss.

Building a long-term portfolio

Coeans build a long-term portfolio based on the following factors:

VOLATILITY AND CORRELATION

Return volatility is generated by emotional reactions of investors to current events. In turn, volatility itself generates an emotional reaction among investors. This means that volatility is created by and stirs up emotions. So when using volatility as a measure of risk, emotion is being placed at the center of your analysis. In particular for building long-term portfolios, volatility contributes little to the chance of underperformance, which is the relevant measure of risk. So focusing on volatility as a risk measure is clearly Coean.

So too is focusing on correlations. Correlations have little impact on long-term portfolio returns, but low correlations reduce short-term volatility. Seeking lower-correlation investments, such as what are referred to in today's markets as alternatives, is Coean. Such efforts usually lead to reduced short-term volatility but also reduced long-term returns.

ELIMINATING TAIL EVENTS

Negative return tail events create strong emotions in investors so it is only natural to attempt to eliminate these emotionally painful aspects of investing. However, it is most frequently the case that for every negative return in a distribution there is an even larger positive matching return that more than offsets the loss. The self-healing nature of return distributions rewards patient long-term investors. The risk in pursuing a strategy that attempts to eliminate short-term losses is that it also eliminates the larger offsetting gain.

On average offsetting gains follow the matching loss, so the biggest risk is getting out of the market to avoid a loss and then not getting back in soon enough to reap the matching gain. Nobody said that investing in the stock market is emotionally easy and tail events test the conviction of even the most steadfast investor.

ASSET ALLOCATION MODELS

The most important drivers of long-term wealth are expected asset class returns. All other statistics pale to insignificance, including short-term volatility and correlations. If you want to maximize long-term wealth, invest the vast majority if not all of the portfolio in the highest expected return asset class. Doing otherwise reduces final wealth.

For example, I've never understood why one should invest in anything other than stocks for building long-term wealth, since all other asset classes are expected to generate lower returns. If I've released my emotional brakes and I am able to tolerate short-term volatility, investing all of my money in stocks will generate the highest long horizon wealth.

The only time it makes sense to diversify across asset classes is if expected returns are high and comparable. Otherwise, for building wealth, diversification is a feel-good strategy and is thus Coean.

EXITING THE MARKET WHEN VOLATILITY INCREASES

Volatility stirs up emotions within investors. As volatility increases, investors get increasingly anxious, sometimes to the point of exiting the market. VIX is a measure of implied stock market volatility and so is often referred to as an index of investor fear. The higher is VIX, the greater is investor fear is the contention. The emotional response by many investors as VIX rises is to exit the market but in fact research shows it makes more sense to stay in the market, and even invest more, as volatility increases. Exiting the market as volatility increases is Coean.

Choosing an investment manager

Coeans choose an investment manager based on the following:

PAST PERFORMANCE

"Past performance is not indicative of future performance." We've all heard and read this many times and so it is surprising how many people continue to use past performance in selecting an investment manager, particularly an equity manager. It's not like there is a group of commentators or academics out there suggesting that indeed past performance is useful. The reality is that the evidence is overwhelming on the side of past performance not being predictive. The one exception is that there is some predictive power in short-term performance.

In spite of these compelling results, the most common approach for selecting managers uses three, five and ten-year past returns. Indeed one of the most popular measures for selecting active managers is Morningstar stars, which are based on these return measures.

Stunningly, in a study reported by Marshall Jaffe, 80% of hiring decisions of large and sophisticated institutional pension funds were the direct result of outstanding past performance, especially recent performance. My own experience in working with individual investors and advisors is that the use of past performance is pervasive when making an investment selection decision. This example alone shows how difficult it is to extract oneself from COE.

Is it possible to select managers without using past performance? The answer is yes. My firm's research shows that manager behavior – in the form of strategy, consistency and conviction – is predictive of future performance. This conclusion is confirmed by a number of other academic studies. So the lesson here is that it is manager behavior which is predictive while past performance is not. In section 3, I will discuss this issue further as an important part of developing a successful investment strategy.

A FUND'S "BRAND"

As I mentioned above, individuals use brands as a shortcut when making decisions. This is no less the case when selecting an investment fund. Funds such as Fidelity, Vanguard and T. Rowe Price are household names among investors. The assumption is that if the name is familiar they must be good. In some cases they are, but the real reason that you're familiar with them is that the firm has made enough money to advertise heavily. This means that the fund family has turned the corner towards distribution and puts less emphasis on performance, or grown so large that it's very difficult for them to perform.

As I mentioned above, manager behavior in the form of strategy, consistency and conviction are predictive of future performance and if a brand fund continues this behavior, there is a good chance of outperforming. However, branding, along with the distribution system, often overwhelms this behavior and instead the manager pursues behaviors that are counterproductive for performance. In particular branding and distribution lead to much larger funds and the larger the fund the worse the performance.

LARGE ACTIVE EQUITY FUNDS

Fund size is another characteristic that helps us feel comfortable. In fact it is one of the criteria that is used to gauge whether a fund is successful by potential investors. The logic is if a fund has attracted a lot of money it must be good – an example of social validation. To the contrary, research shows that the larger the fund, the worse the performance. The reason larger funds underperform is that it becomes increasingly difficult to concentrate on best idea stocks in the face of increasing trading and liquidity constraints. Consequently a larger fund begins to invest in other than best idea stocks, those that tend to underperform. As the fund grows larger, it takes on larger fixed costs, making it susceptible to short-term price declines. Thus it overdiversifies in an attempt to avoid the resulting volatility-driven business disruptions. In short, as the fund grows it increasingly changes its focus away from performance to distribution.

So selecting a larger fund over a smaller one or setting up a system that requires funds to be large in order to be listed on a platform – a common habit among broker-dealers and other platforms – is Coean.

VOLATILITY, BETA, MAX DRAWDOWN

Volatility is largely driven by emotion, a conclusion confirmed by considerable research. Very little of the volatility at the individual stock and even market levels can be attributed to changes in fundamentals. Volatility is driven by emotion and also engenders the emotion of fear within many investors. So if a portfolio is built based on a measure of volatility, emotion is being put at the center of the analysis and is thus Coean.

STYLE DRIFT AND TRACKING ERROR

One of the stranger things that has swept over the investment industry is the style grid. It is based on the idea of categorizing active equity managers, as well as other managers, by the market cap and the PE ratio of the stocks they hold. So a fund is categorized as small-cap value if it holds small market capitalization and low P/E ratio stocks. Never mind that there is no research behind categorizing funds in this way.

Once this concept was introduced, it grew to dominate the industry, driven by a leaderless stampede. Now virtually everyone uses it for categorizing funds and building portfolios. Even worse, research shows that performance is hurt by keeping a manager in a style box. Funds perform best when the manager consistently pursues a strategy and takes high-conviction positions and so by demanding that a manager stay in a style box, the manager is being asked to purchase stocks that may have nothing to do with the strategy being pursued.

Nevertheless, one of the worst sins in the eyes of the industry is manager style drift, in which stocks that are not consistent with the manager's style box are purchased. In fact, style drift is considered risk. So the fund is benchmarked against the arbitrary index and then declared risky if experiencing style drift. It is hard to believe that an industry that is supposedly so smart and so sophisticated has somehow gotten itself tied into this Gordian Knot.

As I've presented these ideas around the industry, there are many who agree with the absurdity of the style grid, but the frequent response is that they need some way to categorize funds. An emotional response indeed.

* * *

Well Tom, you're thinking, you have just thrown out almost everything that is standard practice in the industry. Indeed you are correct. Nobody is more surprised or more disappointed than am I that we have come to the juncture where the MPT paradigm has to be rejected; a paradigm that was so full of promise 40 years ago when it first appeared on the scene. In the next chapter I explore the precursors to MPT's ascendency, only to be followed by its empirically driven fall from grace.

The sad truth is that the financial services industry is full of CEs and MPT has provided the tools with which they ply their trade. Releasing emotional brakes requires effort not only on the part of investors, but also a wholesale change in the way the industry conducts its business. Quite a challenge, but as we will see later it is worth the effort to be free to build high-performance BDI portfolios.

CHAPTER 6: FORTY YEARS IN THE DESERT – THE DISAPPOINTING TALE OF MPT

IN 1738, DANIEL BERNOULLI first proposed that individuals made decisions by rationally maximizing expected utility. Thus was launched the rationality model of human behavior that underpins many of today's theories in the social sciences. It took on a particularly important role in economics, where economic agents were said to make rational decisions and, as a consequence, prices reflected all relevant information.

This model was amenable to mathematical analysis which, over the last hundred years, has grown to dominate economic theory and related empirical testing. Mathematical models provide a veneer of orderliness, thus obscuring the messiness of real-world markets. It was out of this convergence of rationality and mathematics that Modern Portfolio Theory was born.

The launch of MPT was driven by another issue bedeviling university business schools in the 1950s. At the time, business schools were the stepchild of the academy, criticized for being no more than trade schools and lacking a rigorous research underpinning. It's hard to imagine that business schools were held in such low regard, as today they are often among the top programs within universities. However in 1958, Robert Gordon of the University of California, Berkeley and James Howell of Stanford University authored a seminal report arguing that this indictment of business schools was accurate and in order to gain respectability within the academy they would have to beef up their research capabilities. Almost immediately schools began to respond to this criticism.

Back in the early 1960s there were few PhD programs in business and those that existed did not provide the mathematical and research tools so many thought were necessary to upgrade business schools. The solution was to hire economics PhDs to staff business courses, particularly finance courses, so that they could bolster research programs and allow business schools to become more respectable.

Along with the new economics trained faculty came the mathematically-based rationality model of individual, and importantly, investor behavior. In order to publish in top-tier business journals, it became increasingly important to create mathematical market models based on investor rationality. All of the elements necessary for the germination of MPT were in place by the mid-1960s.

THE RISE OF MPT

In 1952, Harry Markowitz of the Rand Corporation published his article on portfolio construction, arguing that portfolios should optimize expected return relative to volatility, with volatility measured as the variance of return. He proposed the now ubiquitous efficient frontier. His mathematical and statistical model gained little traction during the 1950s. But with the growing interest in mathematically-based market models, by the mid-1960s the mean-variance model became a mainstay within academic finance departments.

Meanwhile, at the University of Washington, professor Bill Sharpe recognized Markowitz's mean-variance optimization model as more than a prescriptive model for how to build investment portfolios. Combining it with restrictive assumptions regarding investor rationality, information availability and market trading structure, Sharpe transformed it into a model of capital market equilibrium, capturing the relationship between risk and return. Calling it the Capital Asset Pricing Model, or simply CAPM, he published his seminal work in 1965. Quickly CAPM became a central tenet within MPT.

As a theory of capital market equilibrium, CAPM had a number of important advantages. It was a simple mathematical model whose parameters were, to a large extent, straightforward to estimate using available market data. As a positive theory, it had clearly testable implications for stock market equilibrium. This turned out to be both a strength and a weakness. Clear testable implications make it easy to test the model, but also easy to reject. Another advantage of the CAPM is that it relied on straightforward mathematical equations that could be easily woven into other mathematical financial models. Easily testable and easily integrated into other models, the CAPM became ubiquitous within the finance discipline worldwide.

Joining Markowitz optimization and the CAPM as important pillars within MPT, in the mid-1960s 2013 Nobel laureate Eugene Fama of the University of Chicago put forward the final pillar in what is probably the most famous dissertation of our generation. Extending the mathematical concept of rational investors to its logical conclusion, Fama proposed the efficient market hypothesis, which posited that market prices fully reflected all relevant information and, as a result, it was impossible to earn excess returns by means of active management.

Much as in the CAPM, the implications of EMH were easily testable. If the tests showed that publicly available information could be used to earn excess returns, most notably in the stock market, then EMH should be rejected. Since a measure of risk is necessary in order to determine if returns are excess, all tests conducted over the last 40 years are really joint tests of both a risk model and market efficiency. While this tends to weaken the empirical tests, the results obtained over the last 40 years point to a very clear conclusion, as I will discuss shortly.

MPT was built on Markowitz's mean-variance optimization model, Sharpe's CAPM and Fama's EHM. By the mid-1970s, when I was in the PhD program at the University of Washington, MPT was the ascendant paradigm. My major professor Bill Alberts graduated from the University of Chicago and played a role in getting Sharpe's initial CAPM article published. Another one of my professors, Larry Schall, was a student of Fama. For all intents and purposes, the University of Washington was the University of Chicago West and a hotbed of MPT.

Not that I minded, for as a quantitative person the idea that a simple theory like MPT could explain messy financial markets was very attractive. In fact, as I think back about my PhD program, I realize how seldom we actually talked about real financial markets such as the New York Stock Exchange. This became abundantly clear to me when I began teaching investments at the University of Denver as I had to spend a great deal of time studying real stock markets in order to sound halfway intelligent in the classroom. So in the summer of 1978, as I walked across Red Square at the University of Washington with my defended dissertation in one hand and MPT in the other, I could not have been happier. It seemed that we had a rigorous theory of markets and a rational approach to building investment portfolios.

I could not have been more wrong.

THOSE ANNOYING ANOMALIES

As I graduated from the PhD program, the first shots across the MPT bow were being fired. The initial empirical tests of CAPM had been published and instead of finding an upward slope of returns to beta, studies reported a downward slope. This was just opposite of what was predicted by CAPM, since beta as a measure of risk implies a positive return, beta relationship. One would expect that if the major prediction of a theory turns out to be incorrect, the theory would be rejected.

Surprisingly, this is frequently not the case, as there is an emotional attachment to the theory and a reluctance to reject it in the face of unfavorable evidence. This is not only true in finance but in all of science. So rather than rejecting CAPM, the response of the discipline was to search for statistical problems, such as measurement error, in the tests that had been reported. So as I left the PhD program, the challenge to us as newly minted academics was to uncover the statistical problems in the tests and salvage the theory.

At the same time, the EMH was coming under attack as well. In the late 1970s, Sanjay Basu of McMaster University published his research demonstrating that low PE stocks outperformed high PE stocks.[26] In the early 1980s Rolf Banz of Northwestern University published his research showing that small stocks outperformed large stocks.[27] The problem, of course, is that both PE and firm size are public information and should not allow one to earn excess returns. But they did. So joint hypothesis or not, by the early 1980s both EMH and CAPM were coming under serious attack.

In 1981, 2013 Nobel laureate Robert Shiller of the University of Pennsylvania published his article arguing almost all volatility observed in the stock market, even on an annual basis, was noise rather than the result of changes in fundamentals.[28] Since EMH argues that prices fully reflect all relevant information, volatility driven by other than fundamentals strikes at its very heart. EMH advocates countered by arguing that even though prices were driven by other than fundamentals, as long as one could not use this information for earning superior returns, the EMH held. This represented a *damning with faint praise defense of* EMH. Besides, EMH faced much more serious challenges than excess volatility.

Since Shiller made his claim that volatility was largely noise – or in the terminology of BPM, the result of emotional crowds – a number of studies have tried to refute it without success. It appears that volatility is driven mostly by emotions and very little by changes in fundamentals.

---

[26] S. Basu, 'Investment Performance of Common Stocks in Relation to Their Price-Earnings Ratios: A Test of the Efficient Market Hypothesis', *Journal of Finance* 32:3 (1977), pp. 663-682.

[27] Rolf Banz, 'The Relationship Between Return and Market Value of Common Stocks', *Journal of Financial Economics* 9 (1981), pp. 3-18.

[28] Robert Shiller, 'Do stock prices move too much to be justified by subsequent changes in dividends?', *American Economic Review* 71 (1981), 421-436.

Shiller's noisy market model also creates problems for Markowitz's portfolio optimization. If volatility is the result of emotional crowds, then emotion has been placed at the center of the portfolio construction process. So rather than being a risk-return optimization, it's in reality an emotion-return optimization.

Furthermore, many of the so-called measures used for evaluating portfolio performance are actually emotion measures rather than risk measures. These measures include downside capture, downside risk, R-squared, and most interestingly, the Sharpe ratio. Indeed, the widespread use of the Sharpe ratio by advisors and investment managers alike leads them to focus on emotional catering rather than performance when building a portfolio. The ultimate irony of rationality-based MPT is that it has provided the tools upon which CE's depend. The law of unintended consequences has the last word.

THE DECLINE OF MPT

By the mid-1980s, all three MPT pillars were under serious assault. MPT advocates counter attacked. To save CAPM, a new three factor model was proposed, which included CAPM beta, Banz's small firm effect, and Basu's low PE effect. Later, when Narasimhan Jegadeesh of Emory University and Sheridan Titman of the University of Texas identified a momentum effect, it was also added, resulting in a four factor model.[29] Never mind that it was not determined whether any of these effects were measuring risk or identifying an opportunity. Amazingly the four factor model has become the standard within the industry, even though we have no idea what each factor is capturing. Financial markets theory is truly in disarray.

The response of the EMH supporters was to accept the anomalies that have been uncovered and yet they continued to argue EMH remained a viable theory as long as active equity managers could not use these anomalies to earn excess returns. For the last 20 years, a series of studies

---

[29] N. Jegadeesh and S. Titman, 'Overreaction, Delayed Reaction, and Contrarian Profits', *Review of Financial Studies* 8:4 (1995).

have shown that a large number of active equity managers are superior stock pickers and do indeed earn excess returns. This research has been sidetracked by the better-known research stream focusing on average equity manager performance over long time periods. It concludes the average fund underperforms and goes on to argue that as a result active equity managers lack stock picking skill.

Yes, it is true that the average manager underperforms, but stock picking skill research demonstrates that high-conviction positions taken by active equity managers earn excess returns. The conflict in results can be explained by noting that funds, besides holding high-conviction positions that outperform, also hold many low-conviction positions.

These latter positions are held for reasons other than performance, including getting too large, fitting into style boxes, reducing volatility, and reducing maximum drawdown. For the typical fund, low-conviction positions outnumber high-conviction positions by three-to-one. So the excess returns on the high-conviction positions are more than wiped out by the underperformance of the low-conviction positions. The conclusion to draw from this is that active equity funds are good at stock picking but bad at portfolio management.

So the last pillar supporting EMH has crumbled.

REJECTING THE WORLD RATHER THAN REJECTING THE PARADIGM

Like any good scientific, rational, truth-seeking organization, the finance profession has chosen to reject the world rather than reject the empirically discredited paradigm. You probably find this surprising, as most assume that rational, truth-seeking organizations are empirically based and only accept concepts supported by the evidence. But scientific and professional organizations are human, so are susceptible to the same cognitive errors made by other human organizations.

As I progressed through my academic career, I found this very disappointing. Being an empiricist, I operated under the assumption that if the evidence did not support the theory, then the theory would be rejected, not the world. What I was observing was just the opposite. Rather than rejecting the CAPM, the model was being used widely in studies and showed up in textbooks all over the world. I would query my students from other countries if they had run into CAPM in their home country finance textbooks and indeed they had. The fact that CAPM appeared everywhere in finance confirmed its validity by means of social validation rather than by means of empirical evidence. Emotional decision-making was rampant in what I thought was my rational discipline.

In the mid-1990s, I began to change my teaching, arguing that the evidence was not supportive of CAPM and therefore students should not use it for making investment decisions. This naturally led students to ask why I was the only one in the department making such statements. Of course I would respond by saying that the evidence doesn't support CAPM and so it should not be used. The common response was that everybody else was presenting it and it shows up in lots of different places in finance. I must admit I was baffled by the inconsistency between the evidence and what was widely taught.

The answer to my dilemma came in the form of a book entitled *The Structure Of Scientific Revolutions* by Thomas Kuhn of the University of California, Berkeley. He argued that scientific disciplines are no different than other human organizations that change very slowly. Once a paradigm was accepted, it was a long process before a new paradigm took its place. Most scientists, which Kuhn referred to as normal scientists, did not question the underlying paradigm. The paradigm represented the sand box in which they operated and if the paradigm were rejected, they were no longer scientists, which would be a serious blow to their self-image. So it required a large number of anomalies and lengthy discussion before a new paradigm was accepted. Kuhn recognized that professional pride is a powerful deterrent to change in the sciences.

For example, Copernicus' heliocentric universe was not accepted as the new model of our planetary system until 150 years after it was first proposed in 1543. The idea that meteorites come from outer space was not accepted until 300 years after the first meteorite fragments were collected in France in 1492. Dr. Ignaz Semmelweis, at his 1840s Vienna Austria Hospital, determined that doctors not washing their hands was the major cause of an epidemic of frequently fatal mother and newborn puerperal fever. Distressingly, a recent study concluded 50% of healthcare professionals are still not properly washing their hands. The list goes on.

Just because something is widely used, doesn't mean the evidence supports its usefulness. This is an example of the unreliability of conventional wisdom and the power of social validation within the investment profession.

LET THE TRANSITION BEGIN

Now that we have spent the last 40 years, essentially my entire professional career, waiting for evidence supportive of MPT to appear and seeing none, it is time to move on. Luckily we have an alternative that is emerging: behavioral finance. It should be recognized that normal scientists within the finance industry will fight tooth and nail to preserve MPT, some to the bitter end, but at some point the industry will make the transition from MPT to behavioral finance and the investment world, as we know it, will be forever changed.

As Kuhn observes, when paradigms change, everything changes, including basic concepts, facts, history, tools and methodologies. After the dust settles, virtually nothing of MPT will remain. The debate has begun and will only intensify over the coming years.[30]

---

[30] Andrew Lo, 'The Adaptive Markets Hypothesis: Market Efficiency from an Evolutionary Perspective', *Journal of Portfolio Management* 30 (2004), pp. 15-29, presents an alternative to the EMH that is based on the mistake ridden but adaptive behavior of individuals that helps explain behavioral price distortions. Much as arbitrage plays a central role in the reliability of MPT-based predictions, so too does the speed of adaption play a central role in the AMH. If adaption is slow or non-existent, then AMH will be no more satisfactory than is MPT as a model of the market.

SECTION 2: LEAVING THE CULT OF EMOTION

CHAPTER 7: RELEASING EMOTIONAL BRAKES: A 12-STEP PROGRAM

IN SECTION 1 I discussed the many emotional brakes investors apply when making decisions. I also described the Cult Enforcers – the industry professionals who put in place policies and apply techniques that encourage investors to remain in the Cult of Emotion. So even if the advisor and investor want to release their brakes, the industry is set up to discourage them to do so.

To help you make this transition, in this chapter I present a 12-step program to show you how to release your emotional brakes.

Step 1: Hello my name is _____ and I am a Coean

Like any self-help program, this one starts with admitting there is a problem. That is, you recognize that you make emotional investment decisions and you would like to avoid this going forward.

Step 2: It is OK to be wealthy

This may seem like an unusual step, but I'm amazed at the number of people I run into that don't believe they can be wealthy. Not only is it OK to be wealthy but for many of us it's also possible to be wealthy. Time, discipline and the principles of BPM are the keys to successfully building wealth. If it is possible for you to be wealthy, then don't apply emotional brakes that will prevent you from becoming so.

Step 3: I will strive to eliminate my MLA affliction and reduce my need for social validation

The two most important emotional brakes are MLA and social validation, which are the result of millions of years of evolution. The fight or flight reaction triggered when a saber-toothed tiger showed up was critical to our survival as humans. However, a sudden drop in portfolio value can trigger the same emotions as did that predator thousands of years ago, but without the same life-and-death consequences. So being governed by an ancient set of emotions often leads to poor financial decisions.

Doing the same thing as everybody else, the definition of social validation, also made sense thousands of years ago when life was full of danger. Living in small groups, we depended on others to sense danger and react instinctively. Among other things, you didn't want to be the last or the slowest member of the group when fleeing the tiger. In contrast, today we frequently want to take positions opposite the emotional crowd as a way to harness behavioral price distortions.

Many argue that to overcome such powerful evolutionary emotions is extremely difficult. Kahneman himself is pessimistic about the chances of making such a change. I am familiar with advisors and asset managers who have successfully dealt with these two emotions in themselves as well as in their clients. So I am hopeful that it is possible to make progress in this regard. For example, Don Novick, an extremely successful trader, explains his success as follows:

> "When you are trading, you cannot allow any member of your brain's emotional executive committee to knock on the door of the decision-making boardroom, let alone take a seat at the table. Ruthlessly, remorselessly, relentlessly, you have to stay in the

present. You can't let what happened yesterday affect what happens today."[31]

Step 4: I believe that volatility, along with close cousins the Sharpe ratio, max drawdown and tracking error, are largely measures of emotion and should not be used in constructing and evaluating portfolios

Volatility is driven by the emotional reactions to current events. Consequently, very little of volatility, particularly stock market volatility, can be explained by changes in underlying fundamentals. On the other side of the coin, investors react emotionally to volatility, meaning that emotions both cause volatility and are caused by volatility. To the greatest extent possible, volatility should be taken out of the portfolio management process.

A particularly pernicious impact of volatility is the widespread use of the Sharpe ratio, which is return divided by standard deviation. It suffers from three serious problems. First, returns are historical, and as we know past performance is not predictive of future performance. Second, standard deviation is largely emotionally driven. So rather than being a return-to-risk measure, the Sharpe ratio is a return to emotion ratio. Third, the returns are long term while the standard deviation is annual. This further exacerbates the emotional problems with this ratio. The Sharpe ratio is among the worst measures foisted upon the industry and deserves to be banished.

Second only to the Sharpe ratio, tracking error is a bane within the industry. The first step in calculating tracking error is to assign the equity fund to an arbitrary peer group, for example, small-cap value. It is arbitrary because the assignment has little to do with the strategy of the

---

[31] Kevin Dutton, *The Wisdom of Psychopaths: What Saints, Spies, and Serial Killers Can Teach Us About Success* (Scientific American/Farrar, Straus and Giroux, 2013).

fund. But it gets stranger. Even though the fund is expected to generate alpha, it is also expected to closely track its benchmark. How bizarre is this: as a portfolio manager I am expected to track the index that I am expected to outperform! Finally, in the strangest twist of all, tracking error is considered to be risk.

So let me understand this. As an active manager I am being assigned to an arbitrary peer group, which has nothing to do with the way I manage money, then I am asked to track this group's index while at the same time trying to outperform this same index. If I then generate tracking error, I am considered risky.

The industry can't get rid of these volatility-based measures soon enough.

Step 5: I believe that volatility and risk are not synonymous and that most references to risk are really references to emotion

Risk is the chance of underperformance, while, on the other hand, volatility is a measure of emotion. For short-horizon portfolios, volatility does contribute to risk. For long-horizon portfolios, volatility plays a much reduced role. Since portfolios are often built based on short-term volatility, the paradoxical result is risk is actually increased. This happens because reducing short-term volatility often reduces long-term expected return, which means the chance of underperformance has increased.

A classic example of this is investing in both stocks and bonds in a long-horizon portfolio in an effort to reduce short-term volatility, with the result that it is virtually guaranteed you will underperform a 100% stock portfolio over the long term.

Risk is mentioned frequently in market commentaries and portfolio analysis, but most of the time emotion is what is being referenced, not risk. So when I hear the word *risk*, I mentally cross it out and substitute *emotion*.

Step 6: I believe that increased stock market volatility represents an opportunity for, rather than a risk to, my portfolio

Stock market volatility is particularly problematic in making investment decisions. As market volatility increases, the reaction hardwired by evolution is to exit. Since so many investors do exactly this, a behavioral price distortion results.

Research shows that following a period of heightened market volatility, above average market returns are common. The historical average market return is 10%, which means expected returns exceed 10% after a period of excess market volatility. The typical investor switches into fight or flight mode, exits the market and misses the above average returns. Studies confirm that the typical equity mutual fund investor underperforms the return of the fund, since fund purchases and liquidations are poorly timed.

Step 7: I will divide my portfolio into buckets as a way to reduce emotional sensitivity to volatility

Dividing up a portfolio into buckets, each meeting a different set of client needs, is an important step for reducing the emotional impact of volatility. The bucket approach is also referred to as the endowment model, as endowments construct their portfolios in a similar manner. Typically advisors break the portfolio into three buckets. The first bucket meets liquidity and short-term income needs and is funded using liquid, short-term, low to no volatility instruments. The goal is to eliminate concerns regarding volatility and results in the client being confident that short term needs are being met. The issue of volatility has been removed from this portion of the portfolio.

The second is the capital growth bucket for building long-horizon wealth. It is important to structure client conversations to spend as little time as possible talking about the short-term performance of this bucket in an attempt to maintain a long-term focus. If this can be done successfully, it is more likely long-term expected and excess returns will be the focus for building the capital growth portfolio and, in turn, there will be little focus on short-term volatility and correlations.

The third bucket is comprised of unique investments requiring special management. Such investments include real estate, farms, art, a stock held for other than performance reasons, and other non-traditional assets. These are managed in a unique way based on client guidelines.

Breaking a portfolio into buckets is an alternative to the traditional 60/40 portfolio approach. Each bucket meets a specific client need rather than constructing a single portfolio to meet overall client needs. This divide and conquer approach can have a positive impact on performance, while reducing the emotional impact of portfolio volatility. It is one of the most effective ways for releasing emotional brakes.

The appendix to this book describes how an investment advisor at Cascade Financial Management thinks about and uses the bucket model in building client portfolios.

A creative way to fund short-term income needs without having to devote a large portion of a portfolio to low yield bonds was suggested to me by a seminar participant in Dallas a number of years ago. Let's say that the client wishes to have their next four years of $75,000 annual income needs funded with virtual certainty. To meet this need, one, two and three-year treasury strips, each with a $75,000 maturity value, are purchased. When the one-year strip matures, a new $75,000, three-year strip is purchased. With this rolling investment strategy, four years of income is guaranteed without having to commit an inordinate portion of the portfolio to low yielding bonds.

Step 8: I will focus on expected and excess returns, while largely ignoring correlation and volatility, when building long-horizon portfolios

If a portfolio is divided into buckets, it is easier to focus the capital growth bucket on long-term expected and excess returns. This also provides an opportunity to largely ignore correlation and volatility, which help in dealing with MLA but have little or no positive impact on long-term performance.

Advisors who successfully implement the bucket approach generally hold little or no fixed income in the capital growth bucket, thus avoiding the negative impact of low expected bond returns. Instead, fixed income investments are limited for use in the liquidity and short-term income bucket. This is the power of the bucket approach and allows for constructing separate parts of the portfolio very differently. Being able to ignore volatility in the capital growth portfolio is highly favorable for building long-term wealth.

Step 9: I will forget the price I paid for an investment, as well as its name, to mitigate these emotional anchors

Many will find this suggestion shocking and even irresponsible. Isn't it the responsibility of the manager to know as much as possible about the investments they are making? In particular, the price paid and the name of the investment represent among the most common information gathered. So why would you make an effort to forget both after making an investment?

It is easy for individuals to anchor on a piece of information, even an arbitrary piece of information that has little to do with the investment itself. The price paid is an anchor which impacts subsequent decisions. It is the starting point of many an investment rule, such as stop loss orders, profit harvesting based on X percent price increase, and holding a stock until it gets back up to the price paid. This latter rule is obviously emotional, as are the other two, which is a consequence of MLA.

Hersh Shefrin and Meir Statman of Santa Clara University believe purchase price rules are used by so many investors that it produces market-wide price distortions, something they refer to as the disposition effect.[32] This affect posits that investors sell winners too soon, because of the emotional validation arising from earning a positive return, while hanging on to losers too long, due to loss regret. A straightforward way to avoid the pitfalls of the disposition effect is to forget the price paid.

Reinforcing the disposition effect is the observation that investors fool themselves into thinking that if the stock is not sold it really isn't a loss. The tax code which does not recognize gains or losses until realized supports this too, which is an example of the IRS as CE. The simplest way to avoid this emotional decision is to forget the price paid and thus have no idea whether you have made or lost money.

As Kenny Rogers once wisely advised, "You never count your money when you're sittin' at the table."

The investment's name is another anchor which attracts information, whether useful or not. As I will argue in Chapter 13, the key to successful investing is consistent pursuit of a narrowly defined strategy, which translates into making investment decisions based on a limited information set. This means ignoring everything else about the investment other than what is important in executing the strategy. An investment's name attracts a full range of information that you may have a hard time ignoring, particularly if it comes from what you believe is a credible source. It is only human nature to begin doubting your analysis. One way to avoid experiencing these doubts is to forget the name of your investments.

---

[32] Hersh Shefrin and M. Statman, 'The disposition to sell winners too early and ride losers too long: theory and evidence', *Journal of Finance* 40 (1985), pp. 777-790.

It's only natural that you enjoy talking about your investments. So when asked, you describe them with a sense of pride, since they were selected based on your careful and insightful analysis. The names you mention will trigger in your listener their own emotions and thoughts regarding the company. Often the person will not agree with you and explain why they feel the way they do and you might begin doubting your decision. One way to avoid this problem is to tell people you cannot remember what you've invested in. Better to be thought forgetful than to stray from your investment strategy.

As an example of this concept, for some time I held Deluxe (DLX) in the Athena Pure portfolio. Deluxe manufactures and sells checkbooks and the usage of checks has fallen dramatically in recent years. The conventional wisdom among analysts was that nobody in their right mind would own the stock. However, my strategy surfaced it as a good investment, so it was purchased.

The father of an advisor for which AthenaInvest manages money worked for Deluxe. A couple of years earlier he had some coworkers over for a party and the advisor happened to mention that his investment clients held Deluxe in their portfolio. The Deluxe employees were incredulous, stating in no uncertain terms that Deluxe represented a terrible investment as check usage was tanking.

Deluxe did very well in spite of what everyone else thought and paradoxically even those working at Deluxe did not realize their own company's stock represented a good investment. I sold Deluxe early in 2013, not because check usage was declining but because the company began paying down debt, a no-no in my strategy (I will explain more about this strategy later). The lesson here is to stick with your strategy and don't be unduly influenced by others, even those who know a great deal about the company in which you are investing.

I generally do not remember the stocks I purchase and I do not remember the price paid, because neither is part of my investment strategy. I only learn about gains and losses on individual stocks after the fact, if ever. This does cause problems when current and potential clients ask what is being held in our portfolios and I'm unable to answer. Even if I happen to remember the name of the stock, I am unable to provide a story suitable for their consumption, as I only remember those few things that I believe are important in making the investment decision. This is disconcerting to clients because I don't know the name of the stocks held and I can't tell a feel-good story. What I can do is explain my investment strategy simply and clearly, and strategy is all that matters.

Not only do I make no effort to remember the stocks I currently own, once I sell, I never look back. I don't know how the stock has performed while I hold it and I don't know how it performs after I sell it. It doesn't take much to imagine a bevy of cognitive errors arising as a result of keeping track of previously sold stocks. *Monday morning quarterbacking* doesn't improve portfolio returns.

As I reminded my seminar participants for years, there is only one reason to buy stocks and that is to make money. They are not part of your family. If you conclude that a stock is no longer a good investment, sell it, forget it and move on. Do not fall in love with your stocks and don't think twice when you sell them. Investment management is a cold-blooded, return-maximizing endeavor.

Step 10: I believe past performance is a poor predictor of future performance, so I will not use it when evaluating an investment manager

Past performance is not predictive of future performance. It is not like there is controversy surrounding this conclusion, as it has been confirmed by numerous academic studies. In spite of overwhelming evidence virtually everyone, individuals and professionals alike, uses past performance in selecting managers. In fact, it is frequently the most important criteria when selecting a manager. This is a dramatic example of the emotional power of the representativeness bias. If you release this emotional brake, you will be acting differently than virtually everyone else in the industry. Are you strong enough to do this? If you are, your portfolio performance will improve.

Past performance is best for testing the usefulness of an investment strategy. The larger and longer the sample, the more reliable the results. For this reason, the current effort to ensure the accurate reporting of performance results is worthwhile. Reliable return data leads to more reliable test results.

Step 11: I believe unreasonably constraining a portfolio, such as keeping a manager in a style box, hurts performance and thus will be avoided

Consistent pursuit of a self-declared investment strategy is key to superior performance. Anything that gets in the way of doing this, such as emotional brakes applied by an investor or constraints imposed by the industry, hurts investment performance. One of the major offenders in this regard is the style grid used for active equity fund evaluation and distribution. One way to improve portfolio performance is to remove any requirement for a fund to stay in a style box.

Step 12: I will consistently pursue a narrowly focused investment strategy while taking only high-conviction positions when managing a portfolio

Now that 11 of the 12 steps for releasing emotional brakes have been completed, you are ready to begin building an investment strategy. Successful strategies are narrowly focused on harnessing emotional crowd-driven price distortions by consistently pursuing the strategy over time and by taking high-conviction positions. This is key to implementing BPM.

CHAPTER 8: MITIGATING EMOTIONAL COSTS

TO CATER OR to mitigate, that is the question. It is one of the most important matters for an advisor or asset manager to address. Left to their own devices, investors make poor decisions which end up hurting long-term performance. So financial professionals must decide to what extent they cater and to what extent they attempt to mitigate losses resulting from emotional client decisions.

The path of least resistance, of course, is to cater to client emotions, since trying to modify client behavior is difficult. Be that as it may, one of the most important things an advisor can do is help clients avoid emotional investing mistakes and thus mitigate the resulting losses. In my opinion, this is a top advisor value add.

Having worked with many advisors, I have observed those who do nothing but cater to client emotions, even panicking on a daily basis, all the way up to those who effectively mitigate emotional portfolio losses. It is important for advisors to master mitigation skills rather than cater to clients, but it is certainly much easier to cater as you do not have to deal with highly emotional client issues.

Within the industry, there are firms offering advisor education programs to help clients avoid cognitive errors. I will draw from some of these as I describe how to go about mitigating the damage of emotional errors. This is a rapidly growing field and no doubt there will be new ideas offered in the coming years.

COMMUNICATING WITH CLIENTS

The first important step for the advisor is to release their own emotional brakes. The next step is to implement the critically important bucket model for building client portfolios as described in Step 7 in the previous chapter. If the advisor has accomplished these, the next step is to learn how to communicate with clients so they also release their emotional brakes. As a way to help in this process, below I provide suggestions drawn from my work with the advisors who successfully communicate with clients.

The listening model

A common suggestion for dealing with client anxiety is to listen to their concerns. We are all aware that once we vent, expressing what is bothering us, the emotions surrounding the issue dissipate.

The other thing that helps is that after listening to client concerns, the advisor should not panic and instead should provide reassurances that things will be OK. Many client concerns are the consequence of news stories from TV or the internet, or what has been told to them by neighbors and friends. The calm and soothing response of a financial professional can allay many of these fears. Clearly not everything can be solved in this way, but many issues can be resolved by means of attentive listening followed by a reassuring response.

The planning model

The focus in this approach is on developing and executing an overall financial plan. Client conversations deal with plan progress, involving a wide range of topics, including insurance, estate planning, retirement and investment portfolio. There are two advantages of this approach. First, the more services offered by the advisor, the more likely the client will stay put. Second, a large number of topics discussed are less emotional than investment performance. The result is more time spent discussing planning topics and less time spent on emotional topics such as short-term investment performance.

I'm the boss model

Some advisors develop a relationship with their clients in which the client turns over all decisions to the advisor. This is a product of both the advisor and the client, as some clients, no matter how confident in the advisor, will never relinquish all decision-making. If the advisor is successful in creating a relationship in which the client relinquishes substantially all decision-making, it becomes much easier to mitigate the portfolio impact of emotional errors.

Feathering in investments

Individuals have a difficult time moving quickly when making a decision. This no doubt springs from an internal sense of caution when a decision has to be made. From an evolutionary standpoint, we probably come by it rightly. Have you ever watched a cat step through a door? First they sniff, then they stick one paw out and pull it back in, then sniff some more, then look around some more, and finally step through the door. This sounds a lot like the process many individuals go through when they make investment decisions. If a recommendation is made to invest in stocks, for example, it is highly unusual for the individual to move the entire amount immediately. It is not in our makeup to move quickly.

Besides this built-in caution, there is another emotional reason for staging an investment decision. Let's say somebody wants to put $100,000 in a particular investment. Rather than investing the full amount immediately, have the client invest a third at the beginning of each of the next three months. The advantage of this approach is the client will have a difficult time anchoring on the initial amount. It's easy to remember that you invested $100,000 if it's invested all at once, but more difficult if it's invested over a three-month period. Eliminating the anchor sets the stage for less emotional future conversations.

For many years I railed against dollar cost averaging as being financial nonsense. If you believe stock returns are drawn from a distribution with a historical average return of 10%, then why not invest all of your money right away? It is easy to show the math that justifies investing everything immediately rather than feathering in over time.

I've now changed my mind, as I have done in a number of areas, to the view that dollar cost averaging is an attractive way to get clients to invest. It is much better to have the client invest in the market gradually over time than, for emotional reasons, not invest at all. The emotional benefits of dollar cost averaging outweigh the financial disadvantages.

MOUNTAIN CHART PROBLEMS

Consider the 462 monthly S&P 500 returns from January 1975 through June 2013. If you invested $10,000 on January 1, 1975, you end up with $756,094 on June 30, 2013 (ignoring taxes) as shown in Figure 7.1. This is an annual compound return of 11.9%. This is the traditional *mountain chart* for displaying portfolio performance over time.

FIGURE 7.1: S&P PERFORMANCE, JANUARY 1975 TO JUNE 2013

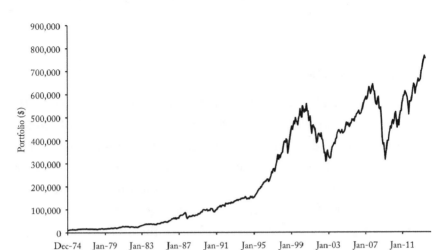

Investors remember and, in turn, understand events by means of stories. Mountain charts facilitate the creation of such market stories. The best known of these are associated with so-called bull and bear markets. I say these are *so-called* markets because, as I will show in the next section, the returns that generated the mountain chart displayed in Figure 1 were drawn from a positive expected return distribution. This means, from a statistical standpoint, stocks always experienced a bull market during this period, since the expected return each month was positive and therefore stocks were expected to go up each month. This is the best known example of the problems associated with mountain charts as a source of misleading stories.

Additional stories are generated by relating market movements to concurrent events. These result from investor desire to understand why the market goes up and down. As I discussed earlier, very little of market up and down movements can be explained by underlying fundamentals, even for annual returns. The stock market is predictive of economic activity six to nine months in the future, so the conventional wisdom has the relationship between the economy and the market running the wrong way. The problem is that mountain charts encourage this faulty analysis and once the stories are created they take on a life of their own, becoming the source of poor investment decisions.

Randomness disguised

You can hear chuckling from the distribution gnomes who generate the randomness that we observe as market movements. A series of random returns are generated and then linked together to form a mountain chart as in Figure 7.1. The resulting patterns are also random, patterns that are turned into stories by market observers. It is the stories that investors remember, not the fact that the patterns were generated randomly. You can hear the gnomes saying "Can you believe the explanation provided for that random return we generated yesterday? Where do they come up with these meaningless stories?"

Let's now look back at Figure 3.1. In that chapter I challenged you to decide which of the four market return series are random and which are real. At least one of the series is real and at least one of the series is random, generated by drawing returns from a normal distribution with the same mean and standard deviation as the real series. What did you determine? The answer is that stock market return series 1 and 4 are real while 2 and 3 are random. How did you do?

A more interesting observation is that series 3 would no doubt generate an extensive discussion of a bear market lasting from month 14 through month 33, the same length as the recent October 2007 through March 2009 market decline. As investors we believe we understand why the market declined in 2008 and place a great deal of importance on that event and the stories surrounding it. In the case of series 3, we know for certain that there is no explanation for why the market went down for 19 months, it just happened, randomly generated. What is more, we know with certainty that throughout this 19-month period we were continuously in a bull market, because the expected return in every month was positive. That is, in every one of the 19 months the market was expected to go up. You can imagine the gnomes chuckling when they hear the silly stories about a bear market during this time.

Both series 1 and 4 in Figure 3.1 are real so we do not know how they were generated. Since random series are so similar to the real series, it gives one pause when hearing a story about why the market went up or down. It makes sense to question stories that are based on what are probably random events.

The most remembered stories are those associated with the strongest emotions. So when examining the mountain chart in Figure 7.1, clients will focus on the market declines of 2000 to 2002 and 2007 to 2009. These were very painful events and, given the 2-to-1 emotional loss-to-gain ratio, these two declines easily dominate this nearly 40-year market history. Lost in the haze of peak-end memories is the impressive fact that the stock market generated an annual compound return of nearly 12%, meaning that wealth doubled every six years over this time period. Truly amazing.

Having presented these results to many clients and advisors, I am struck with how few of them hear, let alone assimilate, the message that the stock market was a powerful generator of wealth over this time period. The market drop stories of the last decade trump any discussion of the benefits of long-term stock market investing. Mountain charts make it much easier to create such decision distorting stories.

I am not arguing that last decade's large market drops were not painful, for indeed they were. What I'm arguing is that how you present performance can have a profound impact on how clients view investments and make subsequent decisions. Given the highly emotional market drops displayed in Figure 7.1, it is very difficult for a client to hear anything else you say after viewing the mountain chart.

The goal is to present performance so that it doesn't trigger these attention blocking emotions and in so doing you are able to lead the client to decisions believed best for them. I now turn to two alternative ways of presenting performance that focus on the essential aspects of an investment without triggering debilitating emotional client reactions: the return histogram and matched returns.

THE RETURN HISTOGRAM ADVANTAGE

Histograms are a well-known statistical tool for representing random variables, such as investment returns. A histogram for the 462 monthly S&P 500 returns – those used to create the mountain chart in Figure 7.1 – is displayed in Figure 7.2. It displays a much different picture than does the mountain chart.

FIGURE 7.2: MONTHLY S&P 500 RETURNS, JANUARY 1975 TO JUNE 2013

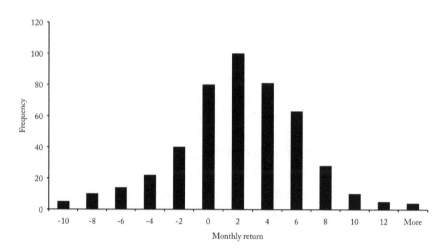

What stories flow from this representation of market returns?

The first is the average monthly return is positive and, in addition, a majority (63%) of the monthly returns are positive. Thus you were able to tilt the odds in your favor by investing in the stock market during this time period. Successful long-term investing is about tilting the odds in your favor, not generating consistent returns over time. Cash equivalents are the only investments yielding consistent returns over time and we all know how good they are for building long-horizon wealth.

The second story is that the matching positive returns on the right side of the distribution are larger than the matching negative returns on the left side. The matching positive returns more than offset the negative market returns. I will demonstrate this in the next section. Naturally, we would like to eliminate the negative returns, but since there is a 63% chance next month's return will be positive, you must correctly forecast at least 63% of the months in order to increase your return relative to buying and holding. Research shows such accuracy in forecasting is very difficult to achieve. The fact that the matching positive return more than offsets the negative return provides a further argument against short-term market timing.[33]

Many will object to viewing market returns as a histogram rather than as the traditional mountain chart. This is largely driven by our desire to be able to tell a story about what has happened and the belief that much of what happens in the stock market is driven by concurrent events. However the truth is the path followed by the market, as represented in Figure 7.1, is one of millions of possible paths. We know that the return in any month is largely driven by the collective emotions existing in the market that month, thus different collective emotions produce a different return. So the actual sequence of returns is, surprise, surprise, random.

Consequently, a histogram provides the most accurate representation of market returns. *The mountain chart is an emotionally driven, random representation of market returns.* This means that the many stories based on the mountain chart are themselves largely random. Histogram trumps mountain chart when discussing investment performance with clients.

THE SELF-HEALING RETURN DISTRIBUTION: MATCHED RETURNS

I often hear presentations about the impact of negative returns on portfolios. If a portfolio drops by 20%, for example, it is pointed out that

---

[33] In Chapter 17 I will discuss behavioral measures of expected market return that can be used for market timing. This methodology is based on time periods longer than a month and so is consistent with the argument that monthly market timing is difficult. As I argued earlier, it is my belief that many of the current market timing services are largely catering to investor MLA and more than likely reduce portfolio returns.

you have to earn a return of 25% or more in order to offset the loss. The implication, then, is that you should do whatever is necessary to avoid the initial 20% decline, because it is difficult to earn 25%. But it turns out the S&P 500 return distribution contains within it a matched positive return that more than offsets virtually every negative return.

If you invested $10,000 at the beginning of January 1975, you ended with $756,094 on June 30, 2013 and earned an annual compound return of 11.9%, regardless of the sequencing of the 462 monthly S&P 500 returns. What if the 462 returns are sorted from largest monthly loss to largest monthly gain and then the largest loss is matched with the largest gain, the next largest loss with the next largest gain, and so forth, creating 231 matched returns. The 231 matched returns are then calculated as two-month compound returns. Multiplying $10,000 times the linked matched returns produces the same final value of $756,094 as shown in Figure 7.1.

The average matched return is 1.9%, which produces the resulting compound annual return of 11.9%. Of most interest is the fact that only five matched returns are negative, which means that for the other 226 matched returns, the negative return is more than offset by the matching positive return. In fact, for 60 of the matched returns, both returns are positive, a consequence of 63% positive monthly returns.

I refer to this preponderance of positive matched returns as the *self-healing nature* of the S&P 500 return distribution. The median number of months the matching positive return occurs after the negative return is nine months, though the range of monthly leads and lags is large.[34]

How can the concept of a self-healing distribution, as confirmed by the matched return analysis, help in client discussions? Let me suggest three ways:

---

[34] The matching positive return occurs a maximum of 440 months before the negative return, up to a maximum 424 months afterwards.

1. Matched returns demonstrate that virtually every negative return has a more than offsetting matching positive return within the distribution. This provides some consolation when a negative return has been experienced. Of course, in the presence of MLA, a client feels twice as bad about the loss as they feel good about the equivalent gain. Helping offset these emotions is the reality that if enough returns are drawn (i.e. there is a sufficiently long investment horizon), the negative return will be more than offset by a matching positive return. Rather than overreacting to a negative return, the client can take comfort in the knowledge that the return distribution is self-healing.

2. Matched returns can be used to counter the pervasive argument that if you experience a 10% loss, for example, you will need a positive return that exceeds 10% to get back to where you were. This is technically correct, but more often than not the implication, often the direct statement, is that you need to avoid negative returns since those offsetting large positive returns are hard to come by. But matched returns show that this is not the case. The stock market return distribution is self-healing, so the offsetting positive return is within the distribution. This means buying and holding automatically generates an offsetting positive return. No special strategy, beyond patience, is required of the investor.

3. It goes without saying that we would like to avoid negative returns and thus only reap positive returns. There is a market timing industry trying to achieve this ideal, a goal which I think is largely a pipe dream. Matched returns present another challenge for the timing crowd, in that on average the matching positive return occurs after the negative return. So if the market is exited as a result of a negative return, you have to be very adept at returning to the market in order to earn the positive return. My impression is that investors have a difficult time getting back in after exiting. Studies reveal that investors tend to get out at the wrong time and back in at the wrong time. Matched returns are another argument for not trying to short-term time the market; just by staying in the market and waiting the negative return will be offset.

MITIGATING EMOTIONAL COSTS

This chapter focused on mitigating emotional costs associated with investing in the stock market. The stock market is the primary growth engine for building long-term wealth and mistakes here have a disproportionately large impact. I believe the lack of stock market investments is a serious problem among today's advisors and investors.

It was recently reported by Blackrock that individual retirement portfolios hold $10 trillion in cash and are invested 48% in cash, 18% in stocks and the rest in bonds. It goes without saying this is a critical challenge facing investment professionals in dealing with client investment decisions. My hope is the suggestions I have provided will help advisors and investment managers in this effort.

MLA is a serious affliction impacting clients and the resulting emotional reaction to short-term losses leads to inferior long-term performance. So anything the advisor and investment manager can do to help lessen this emotional problem will yield more successful portfolios. Mitigating the damage clients do to their portfolio as a result of emotional investment decisions is one of the more important skills advisors and investment managers need to develop. In fact, I feel this skill is a leading reason why individuals need to hire an experienced advisor. As an advisor, the goal is to mitigate as often as possible, while seldom adopting the role of a caterer.

CHAPTER 9: STYLE GRID PERFORMANCE DRAG

LABELS ARE USED to organize the world around us. If something is mislabeled, it can have a profound impact on the quality of the decisions we make. This is the situation in the active equity space, where funds are labeled using the style grid. The resulting mislabeling contributes to fund underperformance, as managers attempt to stay in the style box in which they have been arbitrarily placed. Consequently, managers have to stray from their stated investment strategy, investing in stocks other than their best ideas. Thus mislabeling drives funds to be strategy inconsistent, as well as take low-conviction positions, resulting in poor investment performance.

The mistake made by many is to assume a fund's equity strategy can be defined by portfolio characteristics, such as the average market cap and PE of the stocks held. Strategy is the way a manager goes about analyzing, buying and selling stocks over time, while portfolio characteristics, such as market capitalization and value-growth, describe the equity holdings that result. There is no reason to believe that portfolio characteristics remain constant over time as an equity strategy is successfully executed.

One of the bizarre outcomes of equating strategy and characteristics is the introduction of style drift. Believing that characteristics and strategy are synonymous, the industry requires managers to avoid style drift, or in other words, maintain the same stock characteristics regardless of economic and market conditions. This requirement hurts performance and shortly I will provide the evidence that style drift is part and parcel of superior performance. As a consequence, one of the worst decisions that can be made is to fire a manager for style drift.

A LEADERLESS STAMPEDE

For several years I attempted to identify the origin of the style grid with little success. Then one day I was speaking with a couple of former Russell analysts who claimed that the style grid originated with Russell in 1984 as a result of a proposal provided by Bill Sharpe for categorizing the exploding number of active equity mutual funds. Based on his suggestion, Russell launched the style grid shortly thereafter. They were stunned when other investment professionals, within a year of the launch, were talking about style drift. Today the industry is victimized by style drift, a concept that was not envisioned at the launch of the Russell equity mutual fund categorization system. The law of unintended consequences strikes again.

The style grid gained considerable momentum when, in 1992, Morningstar released its 3x3 style grid. The grid was motivated by an expressed need of investment advisors for a straightforward tool for categorizing mutual funds in order to help individual investors decide on the proper mix of funds. Among other things, advisors were saying they were having a hard time convincing clients to invest in more than one domestic equity fund. Another challenge was that funds often changed strategies, changed names, or had names that mislead regarding the strategy of the fund.

Around the time Morningstar introduced the style grid, others began offering style indices. The S&P 500/Barra Growth and Value index was introduced in 1992, the S&P Mid Cap 400/Barra Growth and Value index arrived in 1993, and the S&P Small Cap 600/Barra Growth and Value index was created in 1996. Also in 1996, Wilshire released new style indexes which were better for benchmarking active management than those released in 1986.

For many years, Lipper, another major player in the industry, categorized funds based on size by looking at the prospectus and the decisions of the fund manager. However, during the 1990s there was a large increase in the number of equity funds, and in addition the concepts of growth and income began to lose their descriptive power as funds were not using them consistently and frequently changed classifications. Lipper clients began requesting new ways to categorize equity funds and, responding to these requests, Lipper released their style classification in 1999. Lipper wanted a system that was easy to duplicate, consistent and transparent, with stable fund classifications. It is interesting to note that Lipper did not want to force style consistency upon flexible fund managers, so they introduced the idea of the multi-cap or all-cap category.

Wilshire was the first consulting firm to introduce a style index in 1986, providing an indication of the direction in which consultants were pushing clients. Consultants do not like managers who style drift because it makes it harder to evaluate them and compare them to other managers. In practice consultants rely heavily on the style grid for selecting and evaluating managers, even to the extent of demanding style purity from the managers hired by their clients. As a consequence, consultants have helped spread the style grid and the accompanying concept of style drift throughout the investment industry.

The move to style-grid constrained investing was undertaken as a matter of convenience and not on the basis of careful analysis and research. So the stampede into the style grid was not only leaderless but lacked any research underpinning.

STYLE DRIFT AND PERFORMANCE

Proponents of style-box constrained investing believe that it is an easy to understand tool for selecting and monitoring investment managers and helps investors control risk at the overall portfolio level. They also believe that significant style drift is grounds for replacing a manager. Style-constrained investing has become an industry standard through the efforts of investment advisors, consultants and organizations such as Morningstar and Lipper, among others.

There is now considerable evidence that truly active equity managers, who experience high levels of style drift, generate superior returns. This is because consistently pursuing a narrowly defined strategy necessitates moving around the equity universe as economic and market conditions change. Thus style drift is synonymous with strategy consistency, a contention that is exactly opposite of what the proponents of the style grid believe. The result of this is that the current industry practice of demanding little or no style drift hurts performance.

In Chapter 14 I present the evidence that shows consistently pursuing a narrowly defined strategy and taking high-conviction positions is key to generating superior returns. The evidence is based on my own research as well as a growing body of academic finance research showing that truly active equity mutual funds outperform and that a large majority of fund managers are superior stock pickers. So it is not a great leap to contend that anything that impedes the consistent pursuit of an equity strategy will hurt performance. The industry focus on style drift is just such an impediment.

Fortunately there is a study dealing directly with the style drift / performance trade-off. In a 2010 working paper, Russ Wermers of the University of Maryland focuses specifically on the causes and consequences of style drift.[35] He categorizes every stock in each mutual fund into one of 125 boxes based on market cap, value-growth and momentum. He then measures both passive and active drift as well as numerous other fund manager attributes and performance in relation to the extent of style drift. Wermers finds that style drift plays a central role in generating superior performance among mutual fund managers. The most important conclusions of his study are:

---

[35] Russ Wermers, 'A Matter of Style: The Causes and Consequences of Style Drift in Institutional Portfolios', University of Maryland working paper (May 2010).

- Mutual fund managers do not attempt to counteract passive style drift by means of active rebalancing. That is, when a portfolio drifts due to changes in the characteristics of the stocks being held, managers do not counteract this drift by means of active rebalancing.

- Those managers who have the best before the fact stock picking performance also experience the greatest amount of drift.

- Furthermore, these same managers produce the best future investment performance.

- Those managers who do not drift produce little or no tilt-adjusted superior performance.

- The greatest drifters outperform the least drifters by roughly 300 bp.

In summary, Wermers finds that among mutual fund managers, style drift is part and parcel of superior performance. **Without style drift, a manager cannot produce superior investment returns.** This conclusion is further support for the contention that the consistent pursuit of an equity strategy produces both superior performance and style drift.

According to Wermers, superior performance and style drift cannot be separated one from the other. Thus one of the best things the industry can do is abandon the style grid and, in turn, eliminate style purity as a sought-after equity manager behavior.

BIZARRE TALE OF THE STYLE GRID

Having just presented the style grid story, several conclusions came to the fore. First, the style grid, and its close relative returns-based style analysis, play a prominent role in the investment management industry and, if anything, the grid's importance has grown in recent years. The style grid is a key aspect of how participants think about and operate in the industry. It is sometimes referred to in favorable terms and sometimes in disparaging terms, but regardless, it is almost always part of the conversation with respect to categorizing and evaluating equity managers.

Second, in spite of its dominance, there is no group that champions the style grid in the multiple ways it is actually used. One of the best-known proponents of the style grid, Morningstar (MS), touts it as an easy to understand way to categorize and evaluate equity managers. MS does not push the idea that managers should be kept in a box and disciplined for drifting. Lipper, although they created their own system for categorizing managers, does not call it a style grid nor do they use the term style box. Both companies, however, do provide programs for determining whether stock purchases cause the fund to be categorized differently.

Regardless, the prevailing expectation is that managers must fit into a specific style box (e.g. small-cap value) and stay there. The movement towards a style police state has occurred in the absence of an overall champion for such an environment within the industry, that is, the widespread adoption of the style grid is a leaderless stampede.

Third, even though the style grid is built along the dimensions of size and value/growth, there is not a strong link between research on the small firm and PE effects, on the one hand, and the style grid on the other. In the 1980s, when the style grid was launched, the size and PE anomalies were in vogue, much as they are today. These provided a convenient and objective framework for categorizing managers. However, there are a number of methods by which managers can be objectively categorized, so why use these particular dimensions? Academic research demonstrates that size and PE impact equity returns, although there is debate whether in fact these effects still exist today. This evidence does not provide any justification for using these characteristics for categorizing and evaluating equity managers.

Fourth, it is clear that the style grid does not capture a specific manager's equity strategy.[36] This question has been pushed aside by the currently popular method of inferring strategy by analyzing the composition and performance of the portfolio. As I argue in Chapter 14, investment strategy is not captured by stock characteristics and so the use of the style grid for categorizing managers and the attendant measure of style drift force the manager to deviate from the fund's investment strategy and thus underperform. The well documented protestations by equity managers about being restricted to a single style box is further confirmation of this misalignment. Russ Wermers' research reveals a link between style drift and performance: the greater the style drift the better the performance.

The bottom line is that the style grid dominates the active equity industry as a result of a leaderless stampede based on convenience rather than on solid research. The resulting industry expectation that managers be style pure leads to underperformance. The best thing the industry can do for investors is to get rid of the style grid and the measurement of style drift, and allow active equity managers to consistently pursue their equity strategy without having to worry about the silly concept of style purity.

---

[36] The first to propose this link was Bill Sharpe in 'Asset Allocation: Management Style and Performance Measurement', *The Journal of Portfolio Management* 18:2 (1992), pp. 7-19. He suggested measuring a manager's style by regressing historical returns on various indices. Since then, others have run with it. As I will argue in the next section, investment strategy is not captured by stock characteristics and so the use of the style grid for categorizing managers ends up hurting performance.

CHAPTER 10: DIVERSIFICATION: APPLYING BUBBLE WRAP

IN THE PANTHEON of investment virtues, diversification is right up there. Nearly everyone in the industry recommends it in one form or another. It is so widely accepted that nary an objection is raised against it. I feel much differently and, in fact, I believe there are very few situations in which diversification makes sense. I will present my arguments below. As I say this, I feel like I have to duck to avoid the wrath of the investing gods. Attacking diversification is akin to attacking motherhood and apple pie. Be that as it may, here I go.

SHORT-TERM VOLATILITY

The primary benefit of diversification is the reduction in short-term volatility. However if the portfolio is broken into buckets, with one of those buckets devoted to liquidity and short-term income needs and another bucket devoted to capital growth, then this benefit is of little value.

In the first bucket, it makes sense to use short-term investments with low or no volatility, so there is little need for diversification. For the second bucket, the primary goal is creating long-horizon wealth and so those asset classes with the highest expected and excess returns should be the focus. In this bucket short-term volatility plays a relatively small role, other than the emotional reaction of clients to short-term changes in value. Diversification actually hurts the performance of this portfolio if funds are allocated to lower expected return asset classes simply to reduce short-term volatility.[37]

A well-known example will help drive home this point. Over long time periods the stock market has generated an average annual compound return of around 10%. On the other hand, bonds have generated an annual compound return of somewhere around 6%. The last 62 years of stock (S&P 500), T-bond, and T-bill returns, along with inflation, is displayed in Figure 10.1.

The most striking aspect of this chart is how stocks dominate both T-bonds and T-bills for growing long-horizon wealth. If $10,000 was invested at the beginning of 1951 in stocks and held until the end of 2012, the portfolio was worth $5.2 million, ignoring taxes. The same $10,000 invested in T-bonds was worth $420,000 and $162,000 if invested in T-bills. No contest.

FIGURE 10.1: STOCKS, T-BONDS, T-BILLS AND INFLATION, 1951 TO 2012

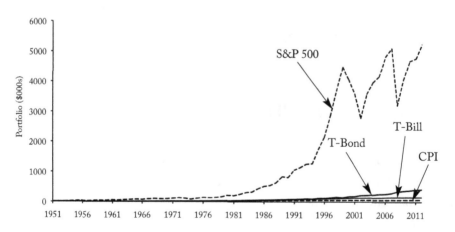

Sources: Thomson Reuters Financial and St. Louis Federal Reserve FRED database.

---

[37] The appendix of this book describes how an investment advisor at Cascade Financial Management thinks about and uses the bucket model in building client portfolios.

Throughout my career I have looked at graphs like Figure 10.1 and concluded that the rational decision, when building long-horizon wealth, is to invest everything in stocks. Why would I ever leave that much money on the table, in this case nearly $5 million? For $5 million I can put up with the emotional roller coaster that is the market. The full commitment to stocks is confirmed by running a model that optimizes long-term wealth by allocating funds across stocks, T-bonds and T-bills. It shows that 100% of the portfolio should be invested in stocks.[38]

If a portfolio is being built for generating long-horizon wealth, why invest anything in bonds? All bonds do is reduce the average portfolio return and therefore terminal wealth. In spite of this, the standard recommendation for a portfolio is to invest 60% in stocks and 40% in bonds. The primary driver of this recommendation is the reduction in emotionally charged short-term volatility. Thus diversification in this case is an example of applying bubble wrap to the portfolio and it leads to a reduction in wealth.

Many investment organizations use computer-based asset allocation models for portfolio construction. A common *problem* with these optimization models is that unconstrained they will often allocate 100% to the highest expected return asset class. This is viewed as a bad thing and so upper and lower allocation bounds are set. I've always thought that these models were working just fine, as I believe 100% allocation to the highest expected return asset class when building long-horizon portfolios is exactly what should be done. This does not fit conventional wisdom, so allocation constraints are imposed.[39]

---

[38] This optimization assumes a strategic asset allocation that does not change throughout this 62-year period. In Chapter 17 I present behavioral measures that can be used for tactical investment decisions in order to avoid steep market declines such as that experienced in 2008. But even with the addition of behavioral tactical movements, investing in stocks is optimal over 80% of the time.

[39] A related problem is error optimization, in which estimation errors in the parameters used for optimization drive the end results. This is a real problem and accurate estimates of future expected returns are particularly important in this regard.

Does diversification ever make sense when building long-horizon wealth?

The only situation in which diversification makes sense is when asset class returns are expected to be roughly the same. This means that when asset classes are combined, the portfolio expected return is unaffected but volatility is reduced, which improves the portfolio's annual compound return. When expected returns differ significantly, there is no argument for applying the bubble wrap that is diversification.

It is well-known that investments with the same arithmetic mean return but differing volatility, as measured by standard deviation, generate different compound returns. The one with the highest standard deviation, even though it has the same mean return, produces a lower compound return and thus lower terminal wealth. However, when combining asset classes with different expected returns, this lower standard deviation benefit plays a much diminished role.

In the previous example based on Figure 10.1, the reduced volatility resulting from combining these two asset classes cannot offset the 4% return advantage of stocks. That is, over long periods of time, a 100% stock portfolio will dominate a mixed stock-bond portfolio.[40]

INFATUATION WITH ALTERNATIVES

Since the 2008 market meltdown, there has been a growing infatuation with *alternatives*. What are alternatives? They are asset classes whose most attractive feature is their lack of correlation with traditional investments, such as stocks, bonds and money markets. The concern being addressed is that during 2008 pretty much all asset classes fell dramatically. This was the largest MLA-driven market spasm in recent memory and still is a topic of discussion by investors. I find it amazing that many investors purchase alternative investments that promise to move differently than traditional investments, but on the other hand generate low returns. How does this make sense?

---

[40] The reduction in compound annual return from the arithmetic return can be approximated by 0.5 times the variance expressed in decimal form.

While the mad search for alternatives was unfolding, the stock market rallied over 140% from its March 2009 low. Explain to me again why I want low correlation in my portfolio. Why is it that I want investments going down when others are going up? I've never understood the rationale behind this argument.

While it is the case in my portfolio that some investments will go up and others will go down, I see no reason to go out of my way to build a portfolio of offsetting returns. As a colleague of mine is fond of saying "Everyone wants negative correlations until they get them." The effort to identify alternatives is largely a search for feel-good bubble wrap.

STOCK PORTFOLIO DIVERSIFICATION

How many stocks does it take to adequately diversify a portfolio?

If you ask financial professionals, the typical answer is 50 or more. There is a widespread belief that a large number of stocks are necessary to obtain the desired level of diversification.

This question has been carefully researched and the conclusion is the number needed is actually quite small. University of Washington professors Stephen Archer and Vince Evans in a 1968 article uncovered what is shown in Figure 10.2.[41]

A major portion of the benefit of diversification, that is the reduction in short-term portfolio volatility, is garnered with as few as 10 to 20 stocks. After 20 stocks, portfolio volatility changes very little with each additional stock. In fact, 83% of the diversification benefit is achieved with ten stocks, 91% with 20 stocks, and the remaining 9% by adding 275 stocks. So there is little argument for more than 20 stocks in a portfolio. This is further reinforced, as I will show later, by the fact that taking a small number of high-conviction positions is key to generating superior returns.

---

[41] John Evans and S.H. Archer, 'Diversification and the reduction of dispersion: an empirical analysis', *Journal of Finance* 23 (1968), pp. 761-767.

FIGURE 10.2: PORTFOLIO STANDARD DEVIATION REDUCTION BY NUMBER OF STOCKS

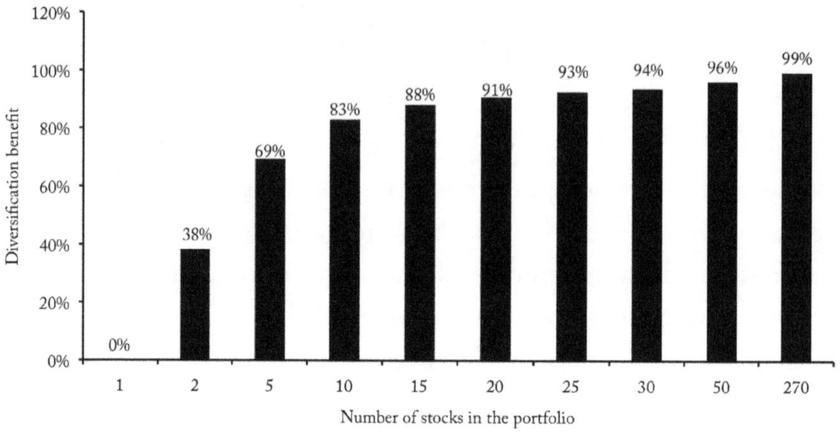

Source: Based on Evans and Archer methodology and using an average individual-stock standard deviation of 45%, an inter-stock correlation of 0.11 and equal weighting.

In the light of this evidence, it is surprising the typical active equity mutual fund holds 100 stocks. Why so many? Research shows that the fund's top 20 or so holdings, based on relative weights, generate excess returns. The diversification analysis just discussed implies roughly the same number, that is, around 20 stocks. It turns out one of the worst things you can add to a stock portfolio is another stock – an example of *deworsification*.

So what about those additional 80 stocks held by the typical fund? This is to a large extent driven by fund size, since it is harder to concentrate in a few good idea stocks as the fund grows large. The 80 or so low-conviction stocks represent bubble wrap for avoiding style drift, holding well-known stocks, and controlling volatility. The result is the fund ends up with two to three times more positions than if the manager focused strictly on performance.[42]

---

[42] This is confirmed by numerous managers telling me they would hold 10 to 15 stocks if it were their own money rather than the fund's.

CAN BUBBLE WRAP BE BENEFICIAL?

The pure finance case for diversification is weak. Diversification makes sense when building long-term portfolios using asset classes with comparable expected returns and when building stock portfolios with 20 or fewer stocks. Other than these situations, there is not a good financial argument for diversifying.

Now that I have made my case, let me climb down from my high horse. While there are few financial arguments for diversification, there are emotional arguments. In the spirit of "it's better to be in rather than completely out of the market," a judicious use of bubble wrap diversification can help build portfolios that encourage clients to stay in their seats. These diversified portfolios will, over the long run, underperform less diversified portfolios, but if clients are less likely to bolt, then diversification is worth it. If an advisor can get clients to invest in what are the best equity portfolios by including additional asset classes such as money markets, bonds and futures, then it is a successful use of bubble wrap. Sometimes emotional catering makes sense.

Our most successful portfolio, Athena Pure Valuation/Profitability, is a highly concentrated individual stock portfolio that is more volatile than the stock market. The truth is, even though we believe it is the best product, very few of our advisors or their clients invest exclusively in it. However, when it is combined with other investments, such as bonds, it has become our most successful portfolio both in terms of AUM and performance. Much like my change in opinion regarding dollar cost averaging, diversification plays an important role in mitigating the emotional costs to client portfolios.

GLOBAL MUSH

It is best to keep diversification to a minimum, using just enough to keep clients in their seats during volatile times. Don't fall into the trap at the other extreme, that is, creating portfolios of *global mush*. These are portfolios that have dozens of different positions comprised of the asset class de jour. Generally both returns and volatility are low in such portfolios. The returns are often so low that these portfolios can be regarded as *expensive savings accounts*. Investors are often willing to pay dearly to reduce or eliminate volatility.

If there is no need to bubble wrap a portfolio then it should be invested in a few high-return strategies or asset classes. Just as in the case of individual stocks, adding additional strategies or asset classes little reduces emotional volatility, but can significantly reduce expected returns. Concentrate the portfolio in a small number of what are expected to be good to very good return opportunities and largely avoid diversification.

Diversification is an approach for trading off lower returns for lower emotions. It is an emotion-return process not a risk-return process. Diversify only in those few situations for which it makes sense. Best of all, help your clients to release their emotional brakes so they don't feel the need for bubble wrap.

Take the less bubble wrap pledge: I will avoid overdiversifying client portfolios.

I see the dark clouds of the investing gods gathering over my head, so before they smite me, I will move on to my next topic.

CHAPTER 11:
THE VOLATILITY TRAP[43]

"Leonard Gerber, a 65-year-old financial planner, has seen plenty of volatile markets during his career. But this one feels different.

"Across the country, investors are fleeing the stock market for the safety of cash. On Tuesday the Standard & Poor's 500-stock index lost as much as 2.2% before a late-day rally sent the index up 2.3% for the session. In the 46 trading days since the beginning of August, the S&P 500 has seen 29 swings of 1% or more.

"Tuesday is a 'perfect example' of why Mr. Gerber has bailed out. 'The market is manic,' he says. 'There's no consistency ... and there's a worrisome amount of volatility.'"

Wall Street Journal, October 5, 2011

THOSE WHO LET emotions drive their investment decisions, as happened with Mr. Gerber and millions of others, missed out on the October 2011 market surge, the largest monthly stock market return in 20 years. These investors have unwittingly fallen prey to the *Volatility Trap*, failing to recognize – as my data shows – that increased volatility is a precursor to higher returns.

Advisors and equity managers are at the center of the volatility firestorm. Panicked clients call demanding relief and the simplest solution is to sell their equity positions. Those advisors who believe stocks are the best long-term investment are forced to talk distraught clients down from rash decisions. The more ammunition advisors have for these heated discussions, the better.

If it is believed that stocks have the best long-term expected return relative to other asset classes, then it is best to stay invested in stocks. So the decision revolves around the issue of short-term anxiety versus long-term benefit. In this chapter I present evidence that there is not only a long-term benefit but *also* a short-term benefit to staying the course.

---

[43] This chapter is based on 'The Volatility Trap: Why Staying the Course Makes Sense' by C. Thomas Howard and Craig T. Callahan that appeared in the November 28, 2011 issue of *Advisor Perspectives*.

The Volatility Trap, portrayed in Figure 11.1, captures the dynamics of market volatility and return over time. Time zero, the present, separates the recent past (the left side of the figure) from the near future (the right). The figure portrays a stock market which has just been through a period of high volatility and below-average returns, the right side represents a near future in which volatility is typically lower and market returns are above average. The long-term average line represents averages for both return and volatility. I will demonstrate that markets routinely work this way. The emotional reaction to volatility turns this into a trap.

FIGURE 11.1: THE VOLATILITY TRAP

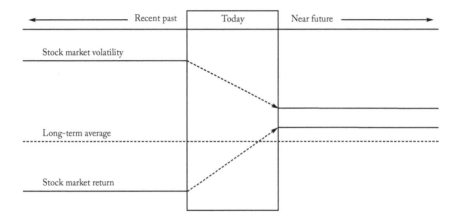

The Volatility Trap is driven by the empirical observation that, even though investors have recently suffered increased volatility and lower or even negative returns, future volatility will most likely lessen and market returns will often be above average. This is often forgotten in the heat of the moment – abnormally high volatility must at some point revert to more reasonable levels, just as below-average returns must rise. As they say, it is hard to remember how to drain the swamp when you are up to your neck in alligators.

As strong as is the urge to bolt the market, the rational decision is to stay the course or even increase equity holdings. If the client falls into the

Volatility Trap by abandoning the stock market, they compound their misery by missing out on higher future returns.

Resisting the impulse to decrease market exposure in the face of increased volatility is against the instinct of the client and everything that received wisdom tells them. It cries out for empirical support, a task to which I now turn.

MARKET VOLATILITY

In order to explore the relationship between market volatility and return represented in Figure 11.1, I gathered weekly values for the S&P 500 index from December 30, 1927 through October 14, 2011. For each week, I calculated trailing 4-, 13-, and 26-week standard deviations – my measure of *weekly* market volatility.

For example, this resulted in 4382 estimates of the trailing 13-week, weekly standard deviation. The average trailing 13-week, weekly standard deviation was 2.16%, reaching a low of 0.41% on 4/10/1964 and a high of 9.52% on 10/07/1932. The most recent value in this sample (10/14/2011) was 4.39%.

I then calculated subsequent 1-, 4-, 13-, 26-, and 52-week S&P 500 price changes (excluding dividends) in order to explore the volatility-return time dynamic of the S&P 500.

For historical perspective, the annual average 13-week, weekly standard deviations from 1928 through 2011 are displayed in Figure 11.2. The 1930s experienced the worst market volatility, with every year at or well above the long-term average of 2.16%. Volatility then declined somewhat during the 1940s, 1950s and 1960s. From the 1970s on, weekly volatility reached a higher plateau, and 1974 and 2008 were particularly volatile. In 2010 and 2011 volatility was a bit higher than average, but these years did not see exceptional weekly volatility by historical standards.

FIGURE 11.2: AVERAGE 13-WEEK S&P 500 INDEX WEEKLY STANDARD DEVIATION BY YEAR

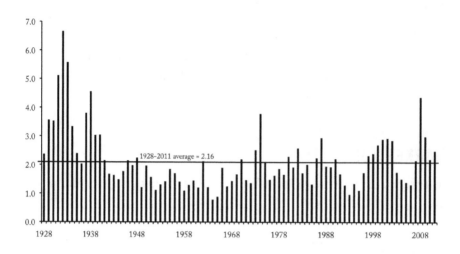

CONTEMPORANEOUS MARKET VOLATILITY AND MARKET RETURNS

> "Volatility is usually associated with market losses, and the current period is no exception. Since April 29 [2011] the Standard & Poor's 500-stock index has fallen by 17.6% – not far from the 20% drop that defines a bear market."

Wall Street Journal, October 5, 2011

Nobody enjoys volatility. When it is combined with a large market loss, it is doubly painful. Highly emotional events are more likely to be remembered, so it is not surprising many investors believe, as the writer states above, that "volatility is usually associated with market losses."

But what does the data tell us? In order to find out, I calculated the average 4-, 13-, and 26-week S&P 500 price changes and matched them with the same-period standard deviation. Figure 11.3 reports these averages in three groups: lower, middle and highest standard deviations from 1928 through 2011.

The results confirm the conventional wisdom: average returns correlate inversely with volatility. In fact, the average price changes were negative for the highest volatility in each sample. The *recent past* aspect of the volatility trap is accurate, as we can see in Figure 11.3; higher volatility is associated with lower returns.

FIGURE 11.3: S&P 500 PRICE CHANGE BY MATCHING STANDARD DEVIATION

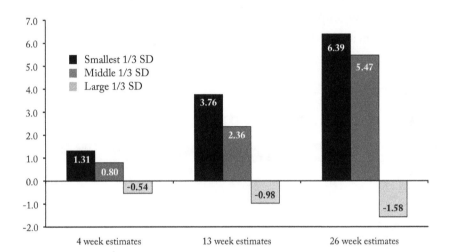

FIGHTING THE URGE TO BAIL

I just showed that there is a strong inverse relationship between contemporaneous market volatility and returns: when volatility increases, returns go negative. No wonder clients are ready to bail as they suffer the dual ignominy of nerve-rattling volatility *and* declining portfolio value.

Putting emotions aside, however, the question is whether rising volatility is a reliable signal for future volatility and returns. If it is, then it can be used to build superior portfolios. If not, then it should be ignored when managing a portfolio.

To test this hypothesis, I regressed subsequent weekly standard deviations (my measure of future volatility) on trailing weekly standard deviations (my measure of recent volatility). The resulting slope coefficients are reported in Table 11.1. A value less than 1.0 means that future weekly volatility is, on average, declining.

A slope coefficient that is less than 1 means high levels of volatility will not persist, but it is possible for future volatility to remain above average. That said, the slope coefficient is less than 1 for each recent-future combination, as the data in Table 11.1 shows, supporting the expectation that volatility will tend to diminish – regardless of how long it has persisted.

TABLE 11.1: REGRESSION SLOPE COEFFICIENT OF SUBSEQUENT SD ON TRAILING SD

	4wk SD	13 wk SD	26 wk SD
	January 1928 - October 2011 (n=4368)		
tr 4 wk SD	0.50	0.49	0.47
tr 13 wk SD	0.69	0.68	0.65
tr 26 wk SD	0.72	0.73	0.71
	January 1950 - October 2011 (n=3224)		
tr 4 wk SD	0.41	0.34	0.30
tr 13 wk SD	0.58	0.51	0.45
tr 26 wk SD	0.60	0.55	0.49
	January 2000 - October 2011 (n=615)		
tr 4 wk SD	0.42	0.31	0.27
tr 13 wk SD	0.56	0.47	0.41
tr 26 wk SD	0.57	0.52	0.46

Next, to test whether volatility signals higher future returns, I regressed future S&P 500 price changes on trailing weekly standard deviations. As can be seen in Table 11.2, 90% of the coefficients are positive, which means that, historically, the higher the recent volatility, the higher were future returns.

During the time period examined, a one-unit increase in four-week standard deviation predicts a 0.03% increase in four-week price change.

Over more recent time horizons – 1950 to 2011 and 2000 to 2011 – a one-unit increase predicts a substantially higher 0.12% and 0.17% increase, respectively.

In other words, future expected returns have risen with an increase in recent volatility, and this relationship has grown stronger over time.

TABLE 11.2: REGRESSION SLOPE COEFFICIENT OF SUBSEQUENT S&P 500 PRICE CHANGE ON TRAILING SD

	1 wk PC	4 wk PC	13 wk PC	26 wk PC	52 wk PC
	January 1928 - October 2011 (n=4368)				
tr 4 wk SD	-0.01	0.03	0.05	0.22	-0.14
tr 13 wk SD	0.00	0.03	0.07	0.19	-0.22
tr 26 wk SD	0.01	0.05	0.17	0.17	-0.31
	January 1950 - October 2011 (n=3224)				
tr 4 wk SD	-0.01	0.12	0.39	1.04	1.02
tr 13 wk SD	0.07	0.19	0.61	1.58	1.51
tr 26 wk SD	0.08	0.33	0.99	1.68	1.39
	January 2000 - October 2011 (n=615)				
tr 4 wk SD	-0.01	0.17	0.27	0.86	1.08
tr 13 wk SD	0.08	0.15	0.20	1.21	2.06
tr 26 wk SD	0.08	0.28	0.77	1.80	2.57

To see this another way, Figure 11.4 depicts future annual S&P 500 returns from 1950 to 2011, broken down by recent volatility. When recent volatility has been low, the average future return is 9.6%, and when recent volatility is high, the average future return is 12.0%. This is further evidence that recent volatility and subsequent returns enjoy an inverse correlation.[44]

---

[44] This is consistent with results reported by French, Schwert and Stambaugh (1987) as well as Bollerslev, Tauchen and Zhou (2009).

FIGURE 11.4: FUTURE ANNUAL S&P 500 RETURN BY RECENT VOLATILITY, 1950 TO 2011

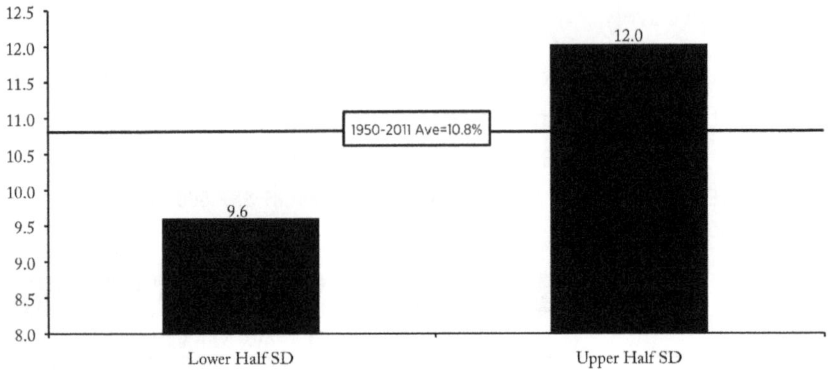

Four-week trailing SD, 13-week subsequent price change, annualized + dividends

STAYING THE COURSE

The data shows that the Volatility Trap is not just logical, it is also observable. High volatility may be accompanied by low and even negative returns, but it is also predictive of lower future volatility and above-average future returns. Though it may be understandable that the joint pain of high volatility and lower returns might increase the urge to bail from the market, clients who do so miss out on the other side of the equation – higher future returns. Essentially you are closing the barn door after the horse gets out.

The Volatility Trap provides no relief for the client over time. Let's say that you have just suffered through four weeks of high market volatility and negative returns, and you are ready to run for the hills. To avoid the Volatility Trap, however, you stay the course in hopes of seeing the predicted lower volatility and high returns.

Instead, volatility worsens and your losses mount. After all, actual results can be much worse or better than expected. At 13 weeks, you are thinking "enough is enough," and prepare to exit the market. Again the evidence reveals that, even though the pain has continued, the empirical facts have not changed: the data still shows that future volatility should decline and returns should rise. With great trepidation, you relent and stay the course. You continue to take a pounding, and after 26 weeks you are at your wit's end. Still the Volatility Trap provides no solace – the evidence still says that most likely things will get better. Thinking that you do not want to miss out when the market turns, you reluctantly stay the course. Boy, is this fun!

There is no time limit to the Volatility Trap. No matter how long recent volatility lasts, the best decision for most clients going forward is to stay the course. In this regard, the Volatility Trap ensnares both rational and irrational investors. The rational investor suffers through all of the indignities thrown at him or her by the market in order to earn the highest possible long-term return, while the irrational investor ends up with an inferior portfolio because he or she bolted the market in times of high volatility. The market does not make it easy to be a successful equity investor.

The relationship between low recent returns, high future returns and recent volatility is driven by the Emotional Crowd. The low recent returns are the result of emotional investors leaving the market as volatility rose, which drives down prices and returns. The higher future returns result when these same emotional investors quit selling or begin to move back into the market. To take advantage of these swings, an investor must be more rational than his or her counterparts in the marketplace. Such self-control is essential to earning the best long-term returns.

While emotions are part and parcel of human nature, responding to gut-wrenching volatility by exiting the stock market, as did Mr. Gerber and millions of other investors, hurts both short-term and long-term portfolio performance. At the very least, clients should stay the course in the face of rising volatility, and maybe even increase equity exposure.

Once we put the initial, instinctive anxiety in perspective and release the emotional brakes, we can see rising volatility for what it is: an opportunity, not something to be feared.

CHAPTER 12: WILL TRUE RISK PLEASE STAND UP!

"As finance academics, we have almost nothing meaningful to say about measuring risk."

OVER THE LAST 15 years or so I made this statement to my classes whenever we covered the topic of CAPM. I was not saying there isn't risk in investing. What I mean is that after all of the effort we as a profession have put into understanding and measuring risk, there is embarrassingly little to say. Admitting this to the students in my classes did not exactly endear me to my academic colleagues.

FAILURE OF CAPM

The CAPM was put forward as a model of investment risk in the mid-1960s by William Sharpe of the University of Washington.[45] In 1990 he, along with Harry Markowitz of CUNY and Robert Merton of the University of Chicago, received the Nobel Prize in economics. As an economic model, the CAPM has much going for it. It is elegantly simple with easily testable implications. It harnessed Harry Markowitz's portfolio optimization model and transformed it into a model of capital market equilibrium. As Gene Fama of the University of Chicago and

---

[45] William Sharpe, 'Capital Asset Prices – A Theory of Market Equilibrium Under Conditions of Risk', *Journal of Finance* XIX, 3 (1964), pp. 425-42.

Ken French of Dartmouth College said in 2004, it was an economic modeling tour de force, worthy of placing on the mantle and admiring for its elegance. Unfortunately, in real-world financial markets, it didn't work as advertised.

The core prediction of the CAPM is a positive relationship between beta, as a measure of risk, and expected return. Many empirical tests of this relationship were conducted, but unfortunately, even after adjusting for many possible statistical problems, virtually all of the studies produced a flat or negative relationship. Based on the preponderance of evidence, beta is not a measure of risk. This led Fama and French in 2004 to recommend CAPM and beta not be used in practical applications.[46]

Malcolm Baker of Harvard, Brendan Bradley of Acadian Asset Management and Jeffrey Wurgler of NYU went even further in a 2010 paper, referring to the negative beta and return relationship as the greatest anomaly of all time.[47] CAPM beta has been transformed from a measure of risk to a measure of opportunity. A painful fall from the pantheon of risk models.

Beyond the lack of empirical support, CAPM has another debilitating problem. Beta is the product of stock return, market return correlation and the stock-to-market standard deviation ratio. Since volatility is mostly the result of emotional investor reactions to current events, it turns out beta is really a measure of emotion. Regardless of how you look at it, beta is not a risk measure.

FALSE HOPE OF FACTOR MODELS

Partly in response to the failure of beta as a measure of risk, other risk measures have been proposed, but again with little success. Arbitrage Pricing Theory, or APT, was the first of the so-called factor models which

---

[46] Eugene F. Fama and Kenneth R. French, 'The Capital Asset Pricing Model: Theory and Evidence', working paper (January 2004).

[47] Malcolm Baker, Brendan Bradley and Jeffrey Wurgler, 'Benchmarks as Limits to Arbitrage: Understanding the Low Volatility Anomaly', working paper (2010).

posited that returns could be explained by broad economic measures, such as changes in interest rates, employment, consumption, and others. These measures are not true return factors, but instead proxy for true factors.

What drives stock returns are the millions of investor buy and sell decisions. What investors are thinking, individually or collectively, and why they make the decisions they do is unobservable. So the best we can do is identify objective measures – in the case of APT these are variables like industrial production – to proxy for these return factors. APT posits that if industrial production increases, increased investor buying pressure is likely and stock prices will rise. An observed positive relationship between industrial production and stock prices is supportive of this contention.

Once factor proxies were introduced in order to explain stock price movements, the issue of measuring risk got muddy. Let's say the relationship between stock prices and industrial production is found to be positive as evidenced by a factor loading (i.e. a slope coefficient in a regression of return on industrial production) and the additional return associated with this factor loading (i.e. additional return earned by investors for being exposed to this factor) both being positive. This means that equity investors react favorably to an increase in industrial production.

The question then becomes does this additional return earned represent a risk premium, an opportunity for enhanced returns, or simply the underlying relationship between the economy and the stock market. There seems no way to untangle these potential explanations. Factor models can uncover relationships between stock prices and other variables, but they are moot on whether risk or some other return driver has been identified.

The most popular model is a four factor model involving the market, market-cap, price-to-book and momentum.[48] It is used widely in academic

---

[48] James L. Davis, Eugene F. Fama and Kenneth R. French, 'Characteristics, Covariances, and Average Returns: 1929 to 1997', *The Journal of Finance* Vol. LV, No. 1 (2000), pp. 389-406; and N. Jegadeesh and S. Titman, 'Overreaction, Delayed Reaction, and Contrarian Profits', *Review of Financial Studies* 8:4 (1995).

studies and for measuring portfolio performance. Like the APT model just discussed, it is unknown what is being measured by these four variables, in that small-cap stocks earning a higher return could be an indication of higher risk or simply an opportunity. The fact that it is unknown whether the four factor model is measuring risk or opportunity makes it all the more bizarre that it is so widely used. This is not an indictment of the industry but a result of the failure to come up with a measure of investment risk.

The newest entry into the factor model race was put forward by Long Chen of Washington University and Lu Zhang of the University of Michigan in 2010.[49] They propose a three factor model involving the market, capital investments by the firm and return on assets. They find this model explains a number of long-standing anomalies, performing the same and, most often, better in this regard than does the four factor model discussed above.

One of the interesting model aspects is two of the measures are based on decisions made by managers of the firm. These can be thought of in the same way as dividend yield and capital structure, both firm decisions previously shown to be predictive of future returns. In other words, these factors are based on manager behavior rather than on inert measures such as market-cap or book-to-market ratios. Another advantage of these two measures is they do not depend on emotionally-driven stock prices.

Alas, this new model does not provide a measure of investment risk, since, as the authors admit, the performance of their three factor model could be the result of either risk premiums or investment opportunities. So it is a step forward that explains more anomalies, but it brings no more clarity with respect to measuring risk.

After many attempts and years of effort, we are no closer to a reliable measure of risk. While no doubt researchers will continue to address this issue, my guess is that not much will come of it. Risk and opportunity

---

[49] Long Chen and Lu Zhang, 'A Better Three-Factor Model that Explains More Anomalies', *The Journal of Finance* Vol. LXV, No 2 (2010), pp 563-594.

are so thoroughly intertwined that untangling them is nearly impossible, with the movement to behavioral finance making this effort even more challenging. It may be that we have extracted all we can by examining the time series and cross-section of stock returns. It is probably time to explore other ways of measuring investment risk.

VOLATILITY AND RISK ARE NOT SYNONYMOUS

In Chapter 1 I reviewed the evidence regarding stock market volatility and argued that most volatility stems from crowds overreacting to information arriving in the market. Indeed, almost no volatility can be explained by changes in underlying economic fundamentals at both the market and individual stock levels. Volatility measures emotions, not necessarily investment risk. This is also true of other currently used measures of risk, such as downside standard deviation, maximum drawdown and downside capture.

Unfortunately, the investment industry has adopted this same volatility as a risk measure that, rather than focusing on the final outcome, focuses on the bumpiness of the ride. A less bumpy ride is thought to be less risky, regardless of the final outcome. This leads to the unintended consequence of building portfolios that result in lower terminal wealth and, surprisingly, higher risk. This happens because the industry mistakenly builds portfolios that minimize short-term volatility relative to long-term returns, placing emotion at the very heart of the long-horizon portfolio construction process. Such an approach is popular because it legitimizes the emotional reaction of investors to short-term volatility. Thus risk and volatility are frequently thought of as being interchangeable.

However, focusing on short-term volatility when building long horizon portfolios can have the unintended consequence of actually increasing investment risk. Based on basic BPM principle 3, risk is the chance of underperformance, which means focusing on short-term volatility will often lead to investing in lower expected return markets with little impact on long-term volatility. Lowering expected portfolio return in an effort to reduce short-term volatility actually increases the chance of underperformance, which means increasing risk.

A clear example of this is the comparison of long-term stock and bond returns. Stocks dramatically outperform bonds over the long run. By investing in bonds rather than stocks, short-term volatility is reduced at the expense of decreasing long-term wealth. Equating short-term volatility with risk leads to inferior long horizon portfolios. Higher return variance lowers an investment's long-term compound return, but this impact is small compared to the impact of investing in lower expected return markets.

The cost of equating risk and emotional volatility can be seen in other areas as well. Many investors pull out of the stock market when faced with heightened volatility but research shows this is exactly when they should remain in the market and even increase their stock holdings, as subsequent returns are higher on average. It is also the case that many investors exit after market declines only to miss the subsequent rebounds. Following the 2008 market crash, investors withdrew billions of dollars from equity mutual funds during a period in which the stock market more than doubled.

The end result is that investors frequently suffer the pain of losses without capturing the subsequent gains. Several studies confirm that the typical equity mutual fund investor earns a return substantially less than the fund return because of poorly timed movements in and out of the fund. Again, these are the dangers of not carefully distinguishing emotions from risk and thus allowing emotions to drive investment decisions.

MEASURING UNDERPERFORMANCE

In order to measure investment risk, it is necessary to properly define underperformance. Underperformance depends on both the time horizon of the investment and the goal of the investor. For example, if the goal is to have $100,000 in two years, risk is measured as the chance of ending up with less than $100,000 in two years. In this case, short-term volatility is an important contributor to risk.

In those cases where there is no specific time horizon, the appropriate benchmark is the highest expected return investment being considered. The actual return should approximate the expected return over long time periods, due to the law of large numbers. Most long-term investment situations fall into this category.

Note that short-term volatility plays an ever-smaller role as the time horizon lengthens. This is because the short-term emotionally and economically driven price changes tend to offset one another over the long run by means of time diversification. Markets experience about one-third to one-quarter of the volatility over the long run as compared to the short run.

ATHENA PURE PORTFOLIO: AN EXAMPLE

I manage the Athena Pure Valuation/Profitability portfolio by consistently pursuing a narrowly defined strategy while taking high-conviction positions of ten or fewer stocks. I consider it the BPM poster child, as my investment decisions harness behavioral factors and the portfolio is managed using BPM principles, with no bubble wrap included.

Pure's mountain performance chart for October 2003 through September 2013 is shown in Figure 12.1, along with the Russell 2000 benchmark performance. Over this ten-year period, Pure generated an annual compound return of 15.4% compared to the 9.6% for the Russell 2000 benchmark.

FIGURE 12.1: ATHENA PURE AND RUSSELL 2000 PERFORMANCE OCTOBER 2003 TO SEPTEMBER 2013

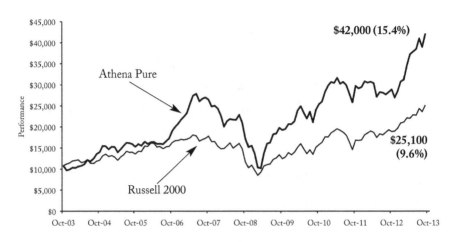

Athena Pure returns are GIPS compliant actual net returns for the period October 2003 through September 2013. Russ 2000 returns are total returns for the Russell 2000 index.

Data Sources: AthenaInvest and Thomson-Reuters Financial.

Reporting such strong performance produces a variety of reactions from my listeners. I actually had an advisor plug her ears with her fingers as I explained these results to her! When I do present these results, I always keep in mind Kahneman's admonition that "mean reversion is just around the corner." Even with these cautions in mind, Pure's results provide evidence of the power of harnessing behavioral factors and applying BPM principles when managing an equity portfolio.

Table 12.1 presents additional Pure performance measures and allows for comparing emotion-based MPT measures in common industry use, and alternative BPM measures that emphasize long-term performance rather than short-term volatility.

TABLE 12.1: ATHENA PURE PERFORMANCE MEASURES, OCTOBER 2003 TO SEPTEMBER 2013

MPT measures		BPM measures	
Annual comp return	15.4	Annual comp return	15.4
Alpha	5.8	Alpha	5.8
Annual SD	36.9	**Matched returns:**	
Upside capture	1.50	# Negative	4/60
Downside capture	1.18	Min	-3.9
Max drawdown	52.9	Ave	2.4
Correlation	0.79	Max	4.0
Beta	1.32	% Months positive	63%
Sharpe ratio	0.34	% Months outperform Russ 2000	58%
Information ratio	1.31	Chance of positive ten year return	96%
		Chance of outperforming Russ 2000:	
		10 years	88%
		30 years	98%

Upside Capture, Downside Capture, Correlation, and Beta are based on the S&P 500. Alpha and Information Ratio based on Russell 2000. Probabilities are based on Student t distribution. Sources: AthenaInvest and Thomson Reuters Financial.

The typical MLA-afflicted investor reacts negatively to the large 2008 drop in value in Figure 12.1 as well as the high short-term volatility revealed in Table 12.1 by an annual standard deviation of 36.9%, a max drawdown of 52.9% and a beta of 1.32. They often jump to the conclusion that Pure is a risky investment.

The BPM measures present a much different picture – that Pure is a high-return, low-risk investment for building long-horizon wealth. The matched return (introduced in Chapter 8) statistics reveal that negative monthly returns are more than offset by the matching positive return, with an average matched return of 2.4%. Only 4 of 60 matched returns are negative, with the lowest being -3.9%. This means that the other 56 of the 60 negative and lowest monthly returns were more than offset by a matching positive return.

Over this ten-year period, 63% of Pure's monthly returns were positive and Pure outperformed the Russell 2000 benchmark in 58% of these months. As strong as the monthly story told by these measures is, the focus should be on the long term, since Pure is intended to build long-horizon wealth. Table 12.1 reveals that there is a 96% chance of generating a positive return over ten years, based on the 15.4% annual return and the 36.9% annual standard deviation. The chance of outperforming the Russell 2000 benchmark is 88% over a ten-year investment horizon and 98% over a 30-year horizon, based on the 5.8% alpha and the 4.4% Russell 2000 tracking error.

Note that measures of short-term volatility, that is standard deviation and tracking error, are not directly reported as BPM performance measures, but instead are included when calculating the chance of outperformance. This correctly focuses attention on the final outcome, the goal of most importance to the investor, and away from the bumpiness of the ride, the most emotional aspect of the portfolio. This moves the discussion away from emotions to the task of growing long-horizon wealth.

Collectively the BPM measures reveal Pure to be a high-return, low-risk investment.[50]

Building long-horizon wealth

When measuring risk as the chance of underperformance, you will have noticed that both expected return and/or alpha become part of the risk measure along with standard deviation or tracking error. The higher the expected return the lower the risk, all other things being equal. This is why the risk of the volatile Pure portfolio is so low.

Some will point out that the Sharpe and Information ratios account for both return and volatility, as does the chance of underperformance risk measure, so using either approach yields good investment decisions.

---

[50] I must add that past performance is not predictive of future performance. The only thing that increases the chances of future outperformance is to generate superior returns by consistently pursuing a narrowly defined strategy while taking high-conviction positions. This is our plan for Pure going forward.

What the ratios neglect is long-period time diversification. As the investment horizon lengthens, expected return stays the same but portfolio standard deviation shrinks. Thus two funds with the same Sharpe or Information ratio look very different over long horizons. The fund with the highest expected return produces the lowest chance of underperformance, that is, the fund with the highest expected return also has the lowest risk. So it is best to choose the higher return fund for building long-horizon wealth, but the ratios incorrectly portray the two as equally attractive.

Replacing standard MPT performance measures with BPM measures leads to a clearer picture of a fund's ability to build long-horizon wealth. It also helps redirect client conversations away from emotionally charged short-term volatility and towards long-term excess returns, which is one of the important drivers of long-horizon wealth. I have successfully used BPM performance measures in client and advisor discussions.

Even with the large 2008 drawdown, Pure easily bested the Russell 2000. Short-term volatility, as unnerving as it is, plays an ancillary role in the generation of long-horizon wealth, unless the investor bolts the stock market as volatility increases or chooses underperforming investments to avoid it. The cost of emotional investing is high, so anything that can be done to divert client attention away from emotionally charged measures such as standard deviation and, instead, towards expected and excess returns will benefit them immensely.

SOURCES OF INVESTMENT RISK

Moving beyond emotions, the sources of investment risk are well known. At the micro level, events such as default, company failure and company mistakes contribute to risk. Diversification can mitigate these to a large extent. At the macro level, the economy and government policies contribute to systematic risks. These risks are more difficult to address since they impact a large number of industries and companies. These micro and macro risks are generally taken into consideration by BDIs but are not necessarily well understood by the emotional crowd.

There is another risk component that actually grows over time – I call this *foundational risk* and it is often overlooked. This is the risk of countrywide economic or stock market failure. History reveals that this risk is real, with numerous economic and market failures occurring though the centuries. Foundational risk increases over time, just as the risk of an earthquake increases as the time period lengthens. One must account for this risk when making investment decisions.

Behavioral science confirms that individuals either underestimate or overestimate foundational risk. The probability of such an event happening is low (neither countrywide economic failure nor stock market failure has happened in the US during its 235+ year history), so many assume this probability to be zero, which of course it is not.

On the other hand, if a low-probability event has happened recently, individuals tend to overestimate these risks. The recession of 2008, while not an economic or market failure, was a reminder that such occurrences are possible even in a country as economically advanced as the US. So now many investors overestimate this risk by building portfolios as if such failures are imminent. It takes real discipline to properly estimate this risk in light of emotionally charged events like 2008.

VOLATILITY AND ADVISOR/FUND BUSINESS RISK

Short-term emotional volatility is potentially more of a problem for the advisor/fund than is investment risk. Advisors and funds see revenues decline when client short-term investment performance is poor and, in extreme cases, investors may leave to invest elsewhere. As a way to protect themselves from client reactions to emotional volatility, the industry lumps emotional risk into currently popular risk measures. So when an advisor or fund states that an investment is risky, based on currently popular measures, they are actually saying three distinctly different things:

1. There is considerable emotionally-charged volatility with this investment.

2. Because of this, there is substantial business risk for my firm.

3. Oh, by the way, there is some amount of investment risk.

Only investment risk matters for making decisions, particularly for long-horizon portfolios. But these three types of risk are emotionally interconnected and it requires considerable effort to pull them apart. The first step is to correctly label each component: *client emotional reaction to volatility*, *advisor or fund business risk*, and *investment risk*.

TOWARD A MEASURE OF RISK

The risk measures currently used within the investment industry are really mostly measures of emotion. In order to deal with what is important, let's redefine investment risk as the chance of underperformance. The suggestion that investment risk be measured as the chance of underperformance is intuitively appealing to many. In fact, this measure of risk is widely used in a number of industries.

For example, in industrial applications, the risk of underperformance is measured by the probability that a component, unit or service will fail. Natural and manmade disasters use such a measure of risk. In each situation, the focus is on the chances that various final outcomes might occur. In general, the path to the outcome is less important and has little influence on the measure of risk than does the outcome itself.

SECTION 3: BECOMING A BEHAVIORAL DATA INVESTOR

CHAPTER 13: INVESTMENT STRATEGY

IN SPRING 2003, my long-time friend and former DU colleague Craig Callahan posed a couple of perplexing questions:

1. Why is it not enough for me to manage equity funds using a highly disciplined strategy?

2. Why is it that people are forever asking me what box I fit into?

Craig is the founder and intellectual force behind ICON funds of Denver. He prides himself on managing money based on an easy to describe, consistently applied valuation strategy. The boxes he referred to are the style boxes widely used by market participants to categorize, evaluate and hire/fire active equity managers. It made no sense to him that knowing ICON's strategy was not enough for advisors, consultants and investors with whom he spoke. They were forever asking about those infernal boxes.

Little did I know my spring 2003 conversation would open up the world of Behavioral Portfolio Management. Back then my view was little different from that of most academics: hiring an active equity manager was the triumph of hope over reality and style boxes were an innocuous way to organize the thousands of equity managers. This was based on a combination of my cursory knowledge of this particular aspect of the industry and the received wisdom of my academic colleagues. My research interests lay elsewhere in 2003, but they were about to change dramatically.

IMPORTANCE OF INVESTMENT STRATEGY

Investment strategy – or process, or methodology, whatever term you would like to use – is critical to successful implementation of Behavioral Portfolio Management. It is the way a manager goes about analyzing, buying and selling investments. The consistent pursuit of a narrowly-defined strategy, as well as taking high-conviction positions in the manager's best ideas, makes it possible to harness the behavioral factors driven by emotional crowds and to generate superior returns. There are dozens if not hundreds of emotional crowds operating in the market at any one time. A narrowly-defined strategy focuses on a small number of these crowds and, in turn, a small number of behavioral factors. Beyond these factors, everything else that goes on in the market is ignored by the manager.

Strategy is not only an intuitive way of thinking about investment management, but also provides a superior framework for understanding investment markets in general. I refer to this as the *intelligent* organization of behavioral factors driving market returns. It is intelligent because it is based on the strategies being pursued by thousands of active equity managers, each attempting to earn superior returns by consistently pursuing a strategy. The resulting framework used to organize, rate and view managers, individual investments and markets is derived from the collective intelligence and substantial resources of thousands of active managers.

This is in contrast to the characteristic-based frameworks such as the style grid. That is, an intelligent framework versus an inert framework. A strategy-based framework yields a clearer picture of the markets and, in turn, investment management. For my company, this intelligent framework is used to identify the behavioral factors upon which our investment methodology is based.

Although the concept of investment strategy is widely known and discussed in the industry, the movement to characteristic-based categorization such as the style grid means that the importance of investment strategy is underappreciated these days. As I discussed in Chapter 9, the ill-informed leaderless stampede into the style grid has inflicted serious damage on the industry and moving the discussion away from strategy is part of that damage. My friend Craig's questions reflected this damage first-hand.

ESSENCE OF STRATEGY

Behavioral return factors are not directly observable. In creating an investment strategy, a manager must identify both quantitative and qualitative stock features, such as return on equity or management quality, that proxy for the unobservable behavioral factors. By tracking and responding to each proxy, the manager is able to take advantage of the unobserved factors. Thus proxies used to implement an investment strategy are not the factors themselves.[51] In the following discussion, these factor proxies are referred to as strategy *elements*, that is, the specific items upon which a manager focuses in order to implement an investment strategy.

Strategy encompasses both the manager's general approach to stock picking as well as the specific elements upon which the manager focuses. For example, a *Valuation* (one of the ten equity strategies to be introduced shortly) manager identifies and invests in undervalued stocks.[52] The

---

[51] Market-cap, PE and other stock characteristics are often referred to as return factors and, in fact, the current four and six factor risk models are based on this convention. But this is technically incorrect. The premise is that observable stock characteristics proxy for important but unobservable return factors. It is clear that stock characteristics are one level removed and are not the return factors themselves. Thus the technically correct name is "factor proxy model".

[52] While I focus on equity investing in this section of the book, many of the concepts can be applied to other asset classes as well. Consistently pursuing a narrowly defined strategy and taking high-conviction positions is a recipe for success regardless of the type of investment portfolio being managed.

elements used by the manager to implement the valuation strategy might include PE ratios, valuing future cash flows, or being a contrarian. Drilling down further, the specific criteria used by the manager, such as purchasing stocks with a PE of less than 15, are the manager's *secret sauce*.[53]

EQUITY STRATEGY FRAMEWORK

In this section the research I have conducted on the strategies pursued by US and international active equity managers domiciled in the United States is presented. If you already have an equity strategy, then this information provides a frame of reference for you. If you do not yet have one, my hope is that this information helps you build a successful strategy of your own.

Identifying the investment strategy being pursued by a manager allows for the formation of meaningful fund peer groups and, in turn, proper performance evaluation. Clustering managers based on self-declared strategy avoids the problem of artificially limiting the stocks which can be purchased and the attendant underperformance. Active managers are expected to consistently pursue their self-declared strategy and, in doing so, generate superior returns.

Identifying the strategy of US and International active equity mutual funds was accomplished by gathering "Principal Investment Strategies" information from each fund's prospectus.[54] The resulting information was input into a strategy identification algorithm. This algorithm was developed using an iterative process involving manager interviews, gathering principal strategy information, eliminating keywords that

---

[53] The strategy database described later in this section includes only the primary and secondary strategies as well as the elements but not the secret sauce of the fund. To fully implement a strategy all aspects, including the secret sauce, are necessary.

[54] The Principal Investment Strategies prospectus statement was first mandated by the SEC in 1998. The strategy identification process described here has been tested on thousands of US and international active equity mutual funds. As is always the case in such situations, there is no way to know that this is the best way to view and organize active equity funds and on some future date someone may come up with a better way to organize the fund universe. Be that as it may, the strategy-based system provides a number of unique insights into how active equity funds are managed.

generated false signals, and creating a manageable number of strategies. In order to ensure accuracy, the strategy identifications assigned by the algorithm are subjected to a series of audits before being included in the fund database.

Over 45,000 pieces of prospectus strategy information were gathered for the 2801 (ignoring share classes) US-based active US and international equity mutual funds. The identification algorithm assigned specific strategy information to one of 40 elements (i.e. behavioral factor proxies), which were then assigned to one of ten equity strategies. The strategy database is updated monthly. This is a self-identification process so the number of funds varies considerably across strategies. The largest strategies, in terms of number of funds, are Competitive Position, Valuation, and Future Growth, while Risk and Market Conditions are the smallest.

The ten US and international equity strategies are described in Table 13.1. From this table, one can see that Competitive Position managers focus on business principles, including quality of management, market power, product reputation, competitive advantage, sustainability of the business model and history of adapting to market changes.

On the other hand, Economic Conditions managers take a top-down approach based on economic fundamentals which might include employment, productivity, inflation and industrial output, then gauge where the overall economy is in the business cycle, the resulting supply and demand situations in various industries, and the best stocks to purchase as a result. And so forth for the other eight strategies.

TABLE 13.1: US AND INTERNATIONAL EQUITY STRATEGIES

Strategy	Description
Competitive Position	Business principles, including quality of management, market power, product reputation and competitive advantage. Considers the sustainability of the business model and history of adapting to market changes.
Economic Conditions	Top-down approach based on economic fundamentals; can include employment, productivity, inflation and industrial output. Gauges where overall economy is in business cycle, the resulting supply and demand situations in various industries, and the best stocks to purchase as a result.
Future Growth	Companies poised to grow rapidly relative to others. The Future Growth and Valuation strategies are not mutually exclusive and can both be deemed important in the investment process.
Market Conditions	Consideration of stock's recent price and volume history relative to the market and similar stocks as well as the overall stock market conditions.
Opportunity	Unique opportunities that may exist for a small number of stocks or at different points in time. May involve combining stocks and derivatives and may involve use of considerable leverage. Many hedge fund managers follow this strategy, but a mutual fund manager may also be so classified.
Profitability	Company profitability, such as gross margin, operating margin, net margin and return on equity.
Quantitative	Mathematical and statistical inefficiencies in market and individual stock pricing. Involves mathematical and statistical modeling with little or no regard to company and market fundamentals.
Risk	Control overall risk, with increasing returns a secondary consideration. Risk measures considered may include beta, volatility, company financials, industry and sector exposures, country exposures, and economic and market risk factors.
Social Considerations	Company's ethical, environmental and business practices as well as an evaluation of the company's business lines in light of the current social and political climate. A manager can look for these criteria or the lack of in selecting a stock.
Valuation	Stocks selling cheaply compared to peer stocks based on accounting ratios and valuation techniques. The Valuation and Future Growth strategies are not mutually exclusive and can both be deemed important in the investment process.

Managers use one of these ten strategies as a primary strategy and then may use another as their secondary strategy. The resulting primary and secondary fund strategies, along with the corresponding elements, make it possible to create broad or granular fund peer groups. These groupings range from the ten primary strategy groups to the 90 primary-secondary peer groups (formed by creating all possible paired combinations of the ten strategies listed in the table), to primary-secondary-elements strategy peer groups.

When broken down by primary-secondary-element groups, only 22 of the 2801 funds have a primary-secondary-elements twin outside their fund family (meaning all those funds managed by a single firm, such as Janus in the US). Including same family funds, the number of funds with a strategy twin is 348.

Thus the typical fund is pursuing a unique strategy when full granularity is taken into consideration. This means that positive alphas are the consequence of highly idiosyncratic investment strategies being pursued by individual managers. That is, there are hundreds of managers pursuing their own unique strategy, while selecting hundreds of different best idea stocks, each generating a positive alpha. The evidence of stock picking skill among active equity managers was presented in Chapter 1 and will be further discussed later.

There is a widely held belief, in both the academic and professional communities, that equity managers frequently deviate from their stated investment approach, which has created a general distrust of what investment managers say versus what they actually do. This begs the question of whether self-declared strategy information has any value. I tested this value proposition in two ways.

First, I tested the ability of strategy statements to cluster funds pursuing similar investment approaches. This is important for creating meaningful peer groups and for proper performance evaluation. Second, I tested the ability of strategy statements to concentrate measurable and persistent behavioral return factors in a single cluster, while distributing those of little interest across clusters. This allows managers to pursue their strategy without facing artificial peer group constraints as well as making it easier to identify superior strategy managers. Based on the results for each of these tests, I concluded that self-declared strategy statements *are* a superior way to view and label active equity managers.[55]

STRATEGY STOCK POOLS

Once the strategy of the manager has been identified, the next step is to create strategy stock pools. Strategy stocks are the ones of collective interest to managers pursuing the same strategy. For example, those stocks most attractive to Competitive Position managers are categorized Competitive Position stocks. In like manner, those stocks most attractive to Economic Conditions managers are categorized Economic Conditions stocks.

Each stock becomes a member of a particular strategy stock pool based on which strategy finds the stock most attractive. Attractiveness is measured by the percentage of the stock held by each strategy, with the highest percent holding used to strategy categorize a stock. Each stock is forced into one and only one strategy stock pool. Note that the collective intelligence of the equity managers is being used to create the stock pools. Thus this is an intelligent categorization of stocks as compared to the inert style grid categorization of stocks.

The composition of each pool is determined by the collective holdings of all of the managers pursuing that particular strategy. Over time, strategy pool composition changes as managers alter their stock holdings in response to changing market and economic conditions. Consequently, strategy stock pools move about the equity universe over time and strategy pool stock characteristics, such as average market cap and PE, change as managers adjust their holdings. This is clearly shown in Figure 13.1.

---

[55] See C. Thomas Howard, 'The Importance of Investment Strategy', working paper (2010) for more information regarding these tests.

Thus it is not possible to describe strategy stock pools using the characteristics of the stocks held. This lack of descriptive power applies to every stock characteristic, not just market cap and PE. Strategy stock pools are defined by the managers that hold them, not by stock characteristics.

FIGURE 13.1 A: US STRATEGY STOCK POOLS, JANUARY 2012

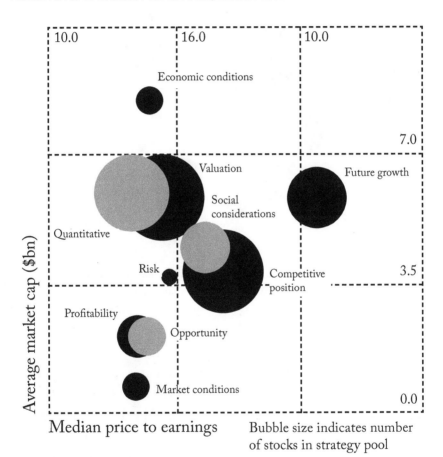

Median price to earnings

Bubble size indicates number of stocks in strategy pool

FIGURE 13.1 B: US STRATEGY STOCK POOLS, JANUARY 2013

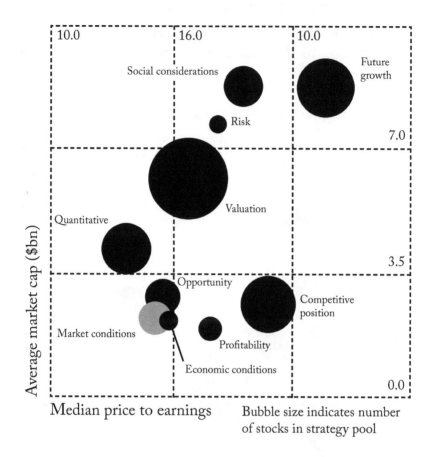

Median price to earnings

Bubble size indicates number of stocks in strategy pool

This approach differs from the representation that is currently dominant in the industry, in which the equity universe is locked in place by the style grid. In this paradigm, managers are categorized by the stocks they hold rather than stocks being categorized by the managers that hold them. In such a world, managers cannot fully respond to changing economic and market conditions as they are tethered to a specific style box.

MEASURING STRATEGY CONSISTENCY

Strategy managers move about the equity universe in pursuit of those stocks which they find most attractive. Over time, managers develop strategy specific stock picking skills which yield the best results when applied to stocks of greatest interest to fellow strategy managers. That is, a strategy manager is most successful when analyzing, buying and selling own strategy stocks. For example, Competitive Position managers are most successful when focusing on Competitive Position stocks. This notion represents a core competency argument and is the basis for the objective fund strategy consistency measure presented next.

The *monthly fund strategy consistency measure* is based on the proportion of own strategy stocks held by the fund and is scaled to range from 1 (fewest own strategy stocks held) to 10 (most own strategy stocks held) within each strategy. The performance of this measure is tested and the results reported in Figure 13.2. The most (10) strategy consistent funds outperform the least (1) consistent funds by a highly statistically significant 2% annually. This means managers who adjust their portfolio to hold as many own strategy stocks as possible outperform those managers who do not. That is, those managers who are most successful in keeping their portfolios centered on the ever-moving own strategy stock pool, as depicted in Figure 13.1, are the top performers.

FIGURE 13.2: ACTIVE EQUITY ANNUAL NET RETURN BY BEGINNING OF THE MONTH FUND CONSISTENCY RATING

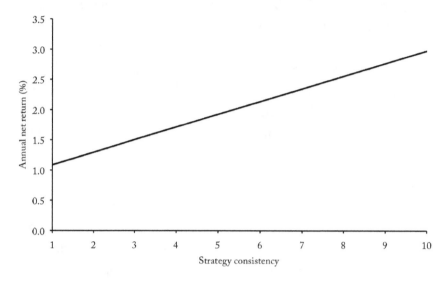

Based on regression results that include all US and International active equity mutual funds domiciled in the US for January 1999 to May 2013. Monthly returns are net of automatically deducted fees and the S&P 500. Data Sources: AthenaInvest, Lipper and Thomson Reuters.

When I first stumbled across this result I was both stunned and perplexed. My first reaction was that this must represent some sort of mathematical tautology. I realized this was not the case, as the strategy identification of the 3000 active equity funds provided a solid foundation for the consistency measure. It also occurred to me that strategy consistency was being judged by the fund's peer group and this judgment was continually revised based on the collective analysis and investment decisions of the group.

This is another example of using collective intelligence to measure an important aspect of strategy execution – that is how consistently strategy is being pursued. What matters in executing the strategy is not consistent returns and not a consistent set of stock characteristics such as market cap and PE, but rather the consistent pursuit of an investment strategy as judged by strategy peers.

CENTRAL ROLE PLAYED BY STRATEGY STOCK POOLS

The consistency results just presented provide strong support for the value of self-declared strategy, in that own strategy stocks are the ones upon which a manager should focus. In essence, this argues for a strategy-based stock screen for the universe of stocks of most interest to the manager, in contrast to the commonly used stock characteristic based screens. The strategy screen is superior because it is based on the collective judgment of skilled stock pickers who are pursuing the same self-declared strategy.

This does not imply that two managers who are pursing, say, a Competitive Position strategy will end up holding the same stocks. There are hundreds of Competitive Position stocks, so it is entirely possible for one strategy consistent Competitive Position manager to hold a completely different portfolio from another strategy consistent Competitive Position manager, and yet both generate superior returns. The consistency results imply strategy managers need to focus on own strategy stocks, but they do not say managers have to pursue identical investment processes nor hold the same stocks.

The strategy consistency results are independent of the strategy being pursued. That is, regardless of what strategy the manager is pursuing, own strategy stocks should be the focus. Stocks in the Competitive Position pool are different from those in the Economic Conditions pool and so forth. Competitive Position managers are looking for stocks with quality management, strong market positions, and which are innovative. Economic Conditions managers are looking for stocks that will most benefit from the current stage of the economic cycle.

These are two different pools, yet each yield superior return opportunities that only a specific group of managers can identify. Competitive Position managers are less successful at finding high return stocks in the Economics Conditions pool, while the Economic Conditions managers are less successful at finding high return stocks in the Competitive Position pool. It is as if each group of active managers views the equity universe through a pair of strategy glasses that allows them and only them to see a unique set of behavioral return factors.

When asked to describe their investment strategy, most managers don't mention the pursuit of own strategy stocks. However, the data reveals that it is indeed important as investing in own strategy stocks is a determinant of portfolio performance. Strategy stock pools change constantly as both the economy and markets evolve over time. While not explicitly attempting to do so, the successful manager is forever pursuing the own strategy stock pool.

A manager who trades more rapidly or slowly than the average of the own strategy stock pool hurts fund performance. The average turnover for each strategy stock pool is presented in Figure 13.3. On average a stock remains in a strategy pool for 14 months. Valuation stocks stay in their pool for an average of 17 months, while Market Conditions stocks remain in their pool for less than half of that time, eight months. This means that a typical Market Conditions manager must generate a turnover rate that is twice that of the typical Valuation manager in order to be as strategy consistent as the Valuation manager.

A fund's optimal turnover rate is dictated by the collective decisions of its strategy peer group. In turn, a strategy pool's average turnover is driven by the elements upon which that strategy focuses and the extent to which changing economic and market conditions impact these elements. Figure 13.3 is thus a crude representation of the dynamic relationship between the economy and markets, on the one hand, and behavioral factors on the other. This is one more example of harnessing active manager collective intelligence in order to better understand financial markets.

FIGURE 13.3: AVERAGE MONTHS IN THE STRATEGY STOCK POOL

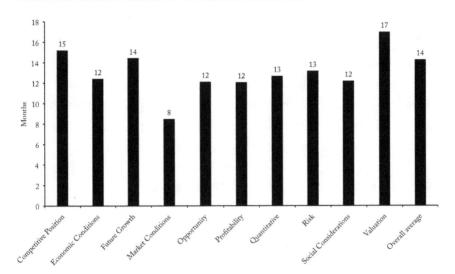

Based on all US strategy identified stocks June 1997 to February 2012. Average number of stocks is roughly 3000. Source: AthenaInvest

SPECIALIST VERSUS GENERALIST

A manager might be tempted to become a generalist by developing the skills needed to fish in several pools rather than in just their own strategy stock pool. After all, superior return opportunities are available in each stock pool, so why not drop a line in each? The results presented in Figure 13.2 suggest against doing this. The greater the percentage of own strategy stocks held, the higher is the return. This percentage can be increased by either investing in more own strategy stocks or decreasing the number of other strategy stocks.

Referring back to the Best Idea results reported in Figure 1.1, we see that portfolio return decreases as stocks are added to a portfolio. Thus the latter choice, decreasing the number of non-strategy stocks, is better, since it both increases the percent of own strategy stocks while decreasing the total number of stocks in the portfolio. The implication is that managers should be specialists and remain strategy focused.

Evidence against becoming a generalist also shows up when manager investment strategy statements are carefully analyzed. Figure 13.4 shows that managers who limit their focus to own strategy elements generate 17.2 bp in annual higher return for each additional own strategy element and 3.3 bp annually for each additional 10% that are own strategy elements. Thus, based on what they say and do, managers should consistently pursue a narrowly defined investment strategy. In other words, managers do best when they are investment specialists.

FIGURE 13.4: ANNUAL GAINS TO NARROWLY DEFINED STRATEGY

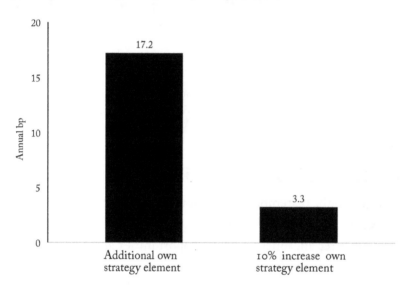

Managers need to be strong willed and relentless in pursuing a narrowly defined strategy. You do not want managers talking to one another and sharing ideas. Each should come to the table with their best idea stocks and not be interested in what other managers think of their choices. Consensus hurts performance, which is the reason why team managed funds underperform.[56] It is desirable to have a collection of strong willed, highly opinionated characters running equity funds.

[56] See J. Chen, H. Hong, M. Huang, and J. D. Kubik, 'Does Fund Size Erode Performance? Organizational Diseconomies and Active Money Management', *American Economic Review* 94:5 (2004), pp. 1276-1302; and Yufeng Han, Tom Noe, and Michael Rebello, 'Horses for courses: Fund managers and organizational structures', working paper (January 2008).

STRATEGY CONSISTENCY AND STYLE DRIFT

The result that strategy consistency pays is just the opposite of the corresponding style grid results, which show that it is better to style drift than be style consistent. It is apparent that strategy and style, as it is currently used in the industry, are not the same. Fund strategy is identified based on the statements made by fund managers, while style is based on the average market-cap and PE characteristics of the stocks held by the fund. When the style grid was launched some 25 years ago, the supposition (hope?) was that managers pursuing the same strategy would end up buying stocks with the same characteristics. Thus, those managers holding small-cap value stocks, for example, were all pursuing the same investment strategy and were placed in the small-cap value style box.

We now know this not to be the case. The most successful active equity managers exhibit the lowest style index correlations, the highest active share and the greatest amount of style drift.[57] So the things that managers do in order to generate superior returns seems to have little to do with style boxes. Strategy, on the other hand, is key to generating superior returns. Jointly, strategy consistency and style drift successfully proxy for the stock picking skill that is so common among active equity managers, the evidence for which will be discussed in the next chapter.

To be successful, a manager needs to be both strategy *consistent* and style box *inconsistent*. Given the importance of the ever changing stock strategy pools, it is no wonder mechanical stock characteristic regimes, such as the style grid, fail to capture the dynamic and largely unobservable interplay between managers and the market in which they invest.

Lest one despair that by jettisoning the style grid the world of portfolio construction and evaluation is forever damaged, be assured there is a strategy alternative for each corresponding style grid tool:

- Funds can be labelled using their identified primary strategy or, if necessary, the secondary strategy and elements.

---

[57] See Amihud and Goyenko (2008); Brands, Brown and Gallagher (2006); Cremers and Petajisto (2009); Kacperczyk, Sialm and Zheng (2005); and Wermers (2010).

- Portfolios can be constructed by diversifying across strategies (this is actually more effective than diversifying across boxes).

- Superior managers within a strategy can be identified using the strategy consistency and conviction measures (to be discussed shortly).

- Fund performance can be evaluated relative to a broadly or narrowly defined strategy peer group.

- Performance attribution can be based on a fund's primary and secondary strategy, and elements.

Thus self-declared strategy can be used to create a rigorous equity portfolio construction and evaluation methodology.

Frequently I am asked whether expecting managers to be strategy consistent is just the latest version of sticking a manager in a box. Not an unreasonable question since there is an expectation that a manager state their strategy and then consistently pursue it. The strategy consistency measure shows that managers should focus on own strategy stocks, which does sound a lot like asking a manager to purchase only stocks within their own style box. But there are critical differences.

First, strategy is self-declared and no doubt represents the core competency of the manager. Second, it is not unreasonable to expect a manager to do what they say. Both of these are opposite of the style grid, in that the style box is externally imposed and then the manager is expected to abide by the resulting external constraints. Third, the strategy stock pools, the basis for strategy consistency, are an economic, market and peer group determined target for fund managers, as compared to the fixed style boxes. What is more, being strategy consistent increases returns, while style box consistency hurts returns. Finally, knowing the manager's strategy tells investors something about how investment decisions are made, while the style box reveals little or nothing about the investment process.

Therefore, expecting a manager to consistently pursue a self-declared strategy is not unreasonable as it provides insight into the management process; provides the metrics needed to analyze, evaluate, and build equity portfolios; and improves returns. It seems a reasonable way to think about the active equity manager universe.

MEASURING STRATEGY CONVICTION AND RATING FUNDS

Consistency is an important part of the successful strategy execution. The other is taking high-conviction positions in best idea stocks. These are the stocks the manager and analysts believe have the best opportunity to appreciate based on their careful analysis. The more heavily these ideas are weighted in the portfolio, the better is portfolio performance. This is demonstrated by the Best Ideas results reported in Figure 1.1 and will be discussed more extensively in the next chapter. Combining this result with the Evans and Archer results reported in Figure 10.1 which show that 90% of the potential volatility reduction is achieved with 20 stocks, gives a strong argument for high-conviction portfolios.

Conviction can be measured in a number of ways, including the number of stocks (the fewer the better), tracking error (the higher the better), R-squared (the lower the better), active share (the higher the better), and industry concentration (the higher the better).

Combining conviction measures with the consistency measure yields a fund rating that is predictive of performance, with both measures contributing roughly equally to predictive power. This means manager behavior, in the form of strategy, consistency and conviction, is predictive of future performance while past performance is not.

Using strategy to organize the active equity universe is not only useful for understanding the dynamics among the economy, markets and investment management, but allows for identifying those managers who have the best chance of outperforming going forward. Funds with the highest levels of consistency and conviction outperform those with the lowest levels by around 5% annually, as shown in Table 13.2.[58] What is more, consistency and conviction are predictive of performance up to five years ahead.[59]

TABLE 13.2: AVERAGE NET RETURNS BY FUND RATING AND RETURN ADVANTAGE

Fund rating	Return count	Average subsequent returns net of S&P 500					
		1 month	1 year	2 year	3 year	4 year	5 year
1	34,856	-0.21	-2.62	-2.75	-2.68	-2.64	-2.55
2	38,643	-0.09	-1.20	-1.55	-1.64	-1.53	-1.38
3	93,317	0.03	0.31	0.12	0.08	0.14	0.22
4	43,200	0.11	2.38	2.07	1.90	1.74	1.53
5	29,602	0.16	2.68	2.25	2.00	1.70	1.42
Total/ Average	239,618	0.01	0.30	0.04	-0.05	-0.09	-0.11
	Annual rating 5-1 return advantage	4.58	5.67	5.45	5.16	4.77	4.34
	Marginal year implied 5-1 return advantage			5.23	4.58	3.62	2.61

Based on subsequent returns for beginning of the month US and International strategy identified, Diamond Rated active equity mutual funds over the April 1997 through July 2009 period. FDR is based on strategy consistency and conviction, with FDR5 being the highest on both scales and FDR1 being the lowest. Fund returns are net of automatically deducted fees and the S&P 500 return. Other than the 1 month return, all returns are annual. The FDR 5-1 return advantage is calculated as the annualized slope from the regression of FDR returns on a variable taking on the values 1 through 5. Data sources: AthenaInvest and Thomson Reuters Financial.

---

[58] This is referred to as a Fund Diamond Rating. To learn more about this rating and its predictive power visit **Athenainvest.com**.

[59] This result is consistent with the work of Jonathan B. Berk and Jules H. van Binsbergen in a 2013 study 'Measuring Skill in the Mutual Fund Industry' that found stock picking skill is not only common among active equity mutual fund managers (they conjecture that up to 80% of these managers are skilled stock pickers), but also persists for up to ten years.

STRATEGY-BASED INVESTING

Consistently pursuing a narrowly-defined investment strategy, while taking high-conviction positions, is the key to successfully implementing Behavioral Portfolio Management. Thinking about the investment markets in the terms of investment strategy rather than the commonly used style grid provides significant benefits. These result from the collective intelligence, skill and resources that active managers bring to bear when making investment decisions.

Objectively measuring outcomes of manager decisions and then aggregating across to managers provides insight into how these managers generate excess returns. These insights will allow you to build a better strategy for managing investment portfolios.

CHAPTER 14: THE BEST (AND WORST) IDEAS OF EQUITY MANAGERS

I N THE PREVIOUS chapter I demonstrated that managers who consistently pursue a narrowly-defined strategy while taking high-conviction positions outperform for up to five years into the future. This seems to imply that managers have superior stock picking skill and indeed there is a growing body of evidence demonstrating that skill. I will first review this evidence and explore how managers can have stock picking skill but yet their funds underperform. This dynamic allows for ranking stocks based on equity fund holdings from best to worst ideas.

After presenting the evidence regarding stock picking skill, I describe how it is possible to rate stocks using fund holdings, which is another example of how the collective intelligence of active equity managers can be used to build superior portfolios.

STOCK PICKING SKILL

Conventional wisdom has the typical active equity mutual fund manager lacking stock picking skill and thus underperforming. There is a well-known body of research that purports to show this.[60] Somewhat

---

[60] For example, see Sharpe (1966), Jensen (1968), Carhart (1997), and Fama and French (2010).

surprisingly, there is a substantial body of manager-decision research, stretching back 20 years, that documents just the opposite – namely the existence of superior equity fund stock picking skill and performance. Recent studies within this research stream report the following:[61]

- Baker, Litov, Wachter and Wurgler (2004): "We uncover new evidence that fund managers have at least some stock picking skill."

- Kosowski, Timermann, Wermers and White (2006): "...a sizable minority of managers pick stocks well enough to more than cover their costs. Moreover, the superior alphas of these managers persist."

- Alexander, Cici and Gibson (2007): "Our analysis reveals that managers making purely valuation-motivated purchases substantially beat the market but are unable to do so when compelled to invest excess cash from investor inflows. A similar, but weaker, pattern is found for stocks that are sold."

- Keswani and Stolin (2008): "... there is a robust smart money effect in the United Kingdom. The effect is caused by buying (but not selling) decisions of both individuals and institutions. Using monthly data available post-1991 we show that money is comparably smart in the United States."

- Cremers and Petajisto (2009): "...the most active stock pickers have enough skill to outperform their benchmarks even after fees and transaction costs." (Where "active" is defined as willingness to look different from an index.)

---

[61] Other articles in this research stream include studies by Hendricks et. al. (1993), Grinblatt and Titman (1993), Goetzmann and Ibbotson (1994), Brown and Goetzmann (1995), Elton et. al. (1996), Daniel et. al. (1997), Chen et. al. (2000), Wermers (2000), Collins and Fabozzi (2000), Pastor and Stambaugh (2002), Wermers (2003), Bollen and Busse (2004), Avramov and Wermers (2005), Cohen et. al. (2005), Kosowski et. al. (2006), Frazzini (2006), Mamaysky (2006), Busse and Irvine (2006), Brands et. al. (2006), Kacperczyk and Seru (2007), Kacperczyk et. al. (2008), and Han et. al. (2008).

- Shumway et. al. (2009): "We measure the differences in beliefs between funds with high BAI and all other funds, the belief difference index (BDI). Sorting stocks based on BDI, we find that the annualized return difference between the top and bottom decile is about two to six percent."

- Pomorski (2009): "…best idea mutual fund trades, likely generated by centralized research of fund management companies, account for about 30% of fund volume and outperform benchmarks and other trades by as much as 47 basis points per month."

- Frey and Herbst (2010): "Positive abnormal returns to buy-side analysts' revisions are also reflected in the performance of mutual fund trades: trades triggered by buy-side recommendations have higher returns than other trades."

- Berk and van Binsbergen (2013): "Using the dollar-value that a mutual fund adds as the measure of skill, we find that the average mutual fund adds about $2 million per year and that this skill persists for as long as 10 years."

Representative of these studies are the Cohen, Polk and Silli Best Idea results reported in Figure 1.1. They find, "… the U.S. stock market does not appear to be efficiently priced, since even the typical active mutual fund manager is able to identify stocks that outperform by economically and statistically large amounts." Their results are based on the performance of the typical manager's ranked best ideas and reveal that not only is the typical manager a superior stock picker, but so are the vast majority of managers.[62]

Collectively these studies reveal a universe of equity mutual fund managers who are very good at identifying profitable investment opportunities and this flies in the face of the conventional wisdom that contends such skill is a rare commodity. Given the size and breadth of

---

[62] Berk and van Binsbergen (2013) suggest that up to 80% of active equity managers are superior stock pickers.

this research stream, it is surprising that it plays such a small role in shaping conventional wisdom regarding active equity stock picking skill.

BEHAVIORAL FACTORS VERSUS INFORMATION MOSAIC

Stock picking is all about collecting the right information and analyzing it correctly, right? This is certainly a belief of many individual as well as professional investors. This requires gathering as much information as possible regarding the company, the industry and the economy, and then applying a unique way of creating a stock's information mosaic. The thought is that if you can do it better than other investors and glean a unique set of insights regarding the stock the result is superior performance.

It is my belief this is very difficult to do. Individuals are competing against other talented individuals, but most importantly against an army of smart, highly paid and elaborately resourced buy-side and sell-side analysts. I've always found it hard to believe that even the professionals are able to be successful in this competitive environment based strictly on superior information. Short of having inside information, it is very difficult to win this contest. On the other hand, behavioral mispricings, if identified, can be used to earn superior returns. This is not a case of outsmarting competitors, but harnessing the emotional mistakes made by others.

In talking with professional portfolio managers, you often hear how they gather large amounts of information and analyze it using a unique, proprietary methodology. I have no doubt this is true, but it is not clear that the excess returns result from a *superior* information mosaic. Could it be that instead they are identifying emotionally-driven price distortions using their methodology and this is why they earn superior returns?

We'll never know for sure because it is virtually impossible to separate an information superiority from an emotion-driven pricing distortion. I have my suspicion that such descriptions by professional managers are a response to the client need for a plausible story of how the portfolio is managed. Talking about markets and financial analysis is easier for clients to accept than is a discussion of uncovering emotionally-driven price distortions.

WHY THEN DO MANAGERS UNDERPERFORM?

If stock picking skill is so widespread, why do so many funds underperform? The typical manager is able to identify a handful of best idea stocks. But rather than limiting the portfolio to these good ideas, managers purchase additional stocks that, by all accounts, hurt portfolio performance. While managers speak passionately about their best ideas, they often speak meekly, even apologetically, about the additional stocks purchased to round out the portfolio, or in our vernacular, bubble wrap the portfolio.

The typical active equity mutual fund holds 100 stocks, which means dramatic over-diversification is common. This creates serious fund performance problems. As a manager moves down best idea rank, stock alphas eventually turn negative (probably somewhere around the 30 rank stock). So as a result, lower ranked stocks morph into "bad" idea stocks. As shown in Figure 1.1, monthly alpha declines to negative 250bp as stock rank approaches "last". Indeed, in the typical fund portfolio bad ideas probably outnumber good ideas by three to one. So in the mutual fund market, over-diversification is the rule while proper diversification is the exception.

INDUSTRY-DRIVEN OVER-DIVERSIFICATION

This raises the perplexing question of why managers purchase so many stocks. Why not hold a small number of stocks, maybe as few as ten as suggested in Chapter 10, thus concentrating the portfolio in best ideas? There are powerful industry incentives encouraging funds to do otherwise.

Funds are compensated based on assets under management (AUM). This provides an irresistible incentive to grow large. As the fund grows in size it becomes increasingly difficult to hold a small number of stocks. Since revenues grow dramatically as size increases, it is easy to see why funds find it to their benefit to invest in a large number of stocks, since the gain to increased AUM easily offsets the loss due to underperformance. Based on this relationship, Jonathan Berk of the University of California, Berkeley and Richard Green of Carnegie Mellon University argue that growing too large and thus over-diversifying represents rational profit maximizing behavior on the part of a fund attempting to extract the economic rents of superior stock picking skill.[63]

The current fund distribution system is based on the style grid, which also encourages funds to purchase many stocks. In order to fit into the style grid distribution system, the fund must be categorized in one of the style boxes, such as small-cap value. Once so categorized, the fund is loath to *style drift* since this is grounds for being excluded from or thrown off highly profitable fund platforms. Style drift is avoided by purchasing the stocks in the style index associated with the fund's style box. Thus in attempting to grow large by fitting into the style grid distribution system, the fund over-diversifies.

Investors, advisors and consultants place considerable importance on fund level volatility, which encourages managers to purchase many stocks. Adding stocks reduces a fund's standard deviation (or maximum drawdown, or downside risk, or other volatility measures), making the fund more attractive with respect to volatility. Adding many stocks in order to reduce volatility leads to over-diversification.

To avoid criticism, or worse yet legal problems, a fund manager will construct the portfolio to look like an index or other fund portfolios. It is well known that investor regret is much higher when a unique or different investment approach does not work as compared to the regret experienced when a traditional approach does not work. This is reinforced by a legal system which at times outright requires over-diversification or leads to the same result by applying "prudent man" concepts.

---

[63] J. B. Berk and R. C. Green, 'Mutual Fund Flows and Performance in Rational Markets', *Journal of Political Economy* 112:6 (2004), pp. 1269-1295.

These rules/regulatory requirements mean that properly diversified portfolios (i.e. small, concentrated portfolios) are more susceptible to regulatory criticism and lawsuits. Managers, often following the advice of legal counsel, over-diversify in order to avoid such potential problems. This is a major issue since, as I discuss below, best ideas are very different from manager to manager and so any pressure to conform to a common portfolio will hurt performance.

Collectively these industry forces lead to dramatic over-diversification by equity fund managers. Without these forces, managers would build small portfolios concentrated in their best ideas and most of them would generate positive alphas. Instead, the vast majority of managers over-diversify to the point of underperformance. So the good news is that the vast majority of equity managers are superior stock pickers, but the bad news is that industry-driven over-diversification wipes out superior returns by encouraging investment in more bad ideas than good ideas.

The evolution of an equity manager looks something like this: The manager starts a fund pursuing a strategy she or he believes in. Not all will succeed, but the ones who do attract assets and grow. As they grow, they add the trappings of a larger company, including annual budget expectations. Now marketing and distribution play an increasingly important role and swings in AUM become a major problem, since fixed expenses must be covered. This is exacerbated by the widespread use of the style grid in fund distribution.

At some point managers succumb to budgetary and distribution pressures and abandon strategy consistency. Underperformance is the result. Having grown to be a large asset management organization, shareholders and cost control become paramount and highly paid portfolio manager superstars are replaced by lower cost team management. This later point argues that portfolio superstars are more likely found at smaller, newer funds. The evidence is consistent with this evolutionary story: large, old, team-managed funds underperform.[64]

---

[64] Berk and van Binsbergen (2013) present an argument similar to this along with supporting evidence.

IDENTIFYING BEST IDEA AND WORST IDEA STOCKS

Collective fund holdings are used to identify best and worst stocks. The resulting ranking is comprised of both quantity and quality dimensions, each market cap adjusted. The quantity component is based on the number of funds holding the stock, with the more funds holding the better. At least five funds must hold the stock for it to be rated. The quality component is derived from the percentage of the stock held by FDR 4 and FDR 5 funds as described in the previous chapter.

The top rating is assigned to those stocks held by the most funds along with the highest percent held by top funds.[65] The quantity measure is more important for smaller stocks, while the quality measure is more important for larger stocks. Smaller funds tend to purchase a stock only for performance purposes, while a larger fund purchases a number of stocks for bubble wrap purposes, thus the need for a quality dimension for larger fund holdings. Top-rated stocks are those most held by funds for alpha generation (i.e. collectively, the best idea stocks), while low-rated stocks are those most held for low-conviction purposes. We refer to these rankings as Stock Diamond Ratings (SDRs).

If investment teams of top-rated funds have skill and if they overweight their best ideas, then top-rated stocks will outperform low-rated stocks going forward. Table 14.1 reveals that this is indeed the case. The average

---

[65] For other approaches to aggregating best idea stocks across funds see Cohen, Coval and Pastor (2005), Cohen, Polk and Silli (2010), Myers, Poterba, Shackelford and Shoven (2000), Shumway, Szeter and Yuan (2009), and Wermers, Yao and Zhao (2007). Each of these studies confirm aggregating holdings across funds results in measures that are predictive of future fund and stock returns. Unlike other studies that use reported holdings as if they are known immediately, our work is based on holdings as made available by Thomson Reuters. Studies show that the value of holdings declines over time and is exhausted a year after reported by the fund (see Cohen, Polk and Silli (2010) and Wermers, Yao and Zhao (2007)). The data in this study is 80% three months or newer and is valuable for identifying stocks that subsequently outperform. Kacperczyk et. al. (2008) find that knowing the trades executed since the most recent holdings report can generate as much as 1.2% additional annual return for the top funds in their sample, i.e. those with the largest unobserved "return gap". So there is additional value to knowing current holdings beyond the reported holdings used in this study.

return advantage of top-rated stocks over low-rated stocks is 6.80% which means that, on average, the best idea stocks outperform worst idea stocks by 6.80% annually. This is both economically and statistically significant and exceeds the top-rated fund advantage reported in the last chapter. The return advantage is only partially explained by the usual size, market-to-book and momentum adjustments, with an adjusted return advantage of 4.76%, which is also economically and statistically significant.[66]

TABLE 14.1: MONTHLY SUBSEQUENT AND ADJUSTED STOCK RETURNS BY STOCK RATING

	Average subsequent month stock return						Annual 5-1 return advantage	
	1	2	3	4	5	Average	Value	p-value
Actual returns	0.74	0.90	0.93	1.10	1.35	0.99	6.80	0.066
Adjusted returns	-0.09	0.10	0.13	0.21	0.35	0.13	4.76	0.018

Based on subsequent monthly returns for beginning of the month US Diamond Rated stocks over the January 1, 1999 through March 31, 2012 period. The Stock Diamond Rating (SDR) is comprised of both quantity and quality components, each market cap adjusted. The quantity component is based on the number of funds holding the stock, with more funds holding the better. At least five funds must hold the stock for it to be rated. The quality component is derived from the percent of the stock held by high quality FDR4 and 5 funds. The quantity measure is more important for smaller stocks, while the quality measure is more important for larger stocks. SDR5 is the highest stock rating while SDR1 is the lowest. The SDR 5-1 return advantage is calculated as the annualized slope from the regression of SDR returns on a variable taking on the values 1 through 5. The standard error used for calculating the p-value is the square root of the sum of the squared values of the SDR1 and SDR5 SE's. Adjusted returns are derived using a four factor Fama and French model based on market, SML, HML and Mom. Data sources: AthenaInvest, Thomson Reuters Financial and Ken French's website: (mba.tuck.dartmouth.edu/pages/faculty/ken.french)

---

[66] Berk and van Binsbergen (2013) argue that the four factor model leads to an upward biased benchmark since they do not include transaction and management costs that the typical investor would have to pay for the mimicking portfolio. Indeed, they find that each of the four factors generate a positive alpha relative to a Vanguard based benchmark, with Vanguard being used because their index funds are the least expensive way to create the mimicking portfolio.

Another observation based on Table 14.1 is that the average monthly adjusted stock alpha is 0.13%, or 1.56% annually. This means the average stock held by active equity mutual funds earns a positive alpha that is roughly equal to average fund expenses. The fact that the average stock earns enough to cover average fund fees is consistent with other studies that find the average active equity fund excess return is zero.[67] The more interesting observation is that the average stock held outperforms, which means investment skill is common among active equity funds.[68]

Clearly the return distribution of stocks held by funds is shifted to the right relative to the complete stock universe. This is consistent with the stated active equity objective of picking stocks that outperform on average. Note the adjusted return of low-rated stocks is a negative 9bps (0.09%) monthly (negative 108bp or 1.08% annually), meaning that these stocks represent underperforming stocks that can be used to build underperforming portfolios.[69]

Some argue stock selection across active equity funds must be a zero sum game. Obviously it is not. Such an assertion is true for the stock market as a whole, as stock selection must be a zero sum game with as many losers as winners, but this does not have to be the case in every segment of the market. Based on World Bank data, the July 2013 US stock market total market value exceeds $22 trillion. Active US equity mutual funds hold less than $2.5 trillion, or about 11% of all equities.

---

[67] See Bollen and Busse (2004), Brown and Goetzmann (1995), Carhart (1997), and Fama and French (2010).

[68] Wermers (2000) also finds that the average stock held by mutual funds outperforms by 1.3%.

[69] Of course, an even clearer signal would be obtained if funds took both long and short positions, with short positions reflecting those stocks that the manager thought would do poorly. This would extend the left tail of the distribution further below zero and might very well provide a boost to top-rated performance. The more manager information impounded in relative holdings, the cleaner are stock rankings.

So it is entirely possible for the average stock held by funds to outperform at the expense of the other 89% of the equity universe.[70] Arguing that stock selection among equity funds must be a zero sum game is akin to arguing that it is impossible to drown in a lake of average depth of 3 feet. Both are indefensible statements.

It is surprising that best idea as well as underperforming stocks can be identified using data from mutual funds that are almost exclusively taking long stock positions. It turns out the ability to identify underperforming stocks is the collateral damage resulting from funds catering to investor emotions by, among other things, over-diversifying in order to reduce volatility and tracking error and also funds responding to the misaligned industry incentive to grow large rather than maximize performance, as revenues are AUM-based.

When a stock is widely held to meet these objectives, rather than as a best idea, the low-conviction motive shows up in the holdings data. Based on revealed low expected return, superior short positions can be constructed. Thus an arbitrage, producing a roughly 7% net return, can be executed by longing the best idea stocks while shorting the worst idea stocks. In essence this represents a skill and industry structure arbitrage. In short, a skill and Cult Enforcer arbitrage.

SOCIAL VALIDATION AND OPINION AGGREGATION

In the last chapter I argued that consensus within a fund hurts performance. This is due to the social validation bias unfavorably impacting investment decisions. However, as I've just shown, aggregating top relative weight decisions of top managers produces superior returns. That is, it is better to aggregate opinions across funds than within funds.

It is much more valuable to know that managers from different funds like a stock than it is to know the collective opinion of analysts within the same organization. Truly independent assessments of a stock provide

---

[70] Berk and van Binsbergen (2013) present a similar argument.

valuable insight into the attractiveness of the stock. Even the professionals can't avoid the cognitive errors associated with social validation unless they are physically separated from one another.

I have worked with many investment organizations and a common structure is that portfolio managers and analysts have offices on the same floor and meet regularly as a large group to discuss their investment ideas. I believe this is a poor structure. As I walk through such offices, I have the urge to tell each of the analysts and portfolio managers to move their offices into physically different locations and not communicate with others. The only investment team structure that makes sense is when you have a clear leader and a supporting cast of analysts – that is vertical integration. This team should be separated from the other investment teams and render their stock opinions without input from these other teams. The final decisions made should not be a vote across different investment teams.

The next thing that should be eliminated is the large meeting rooms where the investment teams gather to discuss their respective ideas. The team should not meet on a regular basis to present their ideas to other investment teams. The pernicious effects of social validation mean that large team-based investment organizations produce inferior returns.

Finally, an investment team should be made up of analysts only, without a separate portfolio manager. The best investment ideas are generated by the analysts since they are the closest to the company and industry and therefore have the best set of information for making investment decisions. A portfolio manager's job is to take these ideas and construct a portfolio based on other considerations. These other non-performance considerations hurt performance, as I described earlier in this chapter. Fire the bubble wrapper, known as the portfolio manager, and keep the analysts.[71]

---

[71] Frey and Herbst (2010) conducted a comprehensive study of a large European mutual fund complex and found that buy-side analyst recommendations produced the highest subsequent stock returns, followed by sell-side analyst recommendations. Portfolio manager driven decisions performed the worst within the fund complex.

CHAPTER 15: BUILDING AN EQUITY STRATEGY

IN CHAPTER 14 I discussed how truly active equity managers are able to earn superior returns and how their best idea stocks, as identified by relative portfolio weights, also earn superior returns. I argued that the most likely source of these superior returns is the identification and harnessing of behavioral return factors that are the result of emotionally-driven price distortions. When building a successful strategy it is necessary to identify those behavioral factors upon which to focus. In this chapter I present ideas on how to build a narrowly-defined equity strategy.

STRATEGY ELEMENTS

Strategy elements, the specific things upon which a manager focuses when executing an equity strategy, proxy for the behavioral factors around which active equity managers build their strategy. The 40 strategy elements identified based on my firm's research are presented in Table 15.1, along with the percentage of the active equity mutual funds that use each particular element, based on what is reported in a fund's prospectus, in executing one of the ten strategies described in Table 13.1 and the annual return gain that can be attributed to each element.

The most popular element is Strong Fundamentals, with 67% of the funds using it, while Religious Issues is the least popular at 0.5%. The return gain in the third column is based on the incremental return earned by adding this element to a strategy. The top return gain element is International Issues, which is also one of the least popular elements. The lowest return ranked element is Time Sensitive Anomalies, which means that focusing on this element hurts returns.

TABLE 15.1: STRATEGY ELEMENTS

Element	Funds using (%)	Annual return gain
Absolute Return	1.6	**0.62**
Accelerated growth	4.4	-0.14
Arbitrage	8.5	**-0.46**
Behavioral considerations	12.4	**0.57**
Business risk	0.8	0.21
Cash flow valuation	32.4	**0.21**
Contrarian	8.5	0.08
Country risk	15.9	**0.50**
Defensible market position	35.0	0.02
Dividend yield	24.5	**-0.23**
Downside risk	2.3	**-0.72**
Earnings surprise	7.6	0.14
Economic output	43.1	**0.14**
Excess volatility	15.5	0.12
Expected return modeling	3.1	**-0.92**
Inflation	4.3	-0.14
Interest rates	6.6	**0.48**
International issues	0.9	**1.30**
Intrinsic valuation	57.5	**0.14**
Management quality	24.4	**-0.20**
Momentum	5.7	-0.22
Overall company growth	48.1	-0.06
Overall market conditions	17.4	0.13

Political issues	15.7	0.22
Price ratios (e.g. P/E, P/S, P/B)	16.7	0.01
Quantitative modeling	20.4	**-0.18**
Relative strength	1.7	-0.26
Religious issues	0.5	-0.71
Return on equity	3.7	**-1.36**
Return on invested capital	2.7	**-0.54**
Social Responsibility	7.2	0.04
Stochastic modeling	0.7	**0.89**
Strong earnings growth	26.6	**-0.56**
Strong financials	16.6	-0.10
Strong fundamentals	67.2	0.04
Strong innovation	10.6	0.21
Sustainable growth	16.0	**-0.32**
Technical analysis/charting	3.0	**1.14**
Themes	14.8	**0.31**
Time sensitive anomalies	0.6	**-2.21**

Based on all strategy identified US active equity mutual funds. Funds Using % is the percent of US funds using this particular element as of October 2013. Annual Return Gain is the fund return net of the primary strategy return averaged over all funds using that element each month, then averaged over all months January 1980 through October 2013. Bold values are statistically significant at the 5% level (two tailed). Sources: AthenaInvest, Thomson-Reuters, Lipper.

The average fund employs seven elements, of which two are own strategy elements and five are other strategy elements. There are a number of ways to execute each element. For example, when speaking with managers who believe the quality of a company's management is important, I have heard different approaches to judging this quality, from quantitative measures based on financials, to speaking with the company's competitors, to reading footnotes to financials. With each element we've observed a variety of approaches to implementing it. This variety is a manager's secret sauce.

ANOMALY RESEARCH

You'll probably not find it too surprising that the source of many of my investment ideas is the academic finance research with which I am familiar and to which I have contributed from time to time. While there are legitimate questions about the relevance of much of this research, I find those studies focused on so-called anomalies to be the most useful for building an equity strategy. The measurable and persistent price distortions uncovered by these studies can be used to build successful portfolios. Or, as the rationality diehards contend, they are capturing risk premiums. The paper I discuss next finds it to be the former.

A 2013 study by David McLean of the University of Alberta and MIT and Jeffrey Pontiff of Boston College analyzed 82 anomalies reported in 68 academic papers.[72] They tested whether the anomalies were statistically significant during the estimation period, during a post-estimation period and during a post-publication period. They find that the anomalies worked as well in the post estimation period as they did in the estimation period, which rules out statistical biases and data mining as explanations for the anomalies.

They found that the returns to the anomalies declined by about 35% in the post-publication period versus the estimation period, which means it is unlikely the anomalies are the result of a risk premium as they should survive into the post-publication period. The average in the sample long-short excess return was 5% while the average post-publication excess return was 3%. Both are statistically and economically significant.

Further confirming that the anomalies are picking up price distortions and not risk premiums, they found that the return decay was less for stocks for which limits to arbitrage are higher. These include smaller stocks with wider bid-ask spreads that do not pay dividends and have higher idiosyncratic volatility. The latter is the strongest predictor of anomaly returns.

---

[72] David R. McLean and Jeffrey Pontiff, 'Does Academic Research Destroy Stock Return Predictability?', working paper (May 2013).

Thus anomalies uncovered by academic studies, even five years after publication, generate superior returns that tend to be higher for those stocks with higher limits to arbitrage. What is more, they found that return decay has not accelerated with the significant decline in transactions costs and the increased percent of trading conducted by institutions. It appears anomaly returns are here to stay, which is further confirmation that emotions trump arbitrage.

It is interesting to note that McLean and Pontiff found no evidence of data snooping nor statistical errors in the anomaly studies in their sample. This seems to suggest that the rigorous statistical methodologies and the pre-publication peer review process have successfully eliminated these problems. This is in contrast to less rigorous practitioner back tests in which such problems are common.

McLean and Pontiff provide the list of articles from which they extracted the 82 anomalies tested. I provide their article bibliography at the end of this book. Think of this list as a price distortion gold mine for building an equity strategy.

BUILDING AN EQUITY STRATEGY

Successfully managing an equity portfolio requires the consistent pursuit of a narrowly-defined strategy that harnesses a handful of measurable and persistent price distortions. I will now suggest some steps in building such a strategy. As I have already mentioned, there are many ways to earn superior equity returns, so what I'm about to present does not represent an exact recipe but a series of suggestions which increase the chances of success.

If you already have your own equity strategy or have a pretty good sense of what that strategy might look like, what follows is intended to help you rethink and possibly modify your strategy:

1. Choose your primary strategy from those listed in Table 13.1. The one you choose will to some extent depend upon your level of experience as well as your personality. Future Growth, Competitive

Position, Opportunity, Quantitative, Profitability, and Valuation are the top six long-term performance strategies, while Market Conditions, Economic Conditions, Social Considerations and Risk are the four worst-performing strategies. But having said this, there are top performing managers in each strategy and each strategy has its turn as a top performer. For example, at the time of the writing, Social Considerations was the top one-year performer in the US as well as internationally.

2. After choosing a primary strategy, choose a secondary strategy from among the ten listed in Table 13.1. The current number of US active equity mutual funds pursuing each primary / secondary combination is reported in Table 15.2. It provides information for helping you select your primary / secondary strategy. It also provides insight into which strategies funds believe are most likely to be successful, along with the corresponding investor demand for each combination. In this regard, Valuation / Competitive Position, Future Growth / Competitive Position and its twin Competitive Position / Future Growth are the three most popular combinations, while no funds are pursuing the six combinations of Profitability / Market Conditions, Social Considerations / Opportunity, and Social Considerations as a secondary strategy along with Market Conditions, Opportunity, Profitability, and Risk.

3. Select the specific elements upon which you wish to focus from Table 15.1. The percentage of funds using these elements and return rank of each provide additional guidance for making this decision. Recall that the typical active equity fund manager uses seven elements. To help further, Table 15.3 reports the top five elements selected by managers in each of the ten strategies. Finally, and most important, limit the number of elements in order to build a narrowly-defined strategy.

4. Decide on how to execute each of the elements. For example, if Strong Fundamentals is one of your elements, will you measure

that by analyzing the firm's financials, by evaluating the strength of the management team, by understanding how effectively and efficiently the company is operated, or by measuring the company's profit margins? Each is an alternative approach for implementing the Strong Fundamentals element. In addition, you will have to decide on the technique for ranking each stock on each element. Collectively these decisions represent your strategy's secret sauce.

5. Peruse the academic finance literature to identify anomalies that can boost your performance. The McLean and Pontiff bibliography has been included at the end of this book as a starting point but new anomalies are being unearthed regularly so you will come across anomalies not included in their study. An initial search can be easily executed on the Social Sciences Research Network (SSRN) website (**ssrn.com**), which is a comprehensive repository of both published and unpublished academic finance articles.

6. Execute your strategy in an unconstrained manner while taking only high-conviction positions. Unconstrained means investing strictly based on your elements and secret sauce while ignoring all other stock characteristics, as well as other economic and market information, that are not part of your strategy. Put your strategy blinders on when managing your portfolio.

TABLE 15.2: US ACTIVE EQUITY MUTUAL FUNDS BY PRIMARY AND SECONDARY STRATEGY

Primary Strategy	Competitive Position	Economic Conditions	Future Growth	Market Conditions	Opportunity	Profitability	Quantitative	Risk	Social Considerations	Valuation	Total
Competitive Position		126	199	10	14	39	48	7	4	164	611
Economic Conditions	31		11	3	1	4	6	3	1	12	72
Future Growth	193	18		12	7	20	12	6	3	72	343
Market Conditions	1	3	2		5	1	5	1		3	21
Opportunity	18	7	10			2	7	8		37	90
Profitability	13	3	13		2		5	2		15	53
Quantitative	16	8	15	9	3	5		18	3	23	100
Risk	6	3	3	4	8	2	4			14	44
Social Considerations	20	3	14	1		4	2	2		16	62
Valuation	293	37	87	14	54	91	48	21	2		647
Total	591	208	354	54	94	168	137	68	13	356	2043

Data as of November 2013. Source: AthenaInvest.

TABLE 15.3: TOP FIVE ELEMENTS BY STRATEGY

Primary Strategy	Element 1	Element 2	Element 3	Element 4	Element 5
Competitive Position	Strong fundamentals	Defensible market position	Intrinsic Valuation	Overall company growth	Management quality
Economic Conditions	Economic output	Strong fundamentals	Themes	Intrinsic Valuation	Overall company growth
Future Growth	Overall company growth	Strong earnings growth	Strong fundamentals	Intrinsic Valuation	Defensible market position
Market Conditions	Momentum	Strong fundamentals	Quantitative modeling	Behavioral considerations	Economic output
Opportunity	Arbitrage	Intrinsic Valuation	Strong fundamentals	Behavioral considerations	Excess volatility
Profitability	Dividend yield	Strong fundamentals	Intrinsic Valuation	Economic output	Strong financials
Quantitative	Quantitative modeling	Intrinsic Valuation	Strong fundamentals	Overall company growth	Economic output
Risk	Excess volatility	Intrinsic Valuation	Strong fundamentals	Quantitative modeling	Economic output
Social Considerations	Social Responsibility	Political issues	Strong fundamentals	Intrinsic Valuation	Overall company growth
Valuation	Intrinsic Valuation	Strong fundamentals	Cash flow valuation	Economic output	Price ratios (e.g. P/E, P/S, P/B)

Data as of November 2013. Source: AthenaInvest.

BUILDING THE PURE STRATEGY

In 2002 I had not yet conducted the active equity mutual funds research reported earlier in this book. So I didn't have the benefit of the framework just described when launching what would become the Athena Pure Valuation/Profitability portfolio. I was familiar with the academic anomaly research, so drew a number of my ideas from this source. I also presented stock analysis seminars throughout the US which provided a basis for my strategy. But looking back, I now realize that I built my strategy in a manner similar to that described above.

I'm an ardent fan of Graham and Dodd and so Valuation was a natural pick as my primary strategy. Value is created by cash flows and not the balance sheet so I chose profitability as my secondary strategy and included the balance sheet as a contrary indicator. Dividends, being the strongest signal management can send regarding the future prospects of the company, were included as an element. And since I was selecting individual stocks and not making specific sector bets, I diversified across sectors. So the Pure strategy ended up looking like this:

Primary strategy: Valuation

Secondary strategy: Profitability

Elements: Dividend Yield, Strong Financials, Contrarian, Price Ratios, Behavioral Factors

Since Pure's July 2002 inception, I have consistently executed this Valuation/Profitability strategy by investing in ten or fewer high-conviction positions. The portfolio has generated a 24.6% annual compound return as compared to the Russell 2000 benchmark annual return of 9.2% from inception to September 2013. The 2013 return exceeded 60%, nearly double the Russell 2000 benchmark return.[73]

While one must be humble as an investment manager, I view this long-term and short-term performance, to a large extent, being driven by the

---

[73] The reported Pure performance is based on monthly GIPS compliant returns net of fees.

consistent pursuit of a narrowly defined strategy, while investing in a small number of high-conviction positions, that were identified based on a small set of measurable and persistent behavioral price distortions. I consider Pure to be a proof of concept for the many BPM ideas presented in this book.

CHAPTER 16: THE POWER OF DIVIDENDS[74]

FUND MANAGER BEHAVIOR in the form of strategy, consistency and conviction is predictive of future equity fund performance. In a similar vein, an announcement by the management of a company that they will pay a dividend is a strong signal regarding future company performance. It turns out that management behavior, in the form of dividend announcements, is predictive of future company and stock performance, thus dividend yield is an important behavioral factor driving equity returns.

Dividend-paying stocks are best known for their income generation on the one hand and their unfavorable tax treatment on the other. Beyond recognizing these well-known features, however, many investors hold a false belief that dividend stocks underperform. High-dividend portfolios are often dismissed as inferior to their high-growth counterparts for several reasons:

- Fear that increasing dividend yield means lower portfolio returns.

- A view that dividend payments are an admission by management that they do not have good reinvestment opportunities.

- A belief that dividends are associated with the end of a company's growth cycle.

---

[74] This chapter is based on my article with the same name that appeared in the January 25, 2011 issue of *Advisor Perspectives*.

- The inferior tax treatment of dividend income relative to capital gains.

The evidence refutes these beliefs. Research shows that the higher a stock portfolio's dividend yield, the greater its return. Just as surprising is that the higher the yield, the lower is portfolio volatility.

Building higher-yield portfolios is a straightforward way to improve returns while simultaneously reducing volatility, notwithstanding the conventional, undue focus on income and tax considerations. Investors should shed this limited view of dividends and let them play a more prominent role in their equity strategy.

DIVIDEND YIELD, RETURNS AND VOLATILITY

At the overall market level, a long line of research shows that higher cash payout and dividend yields lead to higher future market returns.[75] More specifically, this research reveals that dividend yield is a good predictor of future earnings growth, so a period of rising dividend yield bodes well for future market returns. This belies the common belief that executives increase dividend payout when investment and future growth opportunities are poor. Company management, by increasing dividend payout, is actually signaling higher future cash flows, which in turn foretell higher stock returns.

At the individual stock level, too, dividend payout and yield are predictive of future earnings growth and future returns.[76] Among other things, this body of research has found that dividend changes contain information about:

---

[75] See, for example, Rob Arnott and Cliff Asness, 'Surprise! Higher Dividends = Higher Earnings Growth', *Financial Analyst Journal* (January/February 2003) pp. 70-87; and Jacob Boudoukhb, Roni Michaely and Matthew Richardson, 'On the Importance of Measuring Payout Yield: Implications for Empirical Asset Pricing', *Journal of Finance* 62:2 (2007), pp. 877-915.

[76] See, for example, Khaled Hussainey, 'Do dividends signal information about future earnings?' *Applied Economics Letters* 16 (2009), pp. 1285-1288.

1. future earnings that cannot be found in other market data,

2. company profitability, and

3. future positive earnings surprises.

Other research has found that companies experiencing financial distress rely more heavily on dividends for communicating with investors. The overall conclusion is that rising dividends signal improved company performance and, in turn, higher individual stock returns. In essence, dividends represent a measurable and persistent company management behavioral factor that can be used to build superior portfolios.

In order to appreciate the power of dividends, consider the average annual compound returns for S&P 500 stocks over the period 1973 through 2010, which are reported in Figure 16.1 by showing the performance of four portfolios that are variously comprised of dividend cutting stocks, zero dividend stocks, dividend stocks with no change and stocks that grew dividends.

Over this period, S&P 500 stocks that paid growing dividends outperformed dividend-cutting S&P 500 stocks by an astonishing 10% annually. Growing dividends are predictive of strong future stock returns, while zero or reduced dividends are a predictor of poor stock returns.

FIGURE 16.1: ANNUAL COMPOUND RETURN, JANUARY 1973 TO SEPTEMBER 2010

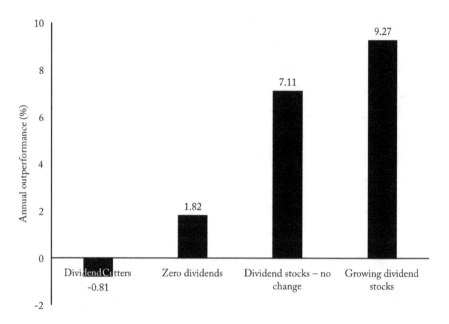

Based on equally weighted compound total returns of dividend and non-dividend paying S&P 500 stocks. Each of the four portfolios were reconstituted at the beginning of each year based on the actual dividends paid over the previous year. **Past performance does not guarantee future performance**. Source: Neil McCarthy and Emanuele Bergagnini of Oppenheimer Funds, Data provided by Ned Davis Research 9/30/2010.

Even more surprising, volatility declines as dividends increase. Figure 16.2 reports the annual standard deviation for the four portfolios reported in Figure 16.1. In general, volatility decreases as dividends – and accompanying stock returns – increase. In particular, the dividend-growing portfolio experiences roughly a third less volatility than the dividend-cutting portfolio.

FIGURE 16.2: ANNUAL STANDARD DEVIATION, JANUARY 1973 TO SEPTEMBER 2010

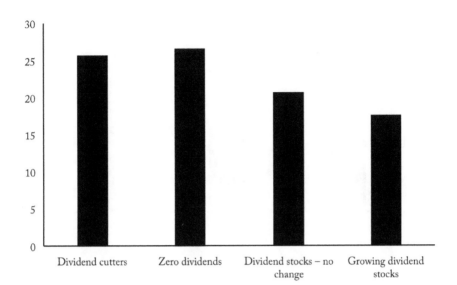

Based on equally weighted compound total returns of dividend and non-dividend paying S&P 500 stocks. Each of the four portfolios are reconstituted at the beginning of each year based on the actual dividends paid over the previous year. **Past performance does not guarantee future performance**. Source: Neil McCarthy and Emanuele Bergagnini of Oppenheimer Funds, data provided by Ned Davis Research 9/30/2010.

DIVIDENDS, MARKET CAP AND TAXES

For a clearer picture of the return and volatility benefits of rising dividend yield (DY), Figure 16.3 shows the after-the-fact, survivor-bias free annual return gain and volatility reduction (as measured by standard deviation) for a 1% increase in dividend yield.

The results reveal that for a large-cap stock portfolio, a 1% DY increase produces an average gain of 22 basis points in annual compound return, along with a 7bp reduction in annual portfolio standard deviation. For example, if DY increases by 3%, then an investor can expect the large-cap portfolio return to increase by 66bp and portfolio volatility to decrease by 21bp. You can have your cake and eat it too: higher dividend yields lead to quantifiably higher returns **and** quantifiably lower volatility.

FIGURE 16.3: ANNUAL RETURN INCREASE AND VOLATILITY REDUCTION PER 1% DIVIDEND YIELD INCREASE

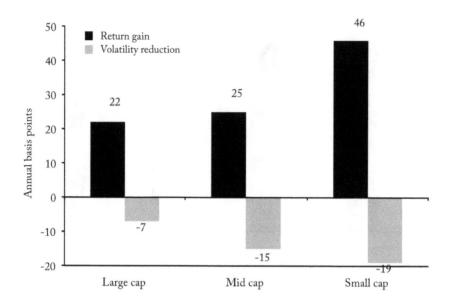

Based on a total of 157,625 stock, month survivor-bias free sample over the March 1997 through December 2009 time period. Dividend yield quintiles and market cap deciles are recalculated at the beginning of each month. Dividend yield is calculated as 12 times the average monthly dividend over the previous 12 months divided by current price and is not calculated when the stock's price is less than $5 or the most recent quarterly dividend is zero. Large Cap stocks are market cap deciles 1-3, Mid Cap stocks are 4-7, and Small Cap stocks are 8-10. Subsequent monthly returns are net of S&P 500. The annual return gain per 1% DY increase is the slope of annual compound return on average DY over the five DY deciles. The annual standard deviation reduction per 1% DY increase is the slope of annual SD on average DY across the five DY deciles. Data sources: CRSP and Thomson Reuters Financial.

Figure 16.3 reveals other interesting results. First, the power of dividends increases as stock size decreases. The return gain increases from 22bp to 25bp to 46bp as one moves from large- to mid- to small-cap stocks, while the volatility reduction improves from 7bp to 15bp to 19bp. Thus, dividend power is not limited to the large-cap S&P 500 stock universe that is the basis of Figures 16.1 and 16.2.

DIVIDENDS AS A MEASURABLE AND PERSISTENT BEHAVIORAL FACTOR

Companies regularly provide information to investors regarding their situation. The confidence with which investors should view such information depends on the incentives facing management when they issue that data. In providing projections regarding a new venture, for example, management has an incentive to present as rosy a picture as possible. If a new venture is perceived as overly bold or expensive, management may experience push-back from sell-side analysts and others, but the cost to management of too optimistic a projection is relatively low.

Some company information, such as quarterly and annual financial statements, is audited. Here investors have additional assurances that the information is accurate, and there are legal penalties for both the company and the auditor for material misrepresentations. Investors will place greater value on such announcements, but, as we know, the auditing process is far from perfect, with some firms able to fool auditors and investors for long periods of time.

The most valuable signals come when company management "puts their money where their mouth is." Specifically this is announcements that are directly tied to changes in current and future investor cash flows. The best examples of such signals are cash dividends, share repurchases and financing decisions. The false signal costs of such announcements are high.

For example, raising dividends to an unsustainable level is costly, since cutting dividends leads to steep price declines. Management, in fact, has incentives to avoid false signals in either direction when it comes to dividends, making dividends a strong two-way signal. Similarly, share repurchases involve promises of current and future cash flows and can lead to disappointment if not fulfilled, and issuing too much debt can put the company at risk of bankruptcy. So management decisions that, like these, bear significant false-signal costs should receive maximum weight in building a strategy.

THE POWER OF DIVIDENDS

Dividends should not be viewed as a source of current income, but as one of the most important stock signals provided by a company's management. Dividends provide valuable information regarding future company performance and, as a result, stock performance, while at the same time providing signals about future volatility. These are good reasons to consider dividends when analyzing, buying and selling stocks, and dividends should play a prominent role in an equity strategy.

CHAPTER 17: BEHAVIORAL MARKET TIMING[77]

I HAVE INTRODUCED THE behavioral factors underlying successful portfolio management, that is strategy, consistency and conviction, and have argued the reason best idea stocks outperform is a result of managers harnessing behavioral price distortions. In this chapter I apply the concept of behavioral harnessing to the challenge of market timing. We are all aware that if we can be in the right markets at the right time, the resulting returns far exceed those of even the most skilled stock picker. For this and MLA reasons, many investment organizations offer products that claim to be able to time markets.

Most timing methodologies are focused on short-term price patterns, such as momentum and mean reversion, or relative valuations across markets. The approach I describe here is based on objective measures of deep behavioral currents in the market, in contrast to trying to time the choppiness on the surface. The goal is to uncover behavioral measures that are predictive of expected market returns. The resulting expected market returns are then used in executing a market timing strategy.[78]

---

[77] This chapter is based on my paper 'Behavioral Measures of Expected Market Return', available at SSRN (**ssrn.com**).

[78] Our company uses the expected return methodology described in this chapter for managing a variety of portfolios, including mutual fund overlay, ETF overlay, hedge fund, and an ETF.

EXPECTED MARKET RETURNS

Expected market returns are the result of time varying premiums driven by the response of Emotional Crowds to ever-evolving economic and market conditions. A number of studies have attempted to relate economic variation to changes in expected returns, but not much has come of these efforts. The most successful is the line of research focused on dividend yield/payout (dividends + share repurchase - share issuance) yield which documents a positive relationship between market payout yield and future returns.

A behavioral *top-down* approach is taken by Malcolm Baker of Harvard and Jeffrey Wurgler of NYU who attempt to identify broad measures that capture investor sentiment and thus make it possible to predict future expected returns.[79] They show that their resulting *Sentiment Index*, based on six individual measures, is predictive of individual stocks as well as market-wide returns.

Beyond the Sentiment Index, I present objective measures of investor behavior based on the relative performance of the US and international equity strategies described in Table 13.1. It turns out that both relative strategy performance and the Sentiment Index are predictive of subsequent expected market returns. These behavioral measures are not based on surveys of investor sentiment, but on variables that can be objectively measured and seem to be driven in a consistent manner by emotional crowds.

---

[79] Malcolm Baker and Jeffery Wurgler, 'Investor Sentiment and the Cross-Section of Stock Returns', *Journal of Finance* (2006), pp. 1645-1680; and Malcolm Baker and Jeffrey Wurgler, 'Investor Sentiment in the Stock Market', *Journal of Economic Perspective* (Spring 2007), pp. 129-151.

SENTIMENT INDEX (SI)

Baker and Wurgler view investor sentiment as either optimism or pessimism about stocks in general. They use these six objective measures for constructing SI:[80]

1. closed-end fund discount,

2. detrended log of share turnover,

3. number of IPOs,

4. first-day return on IPOs,

5. dividend premium, and

6. equity share in new issues.

A low (high) SI implies low (strong) investor sentiment which leads to stock undervaluation (overvaluation) and in turn is predictive of higher (lower) returns going forward. That is, strong sentiment is predictive of lower returns and low sentiment is predictive of higher returns. It is good news for the market when investors are pessimistic and bad news when they are optimistic, another counterintuitive result unearthed by means of careful research.

STRATEGY MARKET BAROMETERS

Equity strategy is the way an active manager goes about analyzing, buying and selling stocks. Put more succinctly, it is the way a manager goes about earning excess returns. In developing a strategy, a set of behavioral factors are identified that the manager can harness. The factors focused upon differ from manager to manager. The manager then develops a strategy around the identified factors and fashions a methodology for implementing the strategy.

---

[80] Malcolm Baker and Jeffrey Wurgler, 'Investor Sentiment and the Cross-Section of Stock Returns', *Journal of Finance* (2006), pp. 1645-1680.

For example, a manager pursing a Competitive Position strategy will develop a methodology for gauging the quality of a company's management team, the defensibility of their product market position, and the level of company adaptability. The fund for which the manager works assembles the resources needed to execute this methodology. The equity strategy is at the core of the investment process and shapes the business and investment decisions of the fund. The consistent pursuit of a narrowly defined equity strategy, along with taking high-conviction positions, is the key to earning excess returns.

Figure 17.1 is a representation of how the ten US equity strategies described in Table 13.1 are being rewarded by investors, with the darker arrows signifying higher returns. Strategies are arranged (from the top of Figure 17.1 clockwise) in their long-term performance order (based on 1988 through 2007 returns).[81]

That is, Future Growth is the top performing long-term strategy, Competitive Position is the next, and so on down to Risk, which is the worst long-term performer. Figure 17.1 presents the situation in which relative strategy performance, as represented by varying arrow shades, matches long-term strategy performance. Strategy performance fluctuates over time, resulting in time periods in which strategies in the lower left of Figure 17.1 are favored by investors. It turns out that the ever-changing pattern of strategy performance ranks are predictive of equity premiums.

---

[81] Strategy performance is calculated as the simple average return across all funds in that strategy that month.

FIGURE 17.1: RELATIVE PERFORMANCE OF US EQUITY STRATEGIES

Several relationships must hold for this to be the case. First, the set of strategies must span the full set of factors driving individual and overall market returns. Second, each factor should be associated, to the greatest extent possible, with a specific strategy, with as few multiple strategy associations as possible. Finally, managers should pursue the same strategy and not change strategies over time.[82] If these relationships hold, strategy

---

[82] Each manager has selected a specific strategy to pursue, most often because they believe that it will allow them to earn excess returns. The fund company then assembles the considerable resources needed to implement this strategy. Over time the portfolio managers and analysts devote considerable time to refining the investment process. Given the large investment of time and money by the manager and the fund, it is unlikely that the fund will incur the cost of switching to a new strategy. Note that it is not necessary to assume active equity managers are superior stock pickers. It is only important that they consistently pursue the same strategy over time, successful or not.

performance ranks will be reliably associated with the return factors driving market returns.

In order to capture the overall response of investors to the ten equity strategies, a Strategy Market Barometer (SMB) for both US and International Markets is calculated. The US Strategy Market Barometer (US SMB) and International Strategy Market Barometer (Intl SMB) are a scaled sum of the absolute difference of each strategy's trailing one-year return rank from its long-term (1988 to 2007) return rank.[83] The resulting US SMB and Intl SMB behavioral measures as well as SI are the basis of the expected return models described next.

AN INITIAL EYEBALL TEST

In order to understand the time pattern of the three behavioral measures – US SMB, Intl SMB and SI – the beginning of the month trailing six-month average for each is graphed for June 1981 through December 2011 in Figure 17.2. Non-shaded time periods represent major S&P 500 bull markets and the shaded time periods represent major bear markets.

There were three major bear markets (June 1981 to July 1982, August 2000 to September 2002, November 2007 to February 2009) for a total of 60 (16%) of the 372 months over this time period, while there were three major bull markets (August 1982 to July 2000, October 2002 to October 2007, March 2009 to December 2011) for a total of 312 (84%) of the months.

---

[83] The out-of-sample (before 1988 and after 2007) SMB prediction performance is better than the in-sample performance. This supports the supposition that SMB's predictive power is not unique to the long-term estimation period. An obvious alternative to ranking strategies based on recent returns is to rank them based on recent fund flows. I have not tested this alternative ranking methodology to determine if it improves on the return ranking methodology.

FIGURE 17.2: BEHAVIORAL MEASURES, JUNE 1981 TO DECEMBER 2011

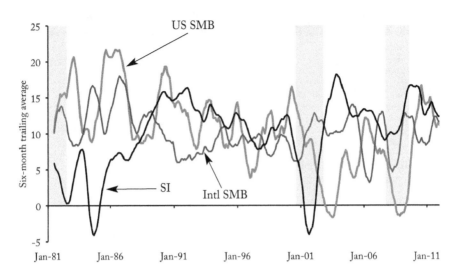

Data Sources: AthenaInvest and Thomson-Reuters Financial. I would like to thank Jeffrey Wurgler for providing the BW Sentiment Index data and Jay Ritter for providing the IPO data.

An eyeball test of the predictive power of each behavioral measure is conducted by examining the level of each during the three major bull and three major bear markets.[84] The results are presented in Table 17.1 and reveal that US SMB and SI are the two best predictors of S&P 500 returns, while Intl SMB is the worst.

Of great interest to many market participants is the ability to predict painful events, such as the 2008 market crash. The only behavioral measure that successfully predicted this crash was US SMB. On the other hand, SI was a better predictor of the August 2000 to September 2002 bear market. The conclusion based on the eyeball test is that both US SMB and SI are good predictors of subsequent S&P 500 market returns, while Intl SMB is the weakest.

---

[84] Baker and Wurgler (2007) provide their own SI eyeball test over a time period extending back to 1963.

TABLE 17.1: EYEBALL TEST OF BEHAVIORAL MEASURE PREDICTION OF S&P 500

Bull/Bear	US SMB	Intl SMB	SI
Bear: January 1981 to July 1982	Poor	Poor	Good
Bull: August 1982 to July 2000	Good	Poor	Good
Bear: August 2000 to September 2002	Good	Poor	Good
Bull: October 2002 to October 2007	Poor	Good	Good
Bear: November 2007 to February 2009	Good	Good	Poor
Bull: March 2009 to December 2011	Good	Good	Good

A striking feature of Figure 17.2 is that behavioral measures vary widely over time. US SMB ranges from a high of 22% to a low of -2%. The SI ranges from a high of 18% to a low of -4%. We will see in the following tests that these wide ranges are consistent with expected market returns varying widely, a feature that makes them useful for behavioral market timing.

The eyeball test involves considerable judgment that might very well be called into question. To provide greater rigor, I now present time series regression results. In spite of the subjective nature of the eyeball test, the regressions produce the same general conclusions: US SMB and SI are best at predicting subsequent equity returns with Intl SMB being the weakest predictor.

PREDICTIVE POWER OF BEHAVIORAL MEASURES

Time series regressions are run to test the ability of US SMB, Intl SMB and SI to predict subsequent equity premiums (i.e. net of T-bill rate) for the US stock market (S&P 500), the US small cap stock market (Russ 2000), and the developed (non-US) international stock markets (MSCI EAFE).[85]

The expected return differences resulting from high versus low behavioral measures are reported in Figures 17.3, 17.4 and 17.5 for the S&P 500, Russell 2000, and US$ EAFE, respectively. If behavioral measures are predictive of subsequent expected returns, we would expect the estimated differences to be positive. Examining Figures 17.3 through 17.5 reveals that indeed this is the case, with 55 of 63 differences being positive.

Furthermore, nearly as many are also economically significant, with 53 of 63 exceeding the 5% threshold and an amazing 21 exceeding 20%. Many of the differences are also statistically significant. The two largest are 39.7% and 35.1% for the one month SI on EAFE and US SMB on S&P 500, respectively. The differences generally decline over longer time horizons, but remain economically significant at both 24 month and 36 month time horizons. Thus the predictive power of behavioral measures persists for many months into the future. These results support the contention that behavioral measures are predictive of future expected returns and that the differences are economically meaningful.

---

[85] The three behavioral measures of US SMB, Intl SMB and SI are included as indicator variables in a single regression for determining the relative predictive power of each. The three behavioral measures are included as month beginning values. To account for fundamental changes, four US economic variables are included, namely: trailing annual growth in US Industrial Production, US total civilian employment growth, and real US Personal Consumption Expenditures along and with the current month NBER Recession Indicator (1 if in recession) are included. Trailing returns are also included in the regressions to account for well documented mean reversion and momentum. See Howard (2013) for more details regarding the regression and robustness tests that I ran.

FIGURE 17.3: S&P 500 ANNUAL EXPECTED RETURN DIFFERENCES BY TIME HORIZON

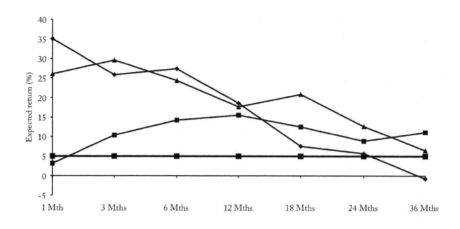

FIGURE 17.4: RUSSELL 2000 ANNUAL EXPECTED RETURN DIFFERENCES BY TIME HORIZON

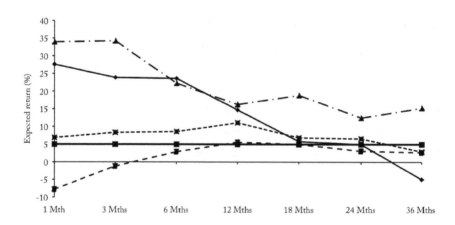

FIGURE 17.5: US$ EAFE ANNUAL EXPECTED RETURN DIFFERENCES BY TIME HORIZON

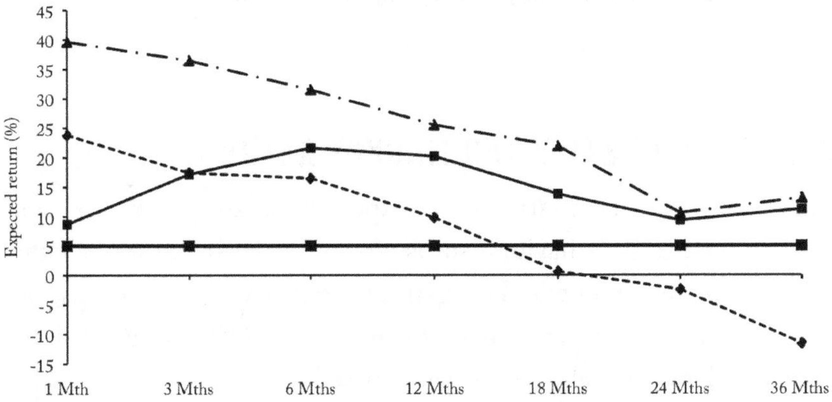

Time period for Figures 17.3, 17.4 and 17.5: June 1981 to December 2011. Data Sources: AthenaInvest and Thomson-Reuters. I would like to thank Jeffrey Wurgler for providing the BW Sentiment Index data and Jay Ritter for providing the IPO data.

Since both trailing returns and current economic variables are included in each regression, it appears that the predictive power of the behavioral measures cannot be explained by return momentum or mean reversion, nor can it be explained by changing current economic fundamentals. The lack of economic variable explanatory power is consistent with a number of other studies that find the stock market returns are little impacted by current economic conditions, but instead returns are predictive of future economic conditions.

This raises the question of how much of the behavioral measure predictive power is explained by future economic activity. In other words, to what extent are the behavioral measures a proxy for future economic activity. To test this, I reran the one month regressions using three month to 15-month-ahead growth in US Industrial Production, US total civilian employment growth, real US Personal Consumption Expenditures, and the six-month-ahead NBER recession indicator.

The general pattern remains the same: SI is both economically and statistically significant and US SMB is economically and sometimes statistically significant, while Intl SMB results are mixed and generally weaker than the other two. Thus it appears that the behavioral measures are capturing something beyond economic conditions, in the present and in the future.

VARIATION IN EXPECTED MARKET RETURNS

I have just shown that variations in expected market returns are mostly due to changes in behavioral measures and, to a much lesser extent, changes in fundamentals. Using these predictive relationships, both expected and subsequent actual returns for the S&P 500, Russell 2000 and EAFE, respectively, are estimated based on beginning of the month US SMB, Intl SMB, SI; trailing returns; and three trailing economic variables, along with the current NBER recession indicator.

The resulting range of expected and actual returns are reported in Table 17.2. On average, the range of expected returns is 61%, while the range of actual returns is 115% over these three markets. The range of expected returns is stunningly large but even with these wide ranges, the subsequent actual return range is nearly twice as wide in each of the three markets.

The overall conclusion is that expected market returns vary dramatically over time and that behavioral measures are important drivers of this variability.

TABLE 17.2: EXPECTED VERSUS ACTUAL ANNUAL RETURN RANGES, JANUARY 1981 TO JANUARY 2011

	Expected return			Actual return		
Market	Min	Max	Range	Min	Max	Range
S&P 500	-18.4	29.4	47.8	-43.9	53.4	97.3
Russ 2000	-21.3	37.1	58.5	-43	63.8	106.7
EAFE	-38.8	36.3	75.1	-52.3	87.4	139.8
Average	-26.2	34.3	60.5	-46.4	68.2	114.6

Time period: June 1981 to December 2011. Data Sources: AthenaInvest and Thomson-Reuters. I would like to thank Jeffrey Wurgler for providing the BW Sentiment Index data and Jay Ritter for providing the IPO data.

BEHAVIORAL MARKET TIMING

The predictive power of the behavioral measures can be used in a number of ways. Such predictions might be used to time among the four markets: large stocks, small stocks, international stocks, and cash. They could be used to determine the extent of long or short leverage in each of these markets.

To test the potential usefulness, Figures 17.6 and 17.7 report the return improvements for investment strategies based on three different expected return predictions:

1. buy & hold,

2. investing in the market when the economic variable only beginning of month return prediction is positive and investing in 3 month T-bills if negative, and

3. the same strategy based on adding behavior measures to the prediction equation.

The economic only prediction sometimes improves subsequent returns and sometimes not. In those cases where there is improvement the gain is small. On the other hand, adding trailing returns and behavioral variables improves subsequent returns in each situation, anywhere from 20bp (36-month Russell 2000) to as much as 313bp (12-month EAFE). So a simple prediction and trading rule, which does not take full advantage of the range of timing/instrument opportunities, generates higher subsequent returns. Most of these gains are driven by changing behavioral measures and not by changes in economic fundamentals.

FIGURE 17.6: 12-MONTH RETURN IMPROVEMENTS BASED ON SIMPLE TRADING RULE VERSUS BUY AND HOLD

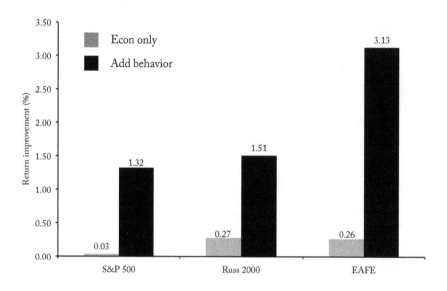

FIGURE 17.7: 36-MONTH ANNUAL RETURN IMPROVEMENTS BASED ON A SIMPLE TRADING RULE VERSUS BUY AND HOLD

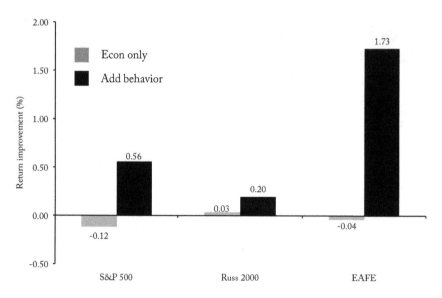

Time period: June 1981 to December 2011. Data Sources: AthenaInvest and Thomson-Reuters. I would like to thank Jeffrey Wurgler for providing the BW Sentiment Index data and Jay Ritter for providing the IPO data.

IMPLEMENTING BEHAVIORAL MARKET TIMING

The behavioral measures just presented provide an estimate of the expected return in each of the three equity markets. Each captures the movement of the return distribution, such as that shown in Figure 7.2, leftward and rightward. If the distribution shifts left, the chance of a negative return increases, while the chance of a positive return decreases. The opposite occurs if it shifts to the right. That is, the timing measures are providing a revised estimate of return probabilities and not whether the market will go up or down in the short run. This means focusing on deep behavioral currents rather than on surface chop.

The resulting tactical call is to invest in the equity market with the highest expected return. If the expected returns are all low, the portfolio is invested in cash or in a short equity position. On the other hand, if the expected return is very high, a leveraged equity position is taken. The tactical concept is to take the best position in light of a low, normal, or high expected returns.

The judicious use of leverage is particularly impactful for generating long horizon wealth, as the stock market generates a positive return in 63% of months and 72% of years. On the other hand, leverage is problematic for those suffering MLA, so releasing emotional brakes is even more critical when implementing a tactical approach.

We have had success using SI and the Market Barometers in managing fund overlay, global tactical ETF, hedge fund, and ETF portfolios. Global tactical is the one portfolio in our lineup that appears to be able to keep up with Pure over the long run. So the behavioral factors being harnessed by Pure appear to generate returns comparable to the deep behavioral currents being harnessed by global tactical. These two funds harness behavioral factors in two different ways, but with similar results.

CHAPTER 18: WHAT FUTURE MAY COME

THE INVESTMENT WORLD is a changing. Empirically discredited MPT is being replaced by behavioral finance. Emotions are replacing rationality as the central tenet of the new paradigm. As happens with such transitions, the current set of concepts for building and evaluating portfolios will be swept away and replaced with new ones. Once this happens, the quaint notions of MPT will quickly be forgotten.

This provides an opportunity to build superior portfolios by mastering your emotions so that they do not drive your investment decisions and implementing the concepts of Behavioral Portfolio Management for building successful portfolios. The key is the consistent pursuit of a narrowly defined strategy by taking only high-conviction positions as identified based on a small number of measurable, persistent behavior price distortions. In short, leave the Cult of Emotion and become a Behavioral Data Investor.

WILL THESE OPPORTUNITIES LAST?

It is only natural to ask if the emotionally-driven price distortions will last or if will they be arbitraged away as have other opportunities. There is good reason to believe that they will indeed last. Behavior is difficult to alter and this is no more true than in financial markets where the emotions triggered are on the upper end of the intensity scale.

The emotionally-driven stock market equity premium has persisted for hundreds of years even though hundreds of articles have pointed out the folly of individuals trying to time the market, which is the source of the emotional component in the equity premium. Anomalies identified by academic studies don't fully disappear even five years after being published, highlighting the limits to arbitrage. Even institutional portfolio managers tend to exacerbate pricing distortions by means of their trades.

My take is that these opportunities will persist for a very long time. Throughout my career, my professional colleagues attempted to explain the anomalies bedeviling the EMH, but things have only gotten worse, with more anomalies than ever. So I've decided to be the student picking up the $100 bill on the sidewalk and not the professor spouting the rationality model.

RATIONAL TO EMOTIONAL

Placing emotions at the center of how we think about markets and investing changes almost everything. At a foundational level, we see movement towards a new behavioral finance paradigm. Viewed as little more than a curiosity in the US, Europe is already moving in this direction. The reason the US is slower to respond is that both MPT and the style grid were invented here. Compounding the problem is that the US creators of MPT received the Nobel Prize in economics in 1990, an external validation that impedes the transition to a new paradigm. However, in 2002 Daniel Kahneman and Vernon Smith shared the Nobel Prize in economics for pioneering research in behavioral science, signaling the legitimacy of this line of inquiry.

Even more intriguing, the 2013 Nobel Prize was shared by Gene Fama of EMH fame and Robert Shiller, of EMH critic fame. Shiller once referred to EMH as "the most remarkable error in the history of economic thought." Maybe this joint award will launch the long needed debate that will finally move us beyond MPT and on to behavioral finance.

One of the ironies of moving to an emotion-based versus rational model of the markets is that we gain a better understanding of the market and the relationships that will be uncovered will be more useful. The reason is that emotional behavior is highly predictable and persistent. Focusing on behavioral factors will provide a superior understanding of markets and will allow for improved investment decisions.

STYLE GRID AND CLOSET INDEXERS

Beyond the emotion-based MPT tools used by investment professionals, the style grid is another damaging concept of the current paradigm. Categorizing active equity managers based on the style grid leads to underperformance. The combination of MLA, MPT and the style grid has led to the most undesirable of investment vehicles: the closet indexer. They represent as much as 80% of the active equity mutual fund universe and no doubt exist in other markets such as hedge funds and institutional portfolios.

My fondest hope is that a focus on strategy, consistency and conviction will drive closet indexers into extinction. I see the active equity universe evolving into a world split between truly active funds and true index funds. The benefit to investors will be the elimination of the dead weight loss of huge active management fees being charged by what are in reality index funds.

DR. SEMMELWEIS: A CAUTIONARY TALE

The evidence is overwhelmingly against MPT, but this does not guarantee a rapid transition to a new paradigm. Dr. Ignaz Semmelweis, at his 1840s Vienna Austria Hospital, determined that doctors not washing their hands was the major cause of an epidemic of frequently fatal mother and newborn puerperal fever. He was able to convince his hospital colleagues to begin washing their hands and the epidemic abated.

He then traveled to other European hospitals, presenting his results and showing the success at his home hospital. But rather than washing their hands, the doctors rejected Dr. Semmelweis's results, labeling him a kook. His results called into question their professionalism and the emotional response was that they were not wrong for not washing their hands so he must be mistaken. Professional pride is a serious roadblock to implementing fundamental change in any industry.

As a result of his futile efforts, Dr. Semmelweis went insane. Two weeks after being admitted to the insane asylum, he died of injuries resulting from a beating administered by guards. This was a terrible end for someone who was only trying to improve the medical care provided to millions of Europeans.

A recent study concluded 50% of US healthcare professionals are still not properly washing their hands. It is distressing to learn that highly educated professionals still don't perform a basic function that can substantially reduce the millions of illnesses and 100,000 patient deaths estimated to result from unwashed hands.

Will investment professionals be as resistant to change as are US healthcare professionals? Only time will tell.

THE FUTURE IS HERE

My company AthenaInvest is practicing BPM today. We have adopted the language of behavioral science when discussing investment decisions. We have released our own emotional brakes and work with advisors and their clients to release theirs as well. Portfolios are built using the bucket model, with as little bubble wrap as possible. Behavioral factors are the basis for selecting active equity funds and individual stocks, as well as for making market timing decisions. Performance and risk are evaluated using BPM measures rather than emotional MPT measures.

Our individual stock, mutual fund allocation, hedge fund, global tactical, and ETF portfolios all beat their benchmarks in 2013 and have generated alpha over longer time periods of up to eleven years. The 60/60/60 concept is never far from our thinking: the stock market produces a positive return in 60% of months, our portfolios beat their benchmark in 60% of the months, and 60% of our stock selections outperform. Thus the odds are tilted in our clients' favor at three different levels. If they remain patient and do not slam on the brakes when emotionally charged events occur, they have an opportunity to grow long-horizon wealth in a superior manner.

As has AthenaInvest, you have the opportunity to enter the brave new world of Behavioral Portfolio Management. Will you choose to be a Cult Enforcer or a wealth builder? Will you choose to be a bubble wrapper or a Behavioral Data Investor? The decision is yours to make. I look forward to seeing you soon outside the Cult of Emotion as a BDI.

APPENDIX: THE BUCKET MODEL – A CASE STUDY

DAVE TURNER OF Cascade Financial Management in Denver is a top investment advisor. His firm has successfully used the bucket model (referred to as Strategy Allocation in this case study) for structuring client portfolios. He has been kind enough to share this document, which he provides to clients, explaining the logic that underlies the process and how it is executed at Cascade.

* * *

With over 20 years of experience as an investment advisor, I've had the opportunity to experience and navigate a number of challenging markets. Since I began my career in 1992, I've seen entire regions collapse financially (the 1997 Asian contagion), world powers default on their sovereign debt (1998 Russian crisis), the brink of the collapse of the US financial markets (1998 Long-Term Capital Management implosion), the dot-com bubble bursting, terrorist attacks in America, the near collapse of the US financial markets for a second time (2008 global financial crisis), the threat of default of the US on its sovereign debt, and the 2013 "shut down" of the US government. Yet, in that time period, the Dow Jones Industrial Average has risen from approximately 3,200, when I started, to over 15,000 (not considering dividends).

To me, the lesson here is investing in the markets works… over time. The key to being a successful investor is to have a comprehensive investment strategy that provides the liquidity, cash flow and security you need, so the component of your portfolio allocated to stocks (capital appreciation assets) is given the time it needs to work for your benefit. You need to be able to "stay in your seats" through the trials and tribulations of the marketplace, allowing you to extract the benefit of your investments. Take a peek at the chart and accompanying table in Figure A1.

FIGURE A1: POTENTIAL MAXIMUM AND MINIMUM RETURNS OF S&P 500 INVESTMENT OVER VARIOUS HOLDING PERIODS

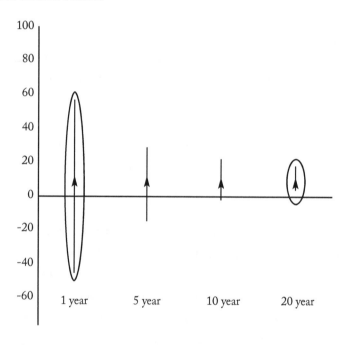

TABLE A1

Return (%)	1 year	5 year	10 year	20 year
Max	56.5	28.6	20.1	17.9
Min	-45.2	-14.5	-1.6	2.8

Based on S&P 500 annual returns from 1926-2012.

This chart, which depicts the volatility of the S&P 500 Index over various holding periods, clearly shows us why staying invested over the long term is important. Using the S&P index as a proxy (which is a representative index, but cannot be directly invested in), holding periods of just one year have historically provided wide swings in potential returns – ranging from great years of as much as 56.5% annual return to dramatic downsides of as much as -45.2%.

By stretching the hold time to only five years, that volatility is dampened dramatically, with a clear bias to positive returns. At ten years, that bias becomes more pronounced and, as the chart shows, there have been no 20-year hold periods that have produced a negative return in more than 80 years of market data. To me, the message is clear: equity investing remains a solid strategy, but your investment plan must be designed to let you stay the course.

Unfortunately, the 2012 Quantitative Analysis of Investor Behavior study from Dalbar, Inc. shows us that most investors don't follow this strategy (see Figure A2). Indeed, average investor hold times are well below five years, with the current average hold of an equity fund investor being a little more than three years.

FIGURE A2: AVERAGE INVESTOR HOLD TIMES

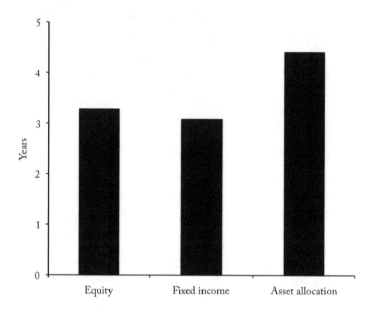

How has this worked out for the average investor? Not too well. See Figure A3.

FIGURE A3: AVERAGE ONE-YEAR RETURNS FOR 2011

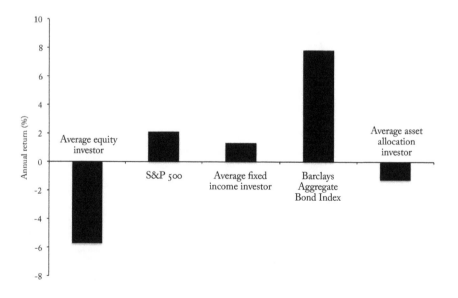

As it has done for many years, the Dalbar study shows that typical investors significantly underperform the markets they invest in. The data show us that improper strategy, and the time commitment to that strategy, lead to less satisfactory results for these investors.

The time has come to start thinking about portfolio construction differently, to allow investors to confidently remain in the markets when current events might challenge your belief in those markets. Traditionally, investment advisors have used "asset allocation" as a method of diversification to stabilize returns in volatile times. We have all seen the pie charts representing "slices" of stocks, bonds, international investments, large-cap, small-cap, value, growth etc., etc., etc. While asset allocation makes some sense, it does little to reassure investors when markets move down in lockstep, as many markets did in 2008.

Given these factors, the way to achieve success in the investment market is just as dependent on "Strategy Allocation" as it is on "asset allocation," and a solid plan of investment must be based on a solid foundation of strategy. This means making sure your "Operating Portfolio," or the money you need to live on – the money that pays the bills, provides liquidity, and funds your "rainy day" account – should be thought of and managed differently from funds dedicated to capital appreciation. In an effort to let the markets work over time, it is important that the timeline for those assets be clearly defined, your liquidity and income needs clearly determined, and your investment strategy built to support those objectives.

STRATEGY ALLOCATION

Strategy Allocation is a design element used in portfolio construction, breaking your overall portfolio into three distinct segments, each with a different purpose:

1. Your Operating Portfolio
2. Your Capital Appreciation Portfolio
3. Your Strategic Portfolio

1. YOUR OPERATING PORTFOLIO

Your operating portfolio comprises the "preservation" portion of your portfolio. This is the amount you will use to provide cash for daily activities, and will serve as your "emergency reserve" should you need it.

When determining your personal allocation to the operating portfolio, take into account your current earnings power and earnings stability, currently planned cash flow needs, and other contingencies you wish to consider.

For a younger couple with high earnings potential and stable employment, an emergency fund of 6 to 12 months of planned expenditures may be adequate to provide a reasonable level of comfort to help you weather market volatility. For a retired person, or an endowment with predictable cash flow needs (and greater emotional sensitivity toward market swings), having an operating portfolio to cover the next three to five years of anticipated cash flow may be more appropriate.

It is critical to make sure you get this number right. Even a retired person may have an investment horizon of 20 years or more, and you need to be able to ride out the gyrations of the market to make sure you take advantage of the long-term return opportunities equity investments provide.

Typical investments in the operating portfolio may include:

- Cash in checking or savings accounts
- Short-term certificates of deposit (CDs)
- Short duration municipal or corporate bonds including mutual funds or ETFs of the same
- Floating rate funds
- Daily liquidity, absolute return or preservation investment strategies

As the objective of the Operating Portfolio is to maintain liquidity for near-term cash flow needs, our return expectations need to be appropriately benchmarked against the goal of maintaining purchasing power, or perhaps slightly outperforming the rate of inflation. In today's market, this does not equate to a particularly impressive number, and we typically suggest using a benchmark of inflation, or inflation plus 1%, for operating portfolios.

2. YOUR CAPITAL APPRECIATION PORTFOLIO

Your Capital Appreciation portfolio is the "market exposure" portion of your investment plan. Typically targeted at five to ten-year investment horizons, this portion of the portfolio will experience volatility along with the market. This portion of your portfolio will be global in design, include multiple asset classes, and will give priority to *liquidity, transparency and tax-awareness*.

Designed to generate the returns associated with the stock market, this portfolio may consist of:

- Stocks and stock mutual funds
- Total return fixed income strategies
- International and emerging market equities
- Tactical or directional trading strategies
- Liquid "alternative" mutual funds

Again, liquidity and transparency are key features of the investments in this portfolio. Fortunately, many new investment options are now available in daily-liquidity mutual funds and ETFs which allow individual investors access to a wide range of investment options which were previously only available to institutional investors. While they are liquid, low cost and (supposedly) transparent, many of these are complex instruments and should only be utilized after you have developed a working knowledge as to how they function, and what role they play in portfolio construction.

Return expectations for this portfolio are generally reflective of "The Market" and thus we tend to lean toward benchmarking to the MSCI All World Index, reflecting the global nature of our portfolios. My preference, however, is to benchmark the long-term performance of the Capital Appreciation Portfolio against the idea of preserving purchasing power while generating a reasonable rate of return. Historically, stock portfolios have delivered somewhere in the neighborhood of 6% in excess of the long-term rate of inflation, thus a benchmark of inflation +6% is appropriate.

3. YOUR STRATEGIC PORTFOLIO

Your Strategic Portfolio represents the portion set aside for more speculative investments. Due to its nature, an allocation to the Strategic Portfolio may not be appropriate for all investors. In the Strategic Portfolio, an investor may trade liquidity and transparency for a higher expected return, a greater cash flow stream, or some measure of principal protection. Types of investments may include:

- Private placements
- Private equity
- Hedge funds
- Option or LEAP strategies
- Real estate

- Oil and gas programs

- Speculative stocks

- Structured products

In this portfolio, many of the investments have liquidity restrictions or other features that require substantially longer holding periods, the potential for future capital calls, or other risks that must be carefully considered by each investor.

Benchmarking the Strategic Portfolio may be challenging at best. Many of the investments may lack pricing transparency, or often have no way of determining a current price. Further, the lack of liquidity may prevent an investor from realizing gains once it appears there has been some appreciation.

Further, some of the assets that qualify for the Speculative Portfolio may not be high return assets. Instead, they may be very stable, predictable cash flow producers, but lack the liquidity to qualify for the Operating or Capital Appreciation portfolios. Others have unique tax benefits that provide real value to the investor, while not offering the price appreciation of other investments. Accordingly, appropriate benchmarks vary by the individual investment, and for each component of the portfolio it may be appropriate to determine expected return prior to investing, and track the investment's success relative to that expectation.

Dave Turner

Cascade Financial Management

Denver, Colorado

BIBLIOGRAPHY

Alexander, G., Cici, G. and Gibson, S., 'Does Motivation Matter When Assessing Trade Performance? An Analysis of Mutual Funds', *Review of Financial Studies* 12:1 (2007), pp. 125-150.

Amihud, Y. and Goyenko, R., 'Mutual Fund's R² as Predictor of Performance', *Review of Financial Studies* 26:3 (2013I), pp. 667-694.

Arnott, R. and Asness, C., 'Surprise! Higher Dividends = Higher Earnings Growth', *Financial Analyst Journal* (January/February 2003) pp. 70-87.

Avramov, D. and Wermers, R., 'Investing in Mutual Funds when Returns are Predictable', working paper, University of Maryland (2005).

Baker, M., Litov, L., Wachter, J. A. and Wurgler, J., 'Can Mutual Fund Managers Pick Stocks? Evidence from Their Trades prior to Earnings Announcements', NBER Working Paper w10685 (July 28, 2004).

Baker, M., Ruback, R. and Wurgler, J., 'Behavioral corporate finance: A survey', in E. Eckbo (ed.), *The Handbook of Corporate Finance: Empirical Corporate Finance* (Elsevier/North Holland, New York, 2007).

Baker, M. and Wurgler, J., 'Investor Sentiment and the Cross-Section of Stock Returns', *Journal of Finance* (2006), pp. 1645-1680.

Baker, M. and Wurgler, J., 'Investor Sentiment in the Stock Market', *Journal of Economic Perspective* (Spring 2007), pp. 129-151.

Baker, M., Bradley, B. and Wurgler, J., 'Benchmarks as Limits to Arbitrage: Understanding the Low Volatility Anomaly', working paper (2010).

Banz, R., 'The Relationship Between Return and Market Value of Common Stocks', *Journal of Financial Economics* 9 (1981), pp. 3-18.

Barberis, N. and Thaler, R., 'A Survey of behavioral finance', in G. Constantinides, R. Stulz, and M. Harris (eds.), *Handbook of the Economics of Finance* (North Holland, 2003).

Basu, S., 'Investment Performance of Common Stocks in Relation to Their Price-Earnings Ratios: A Test of the Efficient Market Hypothesis', *Journal of Finance* 32:3 (1977), pp. 663-682.

Benartzi, S. and Thaler, R., 'Myopic Loss Aversion and the Equity Premium Puzzle', *Quarterly Journal of Economics* 110:1 (1995), pp. 73-92.

Berk, J. B. and Green, R. C., 'Mutual Fund Flows and Performance in Rational Markets', *Journal of Political Economy* 112:6 (2004), pp. 1269-1295.

Berk, J. B. and van Binsbergen, J. H., 'Measuring Skill in the Mutual Fund Industry', working paper (February 2013).

Bollen, N. P. B. and Busse, J. A., 'Short-Term Persistence in Mutual Fund Performance', *Review of Financial Studies* 18:2 (2004), pp. 569-597.

Bollerslev, T., Tauchen, G. and Zhou, H., 'Expected Stock Returns and Variance Risk Premia', *Review of Financial Studies* 22:11 (2009), pp. 4463-4492.

Boudoukhb, J,, Michaely, R. and Richardson, M., 'On the Importance of Measuring Payout Yield: Implications for Empirical Asset Pricing', *Journal of Finance* 62:2 (2007), pp. 877-915.

Brands, S., Brown, S.J. and Gallagher, D.R., 'Portfolio Concentration and Investment Manager Performance', *International Review of Finance* (2006), pp. 149-174.

Brown, G. W., and Cliff, M. T., 'Investor Sentiment and Asset Valuation', *Journal of Business* 78:2 (2005), pp. 405-40.

Brown, S. J. and Goetzmann, W. N., 'Performance Persistence', *Journal of Finance* 50:2 (1995), pp. 679-698.

Busse, J. A. and Irvine, P. J., 'Bayesian Alphas and Mutual Fund Persistence', *The Journal of Finance* Vol. LXI, No. 5, (October 2006), pp. 2251-2281.

Callahan, C. T. and Howard, C. T., 'Outside the Box', *Investment Advisor* (September 2005), pp. 84-88.

Callahan, C. T. and Howard, C. T., 'Boxes are not Asset Classes', *Investment Advisor* (January 2006), pp. 68-70.

Callahan, C. T. and Howard, C. T., 'Risky Business', *Investment Advisor* (February 2006), pp. 78-82.

Callahan, C. T. and Howard, C. T., 'Investing with Style', *Investment Advisor* (February 2007), pp. 54-60.

Callahan, C. T. and Howard, C. T., 'Judgment Day', *Investment Advisor* (September 2007), 82-87.

Callahan, C. T. and Howard, C. T., 'Illusionist', *Investment Advisor* (September 2007), pp. 58-62.

Carhart, M., 'On Persistence in Mutual Fund Returns', *Journal of Finance* 52:1 (1997), pp. 57-82.

Case, D. W. and Cusimano, S., 'Historical Tendencies of Equity Style Returns and the Prospects for Tactical Style Allocation', in R. Klein and J. Lederman (eds.), *Equity Style Management: Evaluating and Selecting Investment Styles* (Irwin, 1995).

Chen, H-L., Jegadeesh, N. and Wermers, R., 'The value of active mutual fund management: An examination of the stockholdings and trades of fund managers', *Journal of Financial and Quantitative Analysis* 35 (2000), pp. 343-368.

Chen, J., Hong, H., Huang, M. and Kubik, J. D., 'Does Fund Size Erode Performance? Organizational Diseconomies and Active Money Management', *American Economic Review* 94:5 (2004), pp. 1276-1302.

Chen, L. and Zhang, L., 'A Better Three-Factor Model that Explains More Anomalies', *The Journal of Finance* Vol. LXV, No 2 (2010), pp 563-594.

Cohen, R. B., Coval, J. D. and Pastor, L., 'Judging Fund Managers by the Company They Keep', *Journal of Finance* 60:3 (2005), pp. 1057-1096.

Cohen, R. B., Polk, C. and Silli, B., 'Best ideas', Harvard working paper (March 2010).

Collins, B. and Fabozzi, F., 'Equity Manager Selection and Performance', *Review of Quantitative Finance and Accounting* 15 (2000), pp. 81-97.

Cornell, B., Landsman, W. and Stubben, S., 'Do Institutional Investors and Security Analysts Mitigate the Effects of Investor Sentiment?', Working Paper (May 2011).

Cremers, M. and Petajisto, A., 'How Active Is Your Fund Manager? A New Measure That Predicts Performance', *Review of Financial Studies* (September 2009), pp. 3329-3365.

Daniel, K., Grinblatt, M., Titman, S. and Wermers, R., 'Measuring Mutual Fund Performance with Characteristic-Based Benchmarks', *Journal of Finance* 52:3 (1997), pp. 1035-1058.

Dutton, Kevin, *The Wisdom of Psychopaths: What Saints, Spies, and Serial Killers Can Teach Us About Success* (Scientific American/Farrar, Straus and Giroux, 2013).

Elton, Edwin J., Gruber, Martin J. and Blake, Christopher R., 'The persistence of risk-adjusted mutual fund performance', *Journal of Business* 69 (1996), pp. 133-157.

Davis, J. L., Fama, E. F. and French, K. R., 'Characteristics, Covariances, and Average Returns: 1929 to 1997', *The Journal of Finance* Vol. LV, No. 1 (2000), pp. 389-406

Elton, E. J., Gruber, M. J. and Blake, C. R., 'The persistence of risk-adjusted mutual fund performance', *Journal of Business* 69 (1996), pp. 133-157.

Evans, J.L. and Archer, S.H., 'Diversification and the reduction of dispersion: an empirical analysis', *Journal of Finance* 23 (1968), pp. 761-767.

Fama, E. F. and French, K. R., 'The Capital Asset Pricing Model: Theory and Evidence', working paper (January 2004).

Fama, E. F. and French, K. R., 'Luck versus Skill in the Cross-Section of Mutual Fund Returns', *Journal of Finance* 65:5 (2010), pp. 1915-1947.

Ferson, W. E. and Khang, K., 'Conditional performance measurement using portfolio weights: Evidence for pension funds', *Journal of Financial Economics* 65 (2002) pp. 249-282.

Frazzini, A., ,The Disposition Effect and Underreaction to News', *Journal of Finance* Vol LXI, No.4 (August 2006), pp. 2017-2046.

French, K., Schwert, G. and Stambaugh, R., 'Expected Stock Returns and Volatility', *Journal of Financial Economics* 19 (1987), pp. 3-29.

Frey, S. and Herbst, P., The Influence of Buy-side Analysts on Mutual Fund Trading', University of Tübingen Working Paper (January 2010).

Glushkov, D., 'Sentiment Beta', unpublished paper (2006), **ssrn.com/abstract862444**.

Grinblatt, M. and Titman, S., 'Performance Measurement without Benchmarks: An Examination of Mutual Fund Returns', *Journal of Business* 66:1 (1993), pp. 47-68.

Goetzmann, W. N. and Ibbotson, R. G., 'Do winners repeat? Patterns in mutual fund performance', *Journal of Portfolio Management* 20 (1994), pp. 9-18.

Goetzmann, W. N., Massa, M. and Rouwenhorst, K. G., 'Behavioral Factors in Mutual Fund Flows', Yale ICF [International Center for Finance] Working Paper 00-14 (2000).

Gordon, R. and Howell, J., *Higher Education for Business* (Columbia University Press, 1959).

Graham, B. and Dodd, D., *Security Analysis*, (McGraw-Hill, 6th Edition, 2009).

Groysberg, B., 'What Drives Sell-Side Analyst Compensation at High-Status Banks', *Journal of Accounting Research* 49:4 (September 2011), pp. 969-1000.

Han, Y., Noe, T. and Rebello, M., 'Horses for courses: Fund managers and organizational structures', working paper (January 2008).

Haugen, R., *The Inefficient Stock Market* (Prentice Hall, 2nd edition, 2002).

Hendricks, D., Patel, J. and Zeckhauser, R., 'Hot hands in mutual funds: Short-run persistence of relative performance, 1974-1988', *Journal of Finance* 48 (1993), pp. 93-130.

Hirshleifer, D., 'Investor psychology and asset pricing', *Journal of Finance* 56 (2008), pp. 1533-1598.

Hong, H., Kubik, J. D. and Stein, J. C., 'Thy neighbor's portfolio: Word of mouth effects in the holdings and trades of money managers', working paper, Stanford University (2002).

Howard, C. T. and Callahan, C. T., 'The Problematic "Style" Grid', *Journal of Investment Consulting* (Winter 2006), pp. 44-56.

Howard, C. T., 'The Importance of Investment Strategy', working paper (2010).

Howard, C. T., 'Behavioral Measures of Expected Market Return', working paper (2013).

Hunter, D., Kandel, E., Kandel, D. and Wermers, R., 'Endogenous Benchmarks', University of Maryland Working Paper (March 2009).

Hussainey, K., 'Do dividends signal information about future earnings?' *Applied Economics Letters* 16 (2009), pp. 1285-1288.

Ivkovic, Z., Sialm, C. and Weisbenner, S., 'Portfolio Concentration and the Performance of Individual Investors', *Journal of Financial and Quantitative Analysis* 43:3 (September 2008), pp. 613-656.

Jegadeesh, N. and Titman, S., 'Overreaction, Delayed Reaction, and Contrarian Profits', *Review of Financial Studies* 8:4 (1995).

Jensen, M. C., 'The Performance of Mutual Funds in the Period 1945-1964', *Journal of Finance* 23:2 (1968), pp. 389-416.

Jones, C. S. and Shanken, J., 'Mutual fund performance with learning across funds', University of Southern California Working Paper (2004).

Jones, R. and Wermers, R., 'Active Management in Mostly Efficient Markets', *Financial Analyst Journal* 67:6 (2011), pp. 29-47.

Kacperczyk, M. T., Sialm, C. and Zheng, L., 'On Industry Concentration of Actively Managed Equity Mutual Funds', *Journal of Finance* 60:4 (2005), pp. 1983-2011.

Kacperczyk, M. T., and Seru, A., 'Fund Manager Use of Public Information: New Evidence on Managerial Skills', *Journal of Finance* (April 2007), pp. 485-528.

Kacperczyk, M. T., Sialm, C. and Zheng, L., 'Unobserved Actions of Mutual Funds', *Review of Financial Studies* 21 (November 2008), pp. 2379-2416.

Kahneman, D. and Tversky, A., 'Prospect Theory: An Analysis of Decision under Risk', *Econometrica* 47:2 (1979), pp. 263-292.

Kahneman, D., *Thinking, Fast and Slow* (Farrar, Straus and Giroux, 2012).

Kamstra, M. J., Kramer, L. A. and Levi, M. D., 'Winter Blues: A SAD Stock Market Cycle', *American Economic Review* 93:1 (2003), pp. 1257-63.

Keswani, A. and Stolin, D., 'Which Money Is Smart? Mutual Fund Buys and Sells of Individual and Institutional Investors', *Journal of Finance* 63:1 (February 2008), pp. 85-118.

Kosowski, R., Timermann, A., Wermers, R. and White, H., 'Can Mutual Fund "Stars" Really Pick Stocks? New Evidence from a Bootstrap Analysis', *Journal of Finance* 61:6 (December 2006), pp. 2551-2595.

Kuhn, Thomas S., *The Structure of Scientific Revolutions* (The University of Chicago Press, 3rd Edition, 1996).

Lakonishok, J., Shleifer, A. Thaler, R. and Vishny, R. W., 'Window Dressing by Pension Fund Managers', *American Economic Review* 81 (1991), pp. 227-231.

Lakonishok, J., Shleifer, A. and Vishny, R. W., 'The impact of institutional trading on stock prices', *Journal of Financial Economics* 32 (1992), pp. 23-44.

Lee, C., Shleifer, A. and Thaler, R. H., 'Investor Sentiment and the Closed-End Fund Puzzle', *Journal of Finance* 46:1 (1991), pp. 75-109.

Lemmon, M., and Portniaguina, E., 'Consumer Confidence and Asset Prices: Some Empirical Evidence', *Review of Financial Studies* 19:4 (2006), pp. 1499-1529.

Levitt, S. D. and Dubner, S. J., *Freakonomics: A Rogue Economist Explores the Hidden Side of Everything* (Harper Perennial, 2009).

Lo, A., 'The Adaptive Markets Hypothesis: Market Efficiency from an Evolutionary Perspective', *Journal of Portfolio Management* 30 (2004), pp. 15-29.

Ljungqvist, A., Nanda, V. and Singh, R., 'Hot Markets, Investor Sentiment, and IPO Pricing', *Journal of Business* 79:4 (2006), pp. 1667-1703.

Mamaysky, H., Spiegel, M. and Zhang, H., 'Improved Forecasting of Mutual Fund Alphas and Betas', Yale ICF working paper (2006).

Markowitz, H., 'Portfolio Selection', *The Journal of Finance* 7:1, pp. 77-91 (March 1952).

McLean, D. R. and Pontiff, J., 'Does Academic Research Destroy Stock Return Predictability?', working paper (May 2013).

Mehra, R. and Prescott, E., 'The equity premium: A puzzle', *Journal of Monetary Economics* 15 (1985), pp. 145–161.

Mehra, R. and Prescott, E., 'The Equity Premium in Retrospect', NBER Working Paper No. 952 (February 2003).

Montier, J., *Behavioural Investing: A Practitioners Guide to Applying Behavioural Finance* (John Wiley & Sons, 2007).

Musto, D. K., 'Portfolio disclosures and year-end price shifts', *Journal of Finance* 52 (1997), pp. 1563-1588.

Musto, D. K., 'Investment decisions depend on portfolio disclosures', *Journal of Finance* 54 (1999), pp. 935-952.

Myers, M. M., Poterba, J. M., Shackelford, D. A. and Shoven, J. B. 'Copycat Funds: Information Disclosure Regulation and the Returns to Active Management in the Mutual Fund Industry', working paper (2001).

Neal, R., and Wheatley, S. M., 'Do Measures of Investor Sentiment Predict Returns?', *Journal of Financial & Quantitative Analysis* 33:4 (1998), pp. 523-48.

Pastor, L., and Stambaugh, R. F., 'Investing in equity mutual funds', *Journal of Financial Economics* 63 (2002), pp. 351-380.

Peck, M. S., *The Road Less Traveled: A New Psychology of Love, Traditional Values, and Spiritual Growth* (Simon & Schuster, 1980).

Phalippou, L., 'Where is the Value Premium?', *Financial Analyst Journal* 64:2 (March/April 2008), pp. 41-48.

Pollet, J. M. and Wilson, M., 'How Does Size Affect Mutual Fund Behavior?', working paper (2006).

Pomorski, L., 'Acting on the Most Valuable Information: Best Idea Trades of Mutual Fund Managers', University of Toronto working paper (March 2009).

Qiu, L. X. and Welch, I., 'Investor Sentiment Measures' (2006), **ssrn.com/abstract589641**.

Sharpe, W. F., 'Capital Asset Prices – A Theory of Market Equilibrium Under Conditions of Risk', *Journal of Finance* XIX, 3 (1964), pp. 425-42.

Sharpe, W. F., 'Mutual fund performance', *Journal of Business* 39 (1966), pp. 119-138.

Sharpe, W. F., 'Determining a Fund's Effective Asset Mix', *Investment Management Review*, Vol. II, no. 6 (Nov/Dec 1988), pp. 59-69.

Sharpe, W. F., 'Asset Allocation: Management Style and Performance Measurement', *The Journal of Portfolio Management* 18:2 (1992), pp. 7-19.

Shefrin, H. and Statman, M., 'The disposition to sell winners too early and ride losers too long: theory and evidence', *Journal of Finance* 40 (1985), pp. 777-790.

Shefrin, H., 'A Behavioral Approach to Asset Pricing', (Elsevier Academic Press, 2008).

Shefrin, H., *Behavioralizing Finance* (Now Publishers Inc., 2010).

Shiller, R., 'Do stock prices move too much to be justified by subsequent changes in dividends?', *American Economic Review* 71 (1981), 421-436.

Shiller, R, 'From Efficient Market Theory to Behavioral Finance', *Journal of Economic Perspectives* 17 (2003), pp. 83-104.

Shumway, T., Szeter, M. and Yuan, K., 'The Information Content of Revealed Beliefs in Portfolio Holdings', University of Michigan working paper (January 2009).

Subrahmanyam, A., 'Behavioural finance: A review and synthesis', *European Financial Management* 14:1 (2007), pp. 12-29.

Taleb, N. N., *Fooled by Randomness* (Random House, 2nd edition, 2004).

Wermers, R., 'Mutual Fund Performance: An Empirical Decomposition into Stock-Picking Talent, Style, Transactions Costs, and Expenses', *Journal of Finance* 55:4 (2000), pp. 1655-1695.

Wermers, R., 'A Matter of Style: The Causes and Consequences of Style Drift in Institutional Portfolios', University of Maryland working paper (May 2010).

Wermers, R., Yao, T. and Zhao, J., 'The Investment Value of Mutual Fund Portfolio Disclosure', University of Maryland working paper (December 2010).

Whaley, R. E., 'The Investor Fear Gauge', *Journal of Portfolio Management* 26:3 (2000), pp. 12-17.

Zweig, M. E., 'An Investor Expectations Stock Price Predictive Model Using Closed-End Fund Premiums', *Journal of Finance* 28:1 (1973), pp. 67-87.

SUPPLEMENTAL BIBLIOGRAPHY

From 'Does Academic Research Destroy Stock Return Predictability?' by David R. McLean and Jeffrey Pontiff, Working Paper (May 2013).

Ang, A., Hodrick, R. J., Xing, Y. and Zhang, X., 'The cross-section of volatility and expected returns', *Journal of Finance* 61 (2006), pp. 259-299.

Amihud, Y., 'Illiquidity and stock returns: Cross-section and time-series effects', *Journal of Financial Markets* 5 (2002), pp. 31-56.

Amihud, Y., and Mendelson, H., 'Asset pricing and the bid–ask spread', *Journal of Financial Economics* 17 (1986), pp. 223-249.

Anand, A., Irvine, P., Puckett, A. and Venkataraman, K., 'Performance of Institutional Trading Desks: An Analysis of Persistence in Trading Costs', *Review of Financial Studies*, forthcoming.

Asness, C. S., Moskowitz, T. J. and Pedersen, L. H., 'Value and momentum everywhere', New York University working paper (2009).

Barberis, N., and Shleifer, A., 'Style investing', *Journal of Financial Economics* 68 (2003), pp. 161-199.

Barberis, N., Shleifer, A. and Wurgler, J., 'Comovement', *Journal of Financial Economics* 75 (2005), pp. 283-317.

Bali, T. G. and Cakici, N., 'Idiosyncratic Volatility and the Cross Section of Expected Returns', *Journal of Financial and Quantitative Analysis* 43 (2008), pp. 29-58.

Bali, T. G., Cakici, N. and Whitelaw, F. R., 'Maxing out: Stocks as lotteries and the cross-section of expected returns,' *Journal of Financial Economics* 99 (2011), pp. 427-446.

Banz, R. W., 'The relationship between return and market value of common stocks', *Journal of Financial Economics* 9 (1981), pp. 3-18.

Blume, M. E. and Husic, F., 'Price, beta, and exchange listing', *Journal of Finance* 28 (1973), pp. 283-299.

Bonferroni, C. E., 'Il calcolo delle assicurazioni su gruppi di teste', in *Studi in Onore del Professore Salvatore Ortu Carboni* (Rome, 1935), pp. 13-60.

Boyer, B., 'Style-related Comovement: Fundamentals or Labels?', *Journal of Finance* 66 (2011), pp. 307-332.

Brennan, M. J., 'Taxes, market valuation, and corporate financial policy', *National Tax Journal* 23 (1970), pp. 417-427.

Chordia, T., Avanidhar Subrahmanyam, and Qing Tong, 'Trends in the cross-section of expected stock returns', Emory University working paper (2011).

Cochrane, J. H., 'Portfolio Advice for a Multifactor World', *Economic Perspectives* 23 (Federal Reserve Bank of Chicago, 1999), pp. 59-78.

Corwin, S. A., and Paul Schultz, 'A Simple Way to Estimate Bid-Ask Spreads from Daily High and Low Prices', *Journal of Finance* 67 (2012), pp. 719-759.

Drake, M. S., Rees, L. and Swanson, E. P., 'Should investors follow the prophets or the Bears? Evidence on the use of public information by analysts and short sellers', *Accounting Review* 82 (2011), pp. 101-130.

Duan, Y., Hu, G. and McLean, R. D., 'When is Stock-Picking Likely to be Successful? Evidence from Mutual Funds', *Financial Analysts Journal* 65 (2009), pp. 55-65.

Duan, Y., Hu, G. and McLean, R. D., 'Costly Arbitrage and Idiosyncratic Risk: Evidence from Short Sellers', *Journal of Financial Intermediation* 19 (2009), pp. 564-579.

De Long, J. B., Shleifer, A., Summers, L. H. and Waldmann, R. J., 'Noise trader risk in financial markets', *Journal of Political Economy* 98 (1990), pp. 703-738.

Dichev, I. D., 1998, 'Is the Risk of Bankruptcy a Systematic Risk?', *The Journal of Finance* 53, pp. 1131-1148.

Dichev, I. D. and Piotroski, J. D., 'The long-run stock returns following bond ratings changes', *Journal of Finance* 56 (2001), pp. 173-203.

Fama, E. F., *Foundations of Finance* (Basic Books, 1976).

Fama, E. F., 'Efficient capital markets: II', *Journal of Finance* 46 (1991), pp. 1575-1617.

Fama, E. F., and French, K. R., 'The cross-section of expected stock returns', *Journal of Finance* 47 (1992), pp. 427-465.

Fama, E. F., and MacBeth, J. D., 'Risk, return, and equilibrium: Empirical tests', *Journal of Political Economy* 81 (1973), pp. 607-636.

Franzoni, F. and Marin, J. M., 'Pension Plan Funding and Stock Market Efficiency', *Journal of Finance* 61, pp. 921-956.

Greenwood, R., 'Excess Comovement of Stock Returns: Evidence from Cross-sectional Variation in Nikkei 225 Weights', *Review of Financial Studies* 21 (2008), pp. 1153-1186.

Goldstein, M., Irvine, P., Kandel, E. and Weiner, Z., 'Brokerage commissions and Institutional trading patterns', *Review of Financial Studies* 22 (2009), pp. 5175-5212.

Hanson, S. G., and Sunderam, A., 'The growth and limits of arbitrage: Evidence from short interest', Harvard Business School working paper (2011).

Harvey, C. R., Liu, Y. and Zhu, H., '... and the cross-section of expected returns', Duke University, unpublished working paper (2013).

Haugen, R. A. and Baker, N. L., "Commonality in the determinants of expected stock returns," *Journal of Financial Economics* 41 (1996), pp. 401-439.

Heckman, J., 'Sample selection bias as a specification error', *Econometrica* 47 (1979), pp. 153-161.

Hedges, L. V., 'Modeling publication selection effects in meta-analysis', *Statistical Science* 7 (1992), pp. 246-255.

Hwang, B-H. and Liu, B., 'Which anomalies are more popular? And Why?', Purdue working paper (2012).

Goyal, A. and Welch, I., 'A comprehensive look at the empirical performance of equity premium prediction', *Review of Financial Studies* 21 (2008), pp. 1455-1508.

Green, J., Hand, J. R. M. and Zhang, X. F., 'The Supraview of Return Predictive Signals', Pennsylvania State University working paper (2012).

Grundy, B. D. and Martin, S. J., 'Understanding the Nature of the Risks and the Source of the Rewards to Momentum Investing', *Review of Financial Studies* 14 (2001), pp. 29-78.

Jegadeesh, N. and Titman, S., 'Returns to Buying Winners and Selling Losers: Implications for Stock Market Efficiency', *Journal of Finance* 48 (1993), pp. 65-91.

Jegadeesh, N. and Titman, S., 'Profitability of momentum strategies: An evaluation of alternative explanations', *Journal of Finance* 56 (2001), pp. 699-720.

Jegadeesh, N. and Titman, S., 'Momentum', Emory University working paper (2011).

LeBaron, B., 'The Stability of Moving Average Technical Trading Rules on the Dow Jones Index', *Derivatives Use, Trading and Regulation* 5 (2000), pp. 324-338.

Leamer, E. E., *Specification Searches: Ad Hoc Inference with Nonexperimental Data* (John Wiley & Sons, 1978).

Lee, C., Shleifer, A. and Thaler, R., 'Investor sentiment and the closed-end fund puzzle', *Journal of Finance* 46 (1991), pp. 75-109.

Lewellen, J., 'The cross-section of expected returns', Dartmouth College, Tuck School of Business working paper (2011).

Lo, A., and MacKinlay, C., 'Data-snooping biases in tests of financial asset pricing models', *Review of Financial Studies* 3 (1990), pp. 431-467.

McLean, R. D., 'Idiosyncratic risk, long-term reversal, and momentum', *Journal of Financial and Quantitative Analysis* 45 (2010), pp. 883-906.

Michaely, R., Thaler, R. and Womack, K. L., 'Price reactions to dividend initiations and omissions: Overreaction or drift?', *Journal of Finance* 50 (1995), pp. 573-608.

Milian, J. A., 'Overreacting to a History of Underreaction?', Florida International University working paper (2013).

Mittoo, U., and Thompson, R., 'Do capital markets learn from financial economists?', Southern Methodist University working paper (1990).

Moskowitz, T, Ooi, Y. H. and Pedersen, L. H., 'Time series momentum', New York University working paper (2010).

Muth, J. F., 'Rational Expectations and the Theory of Price Movements', *Econometrica* 29 (1961), pp. 315-335.

Naranjo, A., Nimalendran, M. and Ryngaert, M., 'Stock returns, dividend yields and taxes', *Journal of Finance* 53 (1998), pp. 2029-2057.

Pontiff, J., 'Costly arbitrage: Evidence from closed-end funds', *Quarterly Journal of Economics* 111 (1996), pp. 1135-1151.

Pontiff, J., 'Costly arbitrage and the myth of idiosyncratic risk', *Journal of Accounting and Economics* 42 (2006), pp. 35-52.

Ritter, Jay R., 'The long-run performance of initial public offerings', *Journal of Finance* 46 (1991), pp. 3-27.

Schwert, G. William, 'Anomalies and market efficiency', in *Handbook of the Economics of Finance*, edited by G.M. Constantinides, M. Harris and R. Stulz, (Elsevier Science B.V., 2003).

Sharpe, William F., 'Capital asset prices: A theory of market equilibrium under conditions of risk', *Journal of Finance* 19 (1964), pp. 425-442.

Shleifer, Andrei, and Robert W. Vishny, 'Liquidation Values and Debt Capacity: A Market Equilibrium Approach', *Journal of Finance* 47 (1992), pp. 1343-1366.

Sloan, R. G., 'Do stock prices fully reflect information in accruals and cash flows about future earnings?', *Accounting Review* 71 (1996), pp. 289-315.

Stein, J. C., 'Presidential address: Sophisticated investors and market efficiency', *Journal of Finance* 64 (2009), pp. 1517-1548.

Sullivan, R., Timmermann, A. and White, H., 'Dangers of data mining: The case of calendar effects in stock returns', *Journal of Econometrics* 105 (2001), pp. 249-286.

Treynor, J. and Black, F., 'How to Use Security Analysis to Improve Portfolio Selection', *Journal of Business* 46 (1973), pp. 66-86.

Vayanos, D. and Woolley, P., 'An institutional theory of momentum and reversal', *Review of Financial Studies*, forthcoming.

Wahal, S. and Yavuz, M. D., 'Style Investing, Comovement and Return Predictability', Arizona State University working paper.

INDEX

CPSIA information can be obtained
at www.ICGtesting.com
Printed in the USA
BVHW03*1510300418
514843BV00005B/15/P

9 780857 193575